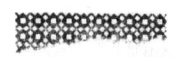

Campion: *On Song*

Stephen Ratcliffe

Campion: *On Song*

Routledge & Kegan Paul
Boston, London and Henley

For Stephen Booth

First published in 1981
by Routledge & Kegan Paul Ltd
9 Park Street,
Boston, Mass. 02108, USA,
39 Store Street,
London WC1E 7DD, and
Broadway House,
Newtown Road,
Henley-on-Thames,
Oxon RG9 1EN

Set in Merganthaler Sabon by Mary Ann Hayden
at the West Coast Print Center, Berkeley, CA, USA
Printed in Great Britain by Biddles Ltd., Guildford, Surrey
Copyright © Stephen Ratcliffe, 1981

British Library Cataloguing in Publication Data

Ratcliffe, Stephen
  Campion on song.
  I. Title
  784.3'0092'4   ML410.C3   80-42265

  ISBN 0-7100-0803-1

The facsimile of Campion's "Now winter nights enlarge" is reproduced by
permission of The Huntington Library; "Canto I" (the first 7 lines) from
The Cantos of Ezra Pound, copyright 1934 by Ezra Pound, is reprinted by
permission of New Directions Publishing Corp. and Faber & Faber, Ltd.

Contents

Preface

This book points out and describes what is obvious. Its purpose is to insist on the obvious and on its aesthetic vitality. The question "What is so good about Thomas Campion?" introduces the double task I have set myself: to answer that question and to demonstrate the validity of certain conclusions about the aesthetics of songs in general. Campion recommends himself for this, first because his own songs are much admired, second because they deserve the admiration, and third because Campion himself thought about aesthetic theory and wrote about it. Chapter 1 presents an account of Campion's improbably high, justifiable, and never satisfactorily justified reputation, and—oddly enough—concludes by suggesting that our ignorance of Campion's music has had something to do with the popularity that Campion's words without their music have enjoyed for the last one hundred or so years; Chapters 2-5 go on to posit, test and illustrate the grounds for the propositions outlined in the paragraphs below.

The way in which a Campion song is good may be illustrated by the simplest but aesthetically most important fact about any song: it is the unification of two detachable identities, made in two different kinds of raw material, words and music. A child of the union of these parents, the new unit is a unit of powerfully separable parts, parts that are at once urgently independent and urgently interdependent. Its wholeness is a scarcely restrained dynamism of components straining to fly apart, components that "rhyme" in the same way the words *enlarge* and *discharge* in these lines do:

> Now winter nights enlarge
> The number of their houres,

> And clouds their stormes discharge
> Upon the ayrie towres.

Although the words are obviously different, they are drawn together phonetically by the *arge* sound of their last syllables (what Campion in his *Observations in the Art of English Poesie* called *similiter desinentia*), their rhythmic similarity, and their similar positions in the line. And though they are phonetically alike, they are logically opposite: the first implies taking in and thus growing bigger, the second implies letting out and thus growing smaller. And though *enlarge* and *discharge* are logical opposites, they are grammatically the same (present indicative transitive verbs), and occur in syntactically equal constructions (subject–verb–object, subject–object–verb). Finally, in addition to these verbal relationships, the two words are set to similarly descending melodic figures that are nonetheless melodically and rhythmically different:

en - large   dis - charge.

Thus, *enlarge* and *discharge* coexist in a number of different relationships simultaneously, according to the various systems of order in which the two words function. The physics of such multiple interaction between rhyming identities can be seen in an even simpler example. The words "cat" and "rat" rhyme phonetically, as three-letter monosyllables sharing the similar ending *at*; they also rhyme psychologically, as mutually antagonistic members of a shared domestic relationship. Pulling together and pushing apart, attracted and opposed at the same time, the words correspond and are unified as components in a dynamic, multi-faceted rhyme: they do both what "cat" and "hat" do and what "cat" and "dog" do.

"Rhyme," then, describes the relationship of identities unified by a strong but strongly imperfect likeness; while maintaining and even emphasizing the separation between the parts, it forces them together, binds them, makes them cohere. In the chapters that follow I argue that what we like about a Campion song is its multiplicity of relationships among parts and patterns whose simultaneous likeness and unlikeness pull them simultaneously together and apart. My topic throughout this book is the *principle of such relationships—the principle of *rhyme*—and my conclusions are (a) that that principle recurs in every artistic relationship in all media, (b) that that principle is the common denominator of aesthetic pleasure, (c) that the simplest fact about any song—that it is the unification of two detachable identities, one in words and one in music—demonstrates the rhyme principle and explains the fact that the pleasure of a Campion song is potentially much greater than the pleasure of either Campion's words or his music separately, and (d) that Campion gets and deserves the special admiration he receives because his words and music together multiply the manifestations of simultaneous likeness and difference to an astonishingly high degree.

What I assert here about Campion's songs is of course true of songs generally. Because a song is composed of all of the structural patterns that organize verse—formal, logical, syntactic, semantic, phonetic, rhythmic, and so on—plus all those that organize music—rhythmic, melodic, harmonic—the number of its structural patterns is necessarily *greater* than the number in either verse or music alone. (Campion's artistic excellence is, for this reason, quantitative as well as qualitative; in writing words-plus-music instead of words only, he was doing the kinds of things that other poets do, only more: there is higher degree of complexity in his work than in the work of other poets because there is another whole set of organized raw materials—musical notes—whose operation complicates an already complex verbal network.) At the same time, while the complexity of verse plus the complexity of music yields what amounts to "complexity squared," a song's complexity necessarily depends upon that genuine simplicity inherent in the combination of its two primary parts, words and music. Such coincidence of genuine complexity with genuine simplicity is essential to what we value in all art.

An investigation of Campion's songs and the aesthetics of songs in general invites so many different expectations that I should clarify at the outset the limits of this book. I do not speculate, first of all, on the psychology of conscious and unconscious perception in the appreciation of art. I have not attempted to make extensive reference to secondary facts and opinions about the nature and causes of aesthetically pleasurable experience. Nor do I take up the usual machinery and concerns of scholarly discourse—particularly matters of difference (e.g. Campion as opposed to this or that earlier, contemporary, or later poet or composer; or this technique and its labels and history as compared to that other technique).

Nor have I tried to talk generally about all or even several of
Campion's songs. What I have attempted in Chapters 2-5 is to
describe in detail the interactions of structures in one Campion
song, "Now winter nights enlarge" (*The Third Booke of Ayres,*
XII). The whole song, reproduced from the first printed edition,
appears on the following page; these are the words:

> Now winter nights enlarge
>   The number of their houres,
> And clouds their stormes discharge
>   Upon the ayrie towres;
> Let now the chimneys blaze
>   And cups o'erflow with wine,
> Let well-tun'd words amaze
>   With harmonie divine.
> Now yellow waxen lights
>   Shall waite on hunny Love,
> While youthfull Revels, Masks, and Courtly sights,
>   Sleepes leaden spels remove.
>
> This time doth well dispence
>   With lovers long discourse;
> Much speech hath some defence,
>   Though beauty no remorse.
> All doe not all things well:
>   Some measures comely tread,
> Some knotted Ridles tell,
>   Some Poems smoothly read.
> The Summer hath his joyes,
>   And Winter his delights;
> Though Love and all his pleasures are but toyes,
>   They shorten tedious nights.

I restrict my discussion to this particular song, first because it
represents Campion at his best, and second because I believe that
the most effective way to prepare a reader for an understanding of
songs in general will be to lead him through an exhaustive analysis,
and an exhaustive analysis of one song is as much as I can hope any
reader will submit to. I use the word *analysis* in its literal sense:
what I am concerned with is, after all, the articulation of parts,

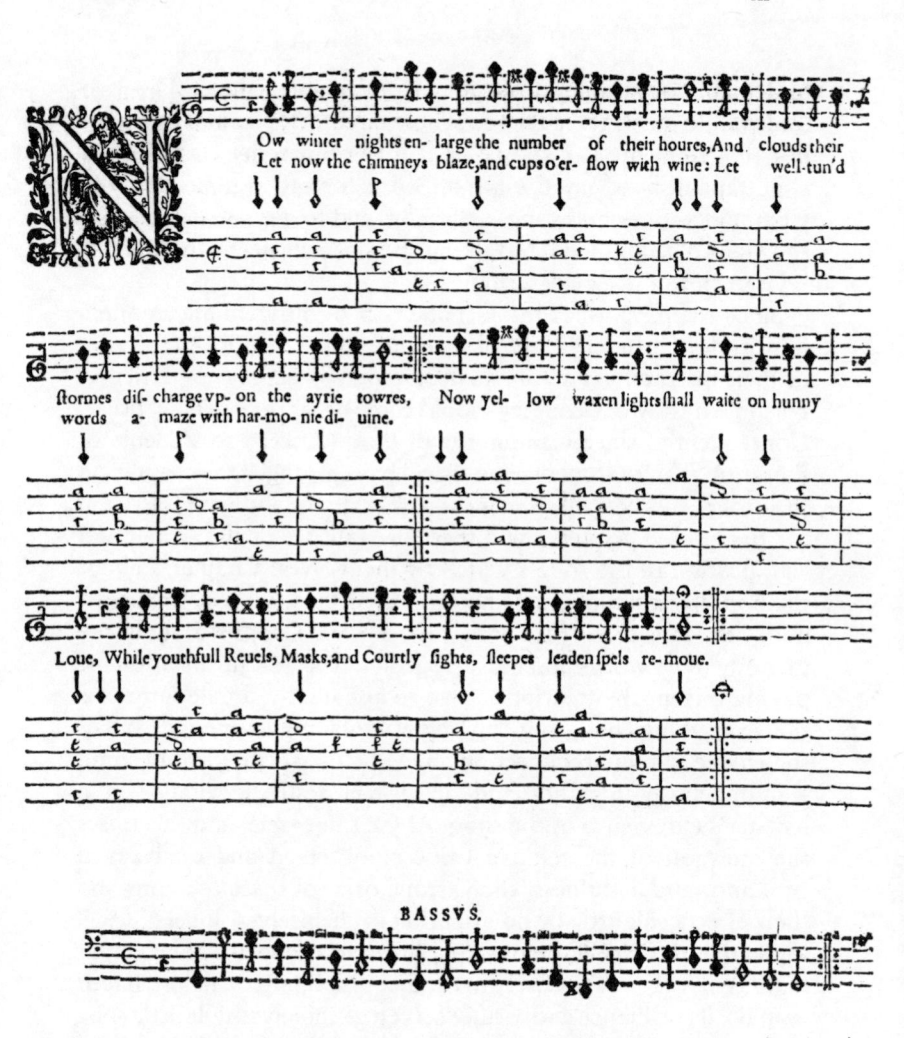

Ow winter nights en- large the number of their houres, And clouds their
Let now the chimneys blaze, and cups o'er- flow with wine: Let well-tun'd

stormes dif- charge vp- on the ayrie towres, Now yel- low waxen lights fhall waite on hunny
words a- maze with har-mo- nie di- uine.

Loue, While youthfull Reuels, Masks, and Courtly fights, fleepes leaden fpels re-moue.

BASSVS.

2 This time doth well difpence
    With louers long difcourfe ;
Much fpeech hath fome defence,
    Though beauty no remorfe.
All doe not all things well ;
    Some meafures comely tread ;
Some knotted Ridles tell ;
    Some Poems fmoothly read.
The Summer hath his ioyes,
    And Winter his delights ;
Though Loue and all his pleafures are but toyes,
    They fhorten tedious nights.

undeniably separable parts, in an undeniable whole. The two undeniable identities, part and whole, are my topic, and by laying out this emblematic example as if for an anatomy class, I hope simultaneously to lay the groundwork for my arguments about Campion's songs and songs generally, and to get a reader used to the kinds of things I will be talking about—particularly the kinds of relationships I will be describing.

Since the purpose of these chapters is to differentiate among a multitude of different kinds of structure and to describe the physics of their interaction and of its effect upon us, there is no particular reason why any one chapter should come before or after any other. Consequently, since Campion is of more concern to students of literature than to students of music, I have arranged the chapters in the order I suspect will seem most natural to the audience I envision for the book. Chapter 2 will therefore talk about the syntax and signification of the song's words by themselves; Chapter 3 about the nonreferential phonetic patterning of those words; Chapter 4 about the structure of the song's music; and Chapter 5 about the prosody of its words and music together. The best justification for paying this much attention to two so apparently simple stanzas is that everything I have found in "Now winter nights enlarge"—all of the rhyme-like interconnections by which separate identities pull simultaneously together and apart—has aesthetic vitality in a listener's experience of the song. At the same time, and this raises the question of the relative value of observed and unobserved brilliance and artfulness, the vast majority of these relations and their effects call little or no attention to themselves. Indeed, I will argue that the excellence of so unobtrusive a song as "Now winter nights enlarge" lies precisely in the fact that Campion has managed to make its brilliance and artifice serve a genuinely simple little song without calling attention to itself. My premises for this argument are that patterns of coherence operate in a work even if they do not impinge on consciousness enough to be recognized as one listens; and that unnoticed effects are more effective—and more valuable—than noticed ones.

I do not attempt similar analyses on other Campion songs for the simple reason that no one would have the patience to go through them: there is no way to examine all of Campion's songs exhaustively and still hope for an audience. Even so, I promise the reader that what I do with "Now winter nights enlarge" can be

done not only with any Campion song but with *any* song, and invite
him to test both the first half of this promise and the efficiency of my
method by referring to the Appendix of Supplementary Notes at
the end of the book. In this Appendix I point out and describe
briefly—by means of selectively annotated lists—effects and
relations that are comparable to the ones I have found in "Now
winter nights enlarge," and that recur throughout the 116
Campion songs printed in *A Booke of Ayres,* Part I (1603), *Two
Bookes of Ayres* (1613), and *The Third and Fourth Booke of Ayres*
(1617), upon which this study and its conclusions are based. I have
provided these Notes both to demonstrate that "Now winter nights
enlarge" is a representative Campion song—to demonstrate that the
multitude of structural patterns that operate in it operate
throughout his work—and to insure that my conclusions about
songs in general will be inductively supported by particular
evidence from all of Campion's songs. While these conclusions
have not been tested systematically and are, therefore, admittedly
speculative, I believe that the interactions of structures in a
Campion song differ in degree but not in kind from those in any
song, and that the interactions described in the book are those from
which one can deduce a theory of the aesthetics of songs in general.

Chapters 2-5 are not ambitious of competing with their subject—are not ambitious of "shorten[ing] tedious nights"—but are
designed to spell out—to spell out leadenly if necessary—*how* the
better tuned words of songs amaze and to analyze the divinity of
harmony. I must warn the reader, however, that to dissect the
maze-like web of interlocking verbal and musical patterns that
operate in "Now winter nights enlarge" will be not only difficult
but extremely tedious. Indeed, though Campion's songs are a
subject most people would consider pure dessert, much of what
follows may well prove rather unpalatable. Be that as it may, since I
do not believe aesthetic analysis should compete with or even try to
be something like the object it analyzes, I do not apologize for what
will probably strike some readers as an unnecessarily dull and
inhumane way of talking about so lively and human a song as
"Now winter nights enlarge." One cannot usefully make this kind
of analysis sound humane. I therefore ask the reader to bear with
me through observations that will at times seem inspired only by a
gratuitously myopic interest in the bits and pieces of poetic and
musical structure. I promise him that his patience will be rewarded

by an ability to comprehend the conclusions—not only about all of Campion but about all verse, all music, all combinations of the two, and art in general—to which such detailed analyses will lead him.

I should in this regard say a few words about the seeming—and, frankly, admitted—innocence with which I describe musical and phonetic patterning in "Now winter nights enlarge." First, while my own background is literary rather than musical, I see no good reason why one cannot talk about music in terms comprehensible to people who do not speak musicology. Since the book is aimed at an audience who will have known Campion primarily as a poet (an audience of musical amateurs), an impressive amount of sophisticated musical scholarship and/or technician's vocabulary would at best tend to complicate an already difficult subject. If, on the other hand, what I describe in as apparently simple a song as "Now winter nights enlarge" seems unduly complex, I must also admit that in musicologists' terms the song is indeed simple. But while Campion is obviously not Bach or even Dowland, my purpose is never comparative. Rather, by attempting to de-monstrate the physics of a multiple interaction of rhyming identities, I want to explain just how and why Campion's songs sound as good as they do and please us as much as they do. I am not therefore talking about musical complexity but about complexity in the absolute, where all music, whatever its *degree* of complexity, is complex.

I suspect that the preceding assertion will raise objections—objections that can be traced to the fact that musical historiography continues to work from casually Darwinian assumptions of the sort that the so-called "whig historians" of the later nineteenth and early twentieth centuries followed when they presented political and social history as an ongoing effort to achieve the laws and order of Victorian or Edwardian England. (For a token example, look at the vocabulary—"second stage in the development of music and poetry," "subsequent development," "an ideal identification of text and melody"—in John Hollander's entry on MUSIC AND POETRY in the *Princeton Encyclopedia of Poetry and Poetics* [Princeton, 1974]). In discussing the interrelation of words and music in songs, musicologists tend to assume that "later is better." In particular, they tend to assume that the historical progress (*progress* in its literal sense) toward increasing musical respon-siveness to the syntactic rhythms and the semantic stresses of song texts is a mark of progress in the metaphoric, qualitative sense of that word. Moreover, they generally assume not only that the congruence between musical stresses and syntactic ones is aesthetically desirable but that greater congruence marks greater aesthetic sophistication. I question the first assumption: I suspect, for example, that Handel's spectacular mutilation of English syntactical rhythms is a major source of delight for audiences of *The Messiah*. And I deny the second outright: if aesthetic pleasure derives from a successful harmony of disparate elements, and if the recently current approbatory sense of *sophistication* describes a high degree of mastery over complexities, then the degree of sophistication in—and exercised by an audience of—a composition is proportionate to the disparity of the elements brought into harmony; the songs of Byrd, Schubert, or Hugo Wolf may be in many respects more sophisticated than the songs of Campion, but in respect of the interrelation of their texts and their music they are less so. I bring up this whole matter here not so much to forestall objections as to inform them.

As for phonetics, everyone knows that it is not easy to talk about what we hear when we hear a poem. What the ear perceives in a moment may take pages to describe in detail, and while an elaborate machinery of symbols, phonetic transcriptions and so on may render the way a poem sounds more readily apparent to some, it has the disadvantage of obscuring the poem itself from anyone not trained to use the tools of linguistic analysis. Since I myself lack that training, and am no more writing this book for linguists than musicologists, I have tried to keep the technical apparatus by which I talk about Campion's sound as simple as possible. To this end, I do not so much try to describe particular sounds as to point out relations among them. This allows me, for example, to refer to a general pattern of assonance between the vowel-plus-*n* sounds in the second and fourth words of "Now *win*ter nights *en*large" without having to discriminate exactly between the precise tonal values of each syllable. Moreover, by simply labeling the phonetic morphology of each syllable "vowel-plus-*n*," I am able to by-pass the need to determine exactly how these two syllables would have been spoken 400 years ago. I have avoided this impossible problem for two reasons. First, and most importantly, in Campion's words as in his music it is not so much the individual particles of sound (syllables, notes) that are important as the relations among them, the correspondences by which they fit together and cohere. Second, while there have been certain definite changes in pronunciation from the various dialects of Renaissance English to those of twentieth-century American (the *Love/remove* and *tread/read* half rhymes in lines 10 and 12 and lines 18 and 20 of "Now winter nights enlarge" may have been exact for Campion), these patterns have remained essentially the same. Campion's poems sounded good when he wrote them and they still do.

*   *   *

There are several people I wish to thank for their help in making this book possible. The book itself is an accurate measure of just how much I owe to Stephen Booth; its virtues are his, its failings mine alone. Raymond Oliver first introduced me to the pleasures of Campion, and in the years since has made some terribly good mint juleps. I am grateful to Thomas Sloane for the cheerful encouragement he offered during a difficult stage in the writing, a time when others were dropping away like flies. I am also grateful to Philip Brett for his expert assistance in matters musical; though his support of the project often came against his own better judgement, he managed to teach me a great deal about how one might talk about Campion's music, and I hope he will not think me impertinent for mentioning his name here. Edward Doughtie and John Stevens each read the entire manuscript with as much attention, insight and good will as any author could wish, and I have made use of nearly all of their many suggestions—a few of which undoubtedly saved me from the embarrassment of foot-in-mouth disease. Not only because they are my neighbors, I also want to thank Bill Berkson, Bill Quist and especially Dave Murray for valuable talents freely shared along the way. To Stephen Brook, my editor at Routledge & Kegan Paul, I owe the debt any writer owes to an editor intelligent and self-confident enough to take on as unlikely a book as this one. Finally, though I have already done so many times, I want again to thank my wife for putting up with me and the ungodly hours I kept during the writing of much of this book; thank you, Ashley Ratcliffe, once again.

S.R.

Bolinas, California

June 4, 1980

Campion: *On Song*

Chapter I

"Silent Musick" : The Aesthetics of Ruins

Praised in his own lifetime, largely forgotten by the eighteenth and most of the nineteenth centuries, resurrected in A.H. Bullen's *Lyrics from the Song-Books of the Elizabethan Age* (1887), Thomas Campion now enjoys a secure but minor reputation as one of the finest poets of the English Renaissance. His verse is valued chiefly for its technical mastery, its management of sound, syntax, rhythm and meter, formal and logical structure. Its virtue–a smoothly polished precision, a gracefully delicate charm which has become synonymous with his name–has most often been accounted for by remembering that Campion himself was a poet-composer who wrote "ayres," or songs, the music as well as the words: "In these *English* Ayres, I have chiefly aymed to couple my Words and Notes lovingly together, which will be much for him to doe that hath not power over both."[1]

The unfortunate result of this tendency to explain Campion's literary excellence in terms of his talent, his "double gift of music and poetry,"[2] has been that for the last eighty-five years Campion criticism has paid surprisingly little attention to either his words by themselves or his words together with their music. Indeed, if Pound is correct ("You can spot the bad critic when he starts by discussing the poet and not the poem"[3]), Campion has attracted more than his share of offenders. Bullen himself set the precedent by implying that Campion's "lyrics" were good because of his unique abilities: "At least one composer, Thomas Campion, wrote both the words and the music of his songs; and there are no sweeter lyrics in English poetry than are to be found in Campion's song-books."[4] Percival Vivian, instead of pursuing what he took to be the distinguishing feature of Campion's verse, was also satisfied to point to its source in Campion's skill as a trained and sensitive musician: "Campion's verse was from the beginning free and musical. This musical quality is indeed the one which distinguishes the whole of his poetry; it is undoubtedly connected with the practice of musical composition and due to a feeling for musical effect, to which, with his trained musical ear, he was peculiarly susceptible."[5] Miles Kastendieck proposed that Campion comes closest to representing the ideal of the lyric poet, again "because he had the talent for both music and poetry."[6] While managing to focus upon certain key attributes of Campion's verse, Roy Fuller still found in his "ingenious mixture of meters" and his "marvellous rhythmic subtleties" the "evidence of an extraordinarily free and beautiful rhythmic talent."[7]

The fact is that by concentrating upon this "talent" as an unusual and remarkable phenomenon, people have made Campion into something of a *wunderkind,* a sacred cow, or, rather, a sacred calf. For his consignment to the rank of minor poet, and the scant critical attention he has received therein, confirms the apparent accuracy of John Irwin's complaint that "the musical qualification which his reputation bears . . . remains a form of special pleading which, whatever its judicious surface appearance, has the effect of protecting Campion from having to compete on the highest poetic levels."[8] People have accorded to Campion a privileged status, Irwin argues, because we have assumed that words originally written for music cannot achieve as much "metaphysical" weight and density of meaning as words originally written by themselves. He discovers, in what is probably the best piece of Campion criticism to date, that this assumption is incorrect at least as applied to Campion, whose verse reveals "a balanced, multi-level meaning other than the metaphysical," one that offers a reader more than enough of its own kind of pleasing complexity.

The claim Irwin makes, that Campion's "richness of meaning" lends itself to analysis as well as that of some of his more widely read contemporaries, has nonetheless been effectively denied by the fact that editors and critics alike, while agreeing that Campion's poems are indeed good, have been generally reluctant or unable to say precisely why. Whether or not Hallet Smith's simple rationalization is true ("Campion is the finest of the Elizabethan poets who wrote for music, and the reason is the obvious one that he was a composer at the same time"), it tells us little about exactly what in the poems makes them so good; nor is the matter so obvious, as Smith himself shows when he confesses that the relation between Campion's verse and music is "difficult to explain for the reason that he wrote both, and quite possibly there was interaction between them in the process of composition."[9] Most critics have headed in the same direction, fixing upon Campion's "musical qualification" as the original mark of his success. The need to return that success back to its source is typified by W.H. Auden's admission that though Campion's words can be enjoyed by themselves, "they would not be what they are or sound as they do if he had not, when he wrote them, been thinking in musical terms."[10]

I do not mean to suggest that these efforts have been entirely misguided. They have not; on the contrary, the fact that it has proved so much easier to discover causes than to describe effects itself suggests something important about the uniqueness of Campion's excellence. It was Pound's conviction that "poetry begins to atrophy when it gets too far from music."[11] The Symbolists before him tried to find a "pure poetry," one which would come as close to music as writing could. Campion himself has been recently named "the greatest master in English poetry of what the French symbolists called la poésie pure,"[12] and if the musical qualification that Campion's reputation carries has discouraged a true estimate of his work, as Irwin claims, the fact still remains that Campion did write songs, did "couple [his] Words and Notes lovingly together." If for no other reason, though Campion may perhaps be "minor" in comparison with certain of his contemporaries (Shakespeare, Jonson, Donne), as a composer of words *and* music he nonetheless stands alone in a lyric tradition that includes not only Shakespeare, Jonson and Donne, but Wyatt, Sydney, Herrick, Blake and Tennyson.

The history of Campion's curious reputation is itself curious. With little or no precedent for the criticism of Elizabethan lyrics except that of Hazlitt ("[they] as often wore a sylph-life form with Attic vest, with faery feet, and the butterfly's gaudy wings"),[13] one can certainly excuse an editor like Bullen for his full-blown account of Campion's famous disclaimer that his poems in *A Book of Ayres* were "eare-pleasing rimes without Arte": "'Ear-pleasing' they undoubtedly are; there are no sweeter lyrics in English poetry than are to be found in Campion's song-books. But 'without art' they assuredly are not, for they are frequently models of artistic perfection . . . . what a wealth of golden poetry . . .!"[14] Nor is it surprising, with the *fin de siecle* appetite for the "sweet" lyric whetted by such poets as Tennyson, Rossetti and Swinburne, to find that Bullen's *Lyrics from the Song-Books,* which included the words to forty songs by Campion, and his privately printed edition of *The Works of Dr. Thomas Campion* three years later, received the highest acclaim. What is surprising, though, is that from this modest debut Campion's popularity should have increased to the point where, only sixteen years after his initial discovery, Bullen felt it necessary to prefix this summary and warning note to his 1903 *Muses' Library* edition: "In 1887 Campion's admirers were few indeed. By critics and by anthologists he had been persistently neglected. I pleaded that the time had come for him to take his rightful place among our English poets; and the plea was so successful that he now runs the risk of becoming the object of uncritical adulation."[15] Ironically enough, Bullen's adjectival enthusiasm in introducing what another early editor called "a poet that he had almost made his own"[16] had made Bullen himself the chief source of the danger he feared.

Even more remarkable is the fact that Campion criticism has continued to employ the kind of adulatory but hollow labels that Bullen first cautioned against. Instead of offering a close and systematic investigation of exactly what in the poems have made them so highly admired and valued by so many readers, when they talk about Campion even good critics begin to sound like dutiful sophomores paying special lip service. To Kastendieck, "Campion was an individualistic artist whose fastidious taste in the combination of words and notes brought to his ayres a certain grace and rare sense of perfection charactristic of all Elizabethan song and, of course, the secret of its spontaneity."[17] Claiming that "his poems can be divided only into the good and the better, or else into the more and less characteristic," C.S. Lewis praised Campion as "the one poet whose loss would leave a chasm in our literature."[18] To Douglas Bush, the poems are "jewels of pure art or artifice which carry no trace of the everyday world."[19] Auden elevates them one step higher, calling the poems "a succession of verbal paradises in which the only element taken from the world of everyday reality is the English language."[20] Though often enough suggestive, these attempts to define Campion's excellence have generally avoided testing his poems with the kind of critical scrutiny exercised on

other poets. Campion criticism to date has remained enthusi-
astically imprecise and, therefore, inadequate.

More than its enthusiasm or its imprecision, however, the main
inadequacy of twentieth-century Campion criticism has been its
failure to perceive that Campion's excellence is embodied in the
principal relationship of his verse to his music as complex parts of
an even more complex whole. This failure is reflected in modern
criticism's wide disagreement on the question of whether Campion's words should be considered with or without his music. The
problem and its implications are serious, and need to be examined
more closely.

From what I have said earlier a reader might guess that Bullen
and the other great English editors, whose work at the end of the
nineteenth century brought to light material which to that time had
been largely unknown, considered Campion's music secondary to
his words. And he would be correct. The praise which these first
editors heaped upon their discovery seems clearly to indicate that
they viewed him primarily as a poet—indeed, as a literary ancestor
of those late Victorian poets whom they themselves most admired.
While they paid token recognition to the fact that Campion's
"poems" were actually songs that could be sung, to them the music
was more or less unimportant. Bullen himself, whose monumental
literary efforts included editions of Marlowe, Shakespeare and
numerous other dramatists, as well as a long list of verse anthologies (*England's Helicon, An English Garner, Lyrics from the
Dramatists of the Elizabethan Age, Speculum Amantis, Musa
Proterva*), was described by Yeats as "a fine scholar in poetry who
hates all music but that of poetry, and knows of no instrument that
does not fill him with rage and misery."[21] Ernest Rhys, whose own
work included editions of Ben Johnson, Dekker, Vaughan and
Keats, indicated a similar literary bias:

> Campion was all but a lost poet when Mr. Bullen so
> fortunately came to his rescue six years ago. His lyrics,
> with the exception of the very few turned to account by
> modern musicians, or given a place in the anthologies,
> lay buried in the old music books in which they were
> first published. And yet, if they had been left to the
> famous obscurity of the British Museum, we had lost
> perhaps the one poet who came nearest to fulfilling, in
> the genre and quality of his work, the lyric canon in
> English poetry.[22]

Percival Vivian's attitude toward music is revealed in this small note to the fourth song in *A Booke of Ayres:* "the air to which this song is set *does duty* also for 'Seeke the Lord and in his wayes persever'"[23] (my italics). The implication here—altogether justified on the evidence Vivian presents—is that music is secondary, subservient, to the poem, the words.

In fact it was. Though Campion's poems had been originally conceived of as songs, and published as a text of words embedded in a musical score (the usual practice for the lute-song was to print the words of the first stanza of each ayre beneath the notes to which they were to be sung; the second and subsequent stanzas were then printed out in metrical form as stanzas beneath the music[24]), modern editors from Bullen on had effectively divorced his words from his music by printing the words only. This was more than a matter of convenience, though it was that too. With both Bullen's and Vivian's editions of Campion containing the words to all of his songs, his four masks, his *Observations in the Art of English Poetry, A New Way of Making Fowre Parts in Counterpoint* (omitted by Bullen), and his Latin epigrams and elegies, and already running to four hundred pages, neither can be blamed for not choosing to include all of Campion's music as well. Nevertheless, Bullen, Rhys and Vivian were primarily literary scholars, editors who made it their business to rescue poets lost "in the famous obscurity of the British Museum"—poets like Campion.

It was against this background, twelve years after publication of the complete Campion song-books in Fellowes' *English School of Lutenist Song-writers* series, that Miles Kastendieck first proposed his radically alternative view. Reacting against the consideration of Campion's songs as poems only, a perspective encouraged by the fact that Campion's early editors had printed only his words, Kastendieck claimed that the lack of attention paid to the music by literary scholars and critics had resulted in a peculiarly limited point of view. Bringing a musical as well as literary background to the first full-scale study of Campion, *England's Musical Poet,* Kastendieck proposed an historically more accurate approach to the matter of Campion's words and music. The fact that Campion was a composer of both words and music, he argued, forces us to extend the meaning of "lyric" back to its etymological origin:

> Campion, then, is to be considered *more* than a poet. He
> was both a poet *and* a musician. He must, therefore, be

introduced again as a *musical poet* in the true meaning
of the words. The music that swayed so many poets was
part of his creative work. He did not write poems, but
"ayres." If, in writing these ayres, he excelled as a lyric
poet, that is all the more to his credit. To call him a lyric
poet while recognizing only his literary achievement is
to present half an artist.[25]

Unfortunately, however much his novel critical perspective may
have gained him, Kastendieck's argument proved to be little more
than another attempt to make Campion's music responsible for
what everyone had already perceived to be the excellence of his
words. The idea that, because he was a musician, Campion's skill as
a poet is "all the more to his credit" is a perfect example of that
familiar kind of lip service which gives in to the temptation to
locate beauty and excellence in its cause, or means, rather than
effects. Even so, while the consensus had in fact always been that
Campion's musical skill was very much "to his credit," was even
somehow directly responsible for the high literary quality of his
work, Kastendieck carried the matter a logical step further by
arguing that the appreciation of Campion's poetic texts must be
broadened to include a consideration of those musical texts with
which they had first been conceived and executed. The measure of
the musical poet's success was to be found only in this "perfect
union of words and notes":

The full charm of this relationship in the ayres can be
appreciated only when they are considered in their
original settings. When read, the lyrics, however refreshing and delightful they may be, are nevertheless
incomplete without the musical setting. The music
brings an added daintiness, a resonant melody, and,
most significant of all, a series of little changes in
meanings and subtle connotations. (p. 70)

Though both the timeliness of his revaluation and the significance
of his reinterpretation should not be denied, the general imprecision that characterizes these remarks points to the limited
success that Kastendieck had in coming any closer to determining
what specifically in Campion's songs makes them so good. Both his
description of the lyrics by themselves ("refreshing," "delightful")
and his explanation of what a musical setting adds to them
("daintiness, a resonant melody . . . . a series of little changes in

meanings and subtle connotations") are nearly as vague and unhelpful as they seem. Like Bullen and the rest, Kastendieck had come not to anatomize and dissect Campion but simply to praise him.

The reaction to Kastendieck followed quickly. Six years after the appearance of *England's Musical Poet,* Ralph W. Short published an article directly opposed to the idea that Campion's poems cannot be fully appreciated without their original settings. On the contrary, Short argued, music can only be an obstacle to the full appreciation of any poem:

> A musical setting is so overpoweringly, determinatively sensuous that in its presence the subtleties of lyric poetry have little chance of making themselves felt. However various music itself may be, it dogmatizes upon any words that accompany it; it dictates one reading and precludes the hearing of any other, whereas for much great poetry there is no one right reading, but several which must be simultaneously apprehended . . . . Campion's tunes rig out his lyrics in pretty but concealing finery; his best poems mean more, as poems, when silently read than when sung or intoned. For this reason, whoever aims at justly appreciating his poetry had best forget his music.[26]

Obviously cast in the wake of Empson's celebration of ambiguity as the main criterion of poetic excellence, which was itself the product of what Walter R. Davis has referred to as Eliot's "domination of the literary scene of the 1920's,"[27] Short's defense of the necessary independence of words and music, and, what is more, of the real necessity of taking words by themselves, has found a far greater following than Kastendieck's argument to the contrary. If critics like Lowbury, Salter and Young admit that "in becoming words for music, poetry, complete in its own right, changes its shape and acquires an apparent incompleteness,"[28] they do not seem to be disturbed by that music's absence. If others admit that by not knowing a Campion song's music they may well be missing a vital part of its wholeness, they justify their ignorance by also admitting that the task of appreciating Campion's words by themselves—however much their music may add to one's appreciation—is more than enough. Indeed, as Catherine Ing explains it, there is good reason why the study of Campion's words without their music is sufficient in its own right, why critics have been willing to accept a part of their subject for the whole:

> hundreds of readers have recognized as poetry, and loved and admired, the verse for songs, who not only have not known the music, but have for various reasons failed to enjoy the music when known. It is, I think, justifiable to look for the causes of such enjoyment of the poetry alone in elements of the poetry alone. There is in this poetry a structure, which contributes to enjoyment, made in words alone, words which cannot do all that music can do, but can in themselves make a purely poetic (or literary) beauty that it is not music's function to make.[29]

Ing's statement is important, first for its attempt to locate the cause of that pleasure which a song's words have given to readers who neither know nor like its music, and second for its effort to distinguish the separate value that verse by itself can have. What she says here needs to be said because it is true. Because it is obvious it needs to be said all the more. Poetry and music *are* two different kinds of things, one made in words and one in notes, each one built upon and exhibiting its own particular structures and beauties which themselves contribute particular pleasures to those who experience them. At the same time, Ing's statement clearly stands in opposition to Kastendieck's assertion that Campion's words cannot be fully appreciated without their original settings, and to that extent it is like Short's defense of studying words and notes separately. But it is a better and stronger argument than Short's, whose somewhat provincial attitudes kept him from granting any but a negative virtue to a song's music. It is a better argument because it reaches further and comprehends more of the essential differences between poetry and music. It therefore is and should be the standard argument, if one is needed, for justifying a consideration of Campion's words apart from his music.

As it turns out, the justification has not been needed. While the fact that Campion "coupled . . . Words and Notes lovingly together" is most certainly crucial to our understanding and appreciation of the unique excellence of his songs, as Kastendieck insisted, most of the admiration and attention that they have continued to receive has been willingly directed toward the words only. This is not really surprising. From Williams to Wordsworth,

from Creeley to Campion, modern readers take their poetry sitting
down, in their classrooms and libraries and studies, from mag-
azines, textbooks, chapbooks, anthologies, edited selections and
complete editions. From Bullen's *Lyrics from the Song-Books* on,
the modern reader has come to Campion's songs as "poems,"[31] as
words—and words only—on the page. He has found them in either
of the two currently available complete editions (Vivian's and
Davis') or, more probably, in the standard anthologies in which
Campion is usually given a generous representation (thirty
selections in the *Oxford Book of Sixteenth Century Verse,* sixteen
in the *Norton Anthology of Poetry*). He has not known Campion's
music, nor has he needed to know it in order to enjoy the words.
Indeed, as Ing suggests, most people who have praised Campion
have probably done so without ever having heard or seen his music.
They have not heard it because it is not easily available; as far as I
know the only recording that gives anything close to a representative sample of Campion (*Deutsche Grammophon Archive
Production,* ten songs on one side only) is long out of print. They
are even less likely to have seen it in either Fellowes' *Lutenist Song
Writers* series or in the Scolar Press facsimile reproductions. What
is more, if they have, they probably have not understood it. It was
one thing for Kastendieck to call for attention to the original
settings of Campion's songs, quite another to give those settings the
wide circulation or the direct and familiar intelligiblity that his
words alone can have.

This was not always the case. Everyone knows that the
Elizabethan Age was also an age of song. The standard reference
books and histories are full of facts, figures, and stories documenting
the musical spirit that pervaded England at the turn of the
seventeenth century:

> Tinkers sang catches; milkmaids sang ballads; carters
> whistled; each trade, and even the beggars, had their
> special songs; the base-viol hung in the drawing room
> for the amusement of waiting visitors; and the lute,
> cittern, and virginals, for the amusement of waiting
> customers, were the necessary furniture of the barber's
> shop. They had music at dinner; music at supper; music
> at weddings; music at funerals; music at night; music at
> dawn; music at work; music at play.[31]

However much a cliché, Chappell's description is remarkable for two reasons. First, this kind of general history was itself largely the product of a mid or late nineteenth-century view of England's romantic past, a view that stands immediately behind people like Kastendieck, people who have taken the truism as their excuse to ground the excellence of Campion's songs in its historical and biographical necessity rather than in the songs themselves. "In the heart of this world of music and poetry lived Thomas Campion.—poet, musician":[32] the talented byproduct of a talented Age. Second, as far as it goes, Chappell's description of the situation is probably accurate.

The weight of evidence indicating the wide popularity of ballads, folk songs, psalms, madrigals and ayres gives substance to the notion that the Elizabethans knew their music. Music actually seems to have been as important to them as Chappell would have had us believe. More likely than not a musical education *was* an essential ingredient in the making of the complete gentleman, as Peachman required: "there is no one Science in the world, that so affecteth the free and generous spirit, with a more delightful and in-offensive recreation; or better disposeth the minde to what is commendable and vertuous."[33] Lute songs and madrigals really *were* printed so that they could be brought out for the guests to sing after supper, and Philomates' often cited inability either to discuss the art or to carry a tune probably *did* make him an uncomfortable member of the party:

> Among the rest of the guests, by chance master Aphron came thither also, who, falling to discourse of music, was in an argument so quickly taken up and hotly pursued by Eudoxus and Calergus, two kinsmen of Sophobulus, as in his own art he was overthrown; but he still sticking in his opinion, the two gentlemen requested me to examine his reasons and confute them; but I refusing and pretending ignorance, the whole company condemned me of discourtesy, being fully persuaded that I had been as skilful in that art as they took me to be learned in others. But supper being ended and the music books (according to the custom) being brought to the table, the mistress of the house presented me with a part earnestly requesting me to sing; but

when, after many excuses, I protested unfeignedly that I could not, every one began to wonder; yea, some whispered to others demanding how I was brought up, so that upon shame of mine ignorance I go now to seek out mine old friend Master Gnorimus, to make myself his scholar.[34]

Thus Philomates. But while he did seek out his Master Gnorimus, and made himself "his scholar," the point is that we in the twentieth century have not. Few of us have heard Campion's music, fewer still have seen it, and one wonders of those who have how many were willing or able to sing or discourse upon it. We are simply not equipped to make the kind of total appreciation called for by Kastendieck a general possibility.

I want to conclude this chapter with a proposition that opens up a whole sub-subject in aesthetic theory: "Heard melodies are sweet, but those/Unheard are sweeter." Keats was not thinking of Campion when he wrote that line. Nevertheless, it may be that our ignorance of Campion's music has had something to do with the popularity that Campion's words without music have enjoyed for the last one hundred or so years. Consider cathedrals. Their murals and frescoes are chipped and faded, the whole of their past is clamoring to speak through them. Mayan temples have gone back to the jungle. The Venus de Milo has no arms. The tapestries at the Cloisters in New York are partially rotted. No one alive has heard the sound of Old English. There are some things so good that we are willing to adore fractions of them. Indeed, by their very incompleteness they are enhanced. Since we are forced to imagine the whole from its part—forced to become artists as audience—and since ruins and fragments include the ideal as nothing else can, whatever is wrong must be the remains of a former right, whatever missing perfect beyond imagining. The Parthenon can never have been as beautiful as it must have been when it was new.

According to Valéry, "Hearing verse set to music is like looking at a painting through a stained glass window."[35] One is suddenly aware of another dimension, a whole new set of impinging complexities and possibilities. As if the painting itself were not enough, there is suddenly the added complication of muted colors, subtly transformed figures and patterns, new surfaces, new light, new shades of meaning. There is suddenly a new painting. But what if to begin with the painting were made in the light of a stained glass window; what if it were made to be hung in the window, made to be seen through thousands of pieces of leaded glass, thousands of colored pieces which themselves were integral parts of the whole: wouldn't the painting in natural light become, however beautiful, a fragment, a fraction of the whole? Wouldn't we find ourselves forced to imagine the glass which was missing? Wouldn't we find ourselves artists as audience?

However beautiful, Campion's words without their music are also fragments, ruins, puzzles with missing pieces. Our experience of them is like our experience of old tapestries, Old English, old cathedrals. When we read them beneath a small block of print that tells us these exquisite poems were really the word-half of songs, we are forced to become artists as audience. We are forced to imagine what is missing, the thousands of pieces of colored glass, the unknown complexities of figures and patterns and surfaces. We are forced to include what we do not hear in what we do. The absence of music where music is known to exist has an effect comparable not only to the absence of Venus' arms but the effects of allusion, echo, and non-comic parody; when he comes to the first song in Campion's *A Booke of Ayres,* for example, what reader does not hear in the background *Vivamus, mea Lesbia, atque amemus* and *Come my Celia, let us prove?* Similarly, knowing that Campion's music is missing, what reader does not feel the need to supply it, to fill in the empty space behind Campion's words on the page? Who does not hear in the disorder that the absent, but allowed-for, missing order shows us—in Campion's metrical flexibility, his shifting rhythms, his beautifully realized stanzaic patterns—who does not hear the music he does not hear, that silent music whose beauty is indeed perfect and smooth:

> Rose-cheekt *Lawra,* come
> Sing thou smoothly with thy beawties
> Silent musick . . . .

Chapter 2

"The World in Harmonie Framed" : Syntax and Substance

In his single attempt at Sapphic meter in a song (*A Booke of Ayres,*
XXI, a free paraphrase of Psalm 19, *Coeli Enarrant*) Campion
praises,

> ... the kings king, th' omnipotent creator,
> Author of number, that hath all the world in
> Harmonie framed.

In this chapter and the chapters that follow I hope to demonstrate
that the array of *Harmonie framed* in a Campion song imitates such
a world, represents the flux of its infinitely various orders by means
of a multiplicity of fixed but (for a listener) fleeting interrela-
tionships among like and unlike parts and patterns which fit
together and pull apart in many different ways at once. I will argue
that the metaphorically physical interaction of harmonizing
components in what I take to be a typical Campion song (*The Third
Booke of Ayres,* XII, "Now winter nights enlarge") manifests the
non-metaphorical but actual interaction of identities in the real
world—what that song itself calls *harmonie divine*. At the same
time, though the substantive meaning of "Now winter nights
enlarge" obviously lies in the denotation and connotation of its
words,[1] I will argue that its meaning in a larger sense—its aesthetic
"meaning"—is likewise to be found in the complex harmony of its
orders, the rhyme-like unity and division embodied not only in the
primary coupling of its words and music but in the correspondence
of materials and structures in every organizing system.

I talk about syntax and signification together because the
ideational content of words is inevitably only delivered in the
sentence structures that contain them. Moreover, since any poem's

sentences are also contained within the matrix of its formal structure (prose is written in sentences, poetry in sentences and lines), the analysis of a poem's syntax and substance must include an analysis of the relation between its syntax and versification. And this raises a problem. For, while the syntax and ideational content of any poem obviously unfolds within or counter to the limits of its formal structure, the arrangement of a song's words must also necessarily conform in some degree to the phrasing of its music. In Campion that degree proves to be remarkably high, partly of course because he wrote his songs against the background of a madrigal tradition in which verbal meaning was often inevitably lost in polyphonic texture, but primarily because his insistence on a single voice part singing the poem's words was designed to emphasize the significance and on-going clarity of those words. Campion outlines this aesthetic in his prefaces to *A Booke of Ayres* and *Two Bookes of Ayres*. One could note in contrast the opening lines of Thomas Morley's three-part canzonet "What ails my darling" (*Canzonets*, 1593), cited by Fellowes in his Preface to *English Madrigal Verse, 1588-1632* (p. xxiii) to illustrate an editor's difficulty in reconstructing even the simplest text from the madrigal part-books. Fellowes transcribed that song's first two lines,

> What ails my darling thus sitting all alone so weary?
> Say why is my dear now not merry?

from the following:

> *Cantus.* What ails my darling, say what ails my darling, what ails my sweet pretty darling, what ails my sweet, what ails mine own sweet darling? What ails my darling dear thus sitting all alone, sitting all alone, all alone so weary? Say, why is my dear now not merry?

> *Altus.* What ails my darling, say what ails my darling, what ails my darling dear, what ails mine only sweet, mine only sweet darling? What ails my darling, what ails my darling dear, sitting all alone, sitting all alone so weary? Say what grieves my dear that she is not merry?

> *Bassus.* What ails my darling, say what ails my darling, what ails my darling, say what ails my dainty dainty darling, what ails mine own sweet darling? What ails

> my dainty darling, my dainty darling so to sit alone so
> weary, and is not merry?

In "Now winter nights enlarge," then, a literary critic's interest
in how any poem's syntax has been made to fit the limits of the
verse-line needs to be expanded to include an awareness of the
dynamics of play between its poetic and musical syntax—the
construction of its sentences in relation to the development of
musical phrases, sections and so on. I will examine the generally
reciprocal agreement between stages in that musical development
and in the poem's formal and syntactic structure in Chapter 4; my
chief concern at this point will therefore be to focus primarily upon
verbal syntax and meaning—with particular attention to how each
develops within the poem's formal boundaries as determined by
rhyme and meter.

Before I begin my analysis of the relation between syntax and
versification in "Now winter nights enlarge," I want to consider
briefly the opening of Pound's *Canto 1*. I assure the reader that I
know he has never thought there is any likeness at all between *The
Cantos* and a Campion song—and that he never, *never* suspected
Campion's syntax of resembling Pound's. That is my point. I am
interested here in what the relation of syntax to versification in
"Now winter nights enlarge" is *not*. This is the opening of *Canto 1*:

> And then went down to the ship,
> Set keel to breakers, forth on the godly sea, and
> We set up mast and keel on that swart ship,
> Bore sheep aboard her, and our bodies also
> Heavy with weeping, and winds from sternward
> Bore us out onward with bellying canvas,
> Circe's this craft, the trim-coifed goddess.

In the Pound passage an elaborately discontinuous syntax imitates
the equally elaborate discontinuity of the events it discloses.
Because the illusion here is one of immediacy, one of the past
brought forward in the rush of what proves to be Odysseus'
recollection of it, Pound has rejected a strict congruency between
the divisions of syntactic and verse-line units. Instead, in order to
represent the speaker's moment-by-moment remembrance of these
things past, individual verse-lines have been made to convey only
fragmentary bits and pieces of information. Line 1 presents one

event complete except for a subject that may be understood to be in the accidentally missing line or lines that precede the first line. (This is arch ultra-literary wit; Pound starts off *in medias res* syntactically as Homer did narratively.) In line 2 there are two parallel (and, inferentially, complete) independent clauses plus a conjunction, *and,* that leaves the series open by telling us there is more to follow. The effect of this two-line series of predicates without an explicit subject is to get the sequence of actions which are being mentioned moving quickly, one action slipping into the next in a syntax that will continue to shift from one to another of the never-made statements in which the phrases seem to be participating. For example, assuming we read these two lines as the continuation of a knowable, but accidentally missing, subject-verb construction, *forth on the godly sea* is still special because it continues the predication of the lost subject *and* modifies *breakers,* which are forth on a godly sea that is itself made all the more godly by them—the tracks of the god Neptune. Notice, however, that the *breakers* both are and are not *forth on the godly sea.* The syntax says they are and they are out in the water, but they are not goers forth but comers in. There is a syntactically dramatized image here of two like forces doing battle: the breakers *versus* the breakable, the immutable force of the home-coming waves and the mutable counter-force of the out-going ships on their way to a home that—in terms of the planet's physics—is merely accidental.

The syntactically regular construction of line 3 (*We set . . .*) supplies the subject which now appears to have implicitly governed the clauses in lines 1-2, and which will continue to govern the following two clauses:[we] *Bore sheep aboard her, and* [we bore] *our bodies also/Heavy with weeping.* Notice that, like the phrase *forth on the godly sea, also* at the end of line 4 fits the sentence in several ways at once. It can apply to *Bore* ("we also bore"). It can also apply to *Heavy* ("like the sheep, our bodies were also heavy—with grief"). But the most probable reading is not syntactically but semantically dictated: the whole phrase is an adjectival ellipsis for "and also our bodies were heavy with weeping"; in this sense, the phrase is syntactically a modifier for *We* and logically an assertion independent of [we] *Bore* (but involved in it because sheep have heavy bodies and were carried on in the preceding phrase). Notice, too, that since line 3, 4 and the first part of 5 together present preembarkation activities—activities that must precede the setting forth mentioned in line 2–one has in fact lost ground: as of line 3, we realize that *forth on the godly sea* has ceased to be possible as part of the temporal sequence X then *went, set,* and [went/set] *forth,* and that *set* has too, and that *went down* . . . has dwindled to "went down to the shore." Line 5, having begun with the tag end of a phrase left hanging from the previous line, in turn closes with *and winds from sternward,* a phrase which, though it echoes the construction of the direct object at the end of line 4 (and therefore appears, though only syntactically, to be yet another direct object) follows the signal inherent in its semantic content and proves in line 6 to be a new subject. Similarly, its verb, *Bore,* is identical to the verb in line 4, thus creating the play of simultaneous likeness and difference between the statements [we] *Bore sheep* and *winds . . ./Bore us* (compare the similar effects of *set keel,* [set] *forth, set up mast, set . . . keel,* and [set sail]; and of *ship,/ Bore sheep* and *winds . . ./ Bore us;* and of *sternward* and *onward*). Finally, this entire series of actions is brought up short and completed in the apposite construction of line 7: *Circe's this craft, the trim-coifed goddess.*

As I have described it, Pound's "sentence" aims to break apart the formal pattern of his verse-line (if it has one) by throwing many things, many grammatical events, into close and often surprising juxtaposition with one another. The individual verse-line has been made not to contain discrete syntactic units but rather to imitate a pattern of continually shifting and irregular syntax which it apparently cannot contain. In this sense, Pound's syntactic pratice is analogous to his purpose in *The Cantos* at large: to write a poem into which the history of many cultures can be fit; or cannot be fit, since it is always spilling over not only from line to line but from the temporal and spacial unity of one subject to that of the next. Jefferson stands beside Confucius, Homer by Cavalcanti and Browning, Greek and Latin and Chinese next to English in a time/space warp that in effect "rhymes" with a syntax of fragments designed to represent, finally, the multiple voices of Ezra Pound breathing into and through the lines of his poem.

The associative structure of Pound's "open" syntax in *Canto I* deliberately asserts itself against any regular pattern of versification; it even more clearly resists the formal confines of rhyme and meter. "Now winter nights enlarge," truly a song because of its music, does the opposite. In varying degrees at the end of each line in Campion's song there is a syntactic pause that coincides with other simultaneous pauses in other systems of organization. Between stanza 1 and stanza 2, for instance, there is a break in every kind of structure (formal, syntactic, ideational, musical) by which the song is made whole and complex, one and many. Everything stops with *Sleepes leaden spels remove*, at least for a moment, after which we hear first the repetition of the entire third quatrain (dictated by the repetition of musical section B), and then the beginning of quatrain 4: *This time doth well dispense*. And though the pause after line 12 is obviously only a temporary close, it is second in degree only to the song's most severe and rigid stop, the one after its final word, *nights*. Notice, however, that one sees the stop after *nights* only on the page. It is not heard because the song's music again requires that the quatrain be repeated. To a listener, a third time through is still possible; so is a third stanza. "Now winter nights enlarge" stops for good only when it stops—when its sound stops—on one of a series of words and notes suitable for syntactic and musical finality.

The final stop after *nights* the second time through quatrain 6 is a gross instance of what happens in the turn between each stanza, quatrain and individual verse-line and the next: the song stops, for a moment, then continues. It stops at the end of *Sleepes leaden spels remove*, then turns back to begin again with *Now yellow waxen lights;* when the third quatrain has been repeated, all systems again stop, then start again with the second stanza. A similar juncture divides each of the song's separate quatrains. One formal, syntactic, ideational and musical period is completed at the end of line 4, a new one begins in line 5—the music starting over, everything else moving on—and concludes with line 8. The next quatrain begins and completes another separate unit, four new rhyme words punctuating a new sentence whose new sounds and ideas are accompanied by new music which, when it repeats, causes the entire quatrain to repeat. So, in varying degrees, do the next and the next.

I say "in varying degrees" because the separation between the individual quatrains is in fact counteracted by a variety of shared similarities that work to pull them together. For example, quatrain 4 is not only sung to music we have already heard (section A–the setting of quatrains 1, 2 and eventually 5) but contains numerous phonetic, ideational and syntactic patterns closely related to ones from earlier quatrains. In *well dispence* we hear a rearrangement of the sounds of *leaden spels; This time* is a pronoun-like substitute for *Now; time doth well dispence/With lovers long discourse* echoes the syntax of *well-tun'd words amaze/With harmonie divine;* and so on. In the same way, the three-fold division of each stanza into distinct but variously related quatrains is reflected in the local division of each quatrain into four individual verse-lines whose formal separation is also counteracted by similarities of sound, syntax and ideas.

And so I come again to the relationship of syntax and substance—how the poem says what it says. In the pages that follow I plan to analyze how the syntactic units in "Now winter nights enlarge" are informed by its formal verse-line structure, how those units convey meaning, and what that meaning is. My purpose is to demonstrate that "Now winter nights enlarge" coheres in many relationships at once, and, specifically, to point out how the rhyme-like interaction of a multiplicity of syntactic and ideational patterns works to pull those patterns simultaneously together and apart. For example, as I have suggested, there is an apparent likeness between the subject-predicate constructions of lines 7-8 (*Let well-tun'd words amaze/With harmonie divine*) and lines 13-14 (*This time doth well dispence/With lovers long discourse*) by which they are mutually attracted. At the same time, there are even more obvious unlikenesses by which they are opposed: the first is an imperative command and the second an indicative statement of fact; the first adverb *well* is part of an adjectival phrase modifying its subject, *words,* and the second qualifies the verb *dispence;* the first prepositional phrase indicates a relation between its object, *harmonie,* and the verb *amaze* and the second becomes the explicit direct object of the verbal combination *dispence/With;* finally, and most obviously, they come at different points in their respective quatrains and are set to different music.

But—in order fully to describe how the complex interrelationship of its formal, syntactic and ideational patterning gives "Now winter nights enlarge" a range of different but simultaneous unities—let me go through it more closely:

> Now winter nights enlarge
>   The number of their houres,
> And clouds their stormes discharge

Upon the ayrie towres;
Let now the chimneys blaze
   And cups o'erflow with wine,
Let well-tun'd words amaze
   With harmonie divine.
Now yellow waxen lights
   Shall waite on hunny Love,
While youthfull Revels, Masks, and Courtly sights,
   Sleepes leaden spels remove.

This time doth well dispence
   With lovers long discourse;
Much speech hath some defence,
   Though beauty no remorse.
All doe not all things well:
   Some measures comely tread,
Some knotted Ridles tell,
   Some Poems smoothly read.
The Summer hath his joyes,
   And Winter his delights;
Though Love and all his pleasures are but toyes,
   They shorten tedious nights.

Although, since *enlarge* has momentary potential as an intransitive verb, line 1 could stand alone had the otherwise fragmentary second line not redefined it, the poem completes its first actually independent clause in the first two lines. Set to a complete musical phrase, this two-line syntactic unit is both one-half of a formal four-line unit (the first quatrain) and is itself divided into two formally equal one-line units—subject and verb in line 1, direct object in line 2. Because the clause runs on from one line to the next, syntax and verse structure are imitative of one another (compare Pound); in turn, the continuation of both patterns physically represents the literal meaning of the verb *enlarge*. Moreover, the unpunctuated enjambment at the end of line 1 adds a new dimension to what the two lines are talking about: both together simply assert the increasing length of winter nights prior to the solstice, but, as Yvor Winters has pointed out, "the firm stop at the end of the first line gives us a momentary illusion of a spacial image, as if the nights were expanding visibly."[2] That is the point: since *enlarge* by itself suggests physical rather than temporal increase, the magnification of objects in space, and since both *Now,* the line's initial adverb, and *winter nights,* its subject, denote temporal states (which are here variously connected—*Now* is the present, *winter nights* indicates a time both of the year and of the twenty-four hour day), there is a rhyme-like tension in the coupling of *Now winter nights* with *enlarge:* they both do and do not fit together. Their divergence is underscored by the song's music, this rising sequence,

opposed to this falling one,

at the same time, it is also concentrated and counteracted by syntax: *Now,* the temporal adverb, modifies *enlarge,* a verb that primarily suggests spacial rather than temporal increase. Furthermore, when we come to the object of *enlarge/The number of their houres,* we are brought back to the idea of temporality in several ways at once: though *number* by itself suggests neither time nor space but quantity, together wth *houres* it becomes a unit for counting time; at the same time, *houres* shares the vowel sound of the temporal adverb, *Now,* and defines periods of the twenty-four hour day. (Notice that *nights* and *houres,* both temporal nouns, are also both set to the fifth note of the scale, D—see Chapter 4, Note 12.)

What I describe here—a multiplicity of fixed but fleeting connections among several words, a simultaneous attraction and opposition of like and unlike elements moving in and out of different patterns of relationship—manifests in little what takes place throughout "Now winter nights enlarge" between elements in every structural system. These kinds of relations are of the essence not only in Campion's art but all art: they define the real by imitating its flux, by representing within set limits the constantly shifting, infinite variety of its orders.

Like the initial *And* of Pound's *Canto* repeated four times in the
first sentence, the opening word of "Now winter nights enlarge"
recurs again throughout its first stanza, twice explicitly (lines 5 and
9) and four more times by implication (lines 3, 6, 7 and 12). As
such, the implied syntax of the poem's second independent clause,

> *And* [now] *clouds their stormes discharge*
> *Upon the ayrie towres*

makes the construction of lines 3 and 4 recognizably similar to that
of lines 1 and 2: verbal action stated at the end of the first line in
each pair is qualified by the temporal adverb occuring directly or
indirectly at or near its beginning. But the syntax of this second
clause is also quite different from that of the first: the first direct
object, *The number of their houres,* follows the verb and the
second, *their stormes,* precedes it. (This is not in any way an
uncommon event in English, but not an untrue one for that.
Criticism too often assumes the usual to be inconsequential.)
Campion's reason for ending lines 1 and 3 as he did—phonetic and
grammatic rhymes—thereby also results in a pattern of syntactic
theme and variation. By rearranging the subject-verb-object word
order of normal English established in the first clause (the
"theme") to a Latin subject-object-verb order in the second (the
"variation"), he subtly but effectively plays down the syntactic
likenesses of the two clauses.

Embedded in this syntax, there are a number of ideational
symmetries informing the two pairs of lines. To *enlarge,* grow
bigger, opposes to *discharge,* which leaves its subject smaller;
winter nights and *clouds* are therefore engaged in another opposition, one expanding and the other contracting. But *clouds* also
has strong connections to *winter nights,* as a parallel grammatical
subject, as a meteorological phenomenon appropriate to this time
of year (and all others) and, crucially, as another source of
darkness. Objects of opposite actions, *houres* and *stormes* are
nonetheless also alike, not only because the enlarging of *winter
nights* produces more of one and the discharging of *clouds* more
wind, rain and/or snow but because each depends upon (and is
literally possessed by: *their*) its subject. Furthermore, sounding
like these two identical possessive pronouns (*their*), *ayrie* is also
capable of a number of suggestive meanings. It suggests the
atmosphere, therefore *clouds* and the *stormes* that now strike upon

the ayrie towers. (*Ayrie towres* is a near tautology: both are by nature high up, in the air; but notice that clouds *do* release their stormes upon the air and then on towers, etc. below; the syntax thus includes a description of the sequence of events from discharge to solid target–towers which are high.) An "aerie" can also be the nest of any bird of prey, again built high in the air, again like *towres* in the storm a home, a place to get into.[3] Despite this reciprocal attraction between *ayrie* and *towres,* however, there is at the same time a strong sense of opposition between them: though *towres* stick up they are heavy, usually made of stone, earthbound; *ayrie* things are like the air in its lightness and buoyancy, are lively and lofty, ethereal and even heavenly, are really not "things" at all. Finally, and not incidentally, "Now winter nights enlarge" is also an air, a song not unlike the one we will hear about in lines 7-8.

With its first quatrain bound together into two pairs of syntactically and ideationally related lines, the poem continues into quatrain 2:

> Let now the chimneys blaze
> And cups o'erflow with wine,
> Let well-tun'd words amaze
> With harmonie divine.

Switching to the imperative mood in *Let,* the syntax of these lines is again punctuated by the adverb *now* (nearly initial, elliptically repeated near the beginning of each of their three independent clauses). The direct or indirect temporal qualification that introduces each of these syntactic units coincides with a direct or indirect announcement of the imperative in *Let: Let now; And* [let now] *cups; Let* [now] *well-tun'd.* These patterns in *Let* and *now* are complimented by another syntactic pattern in *with* in lines 6, 8 and (by implication) 5: *with wine; With harmonie divine; Let now the chimneys blaze* [with fire]. The formal rhyme pairing of the two prepositional phrases in lines 6 and 8 is offset by the understood syntactic pairing of [*with fire*]/*with wine*–phrases that are in some ways more similar to one another than the two explicit *with* phrases in lines 6 and 8, first because their objects– [fire] and *wine*–make up ideationally opposed rhyme pair,[4] and second because they each stand as direct objects to their immediately preceding verbs–*blaze* and *o'erflow,* again ideationally opposed. (Notice the two different senses of *with* in lines 6 and 8: in line 6 it indicates what overflows, in line 8 the means by which the amazing is done.) The quatrain's three syntactic units are thus introduced and concluded by two sets of three implicitly parallel constructions whose subtle variations again manage to suggest but transcend a merely perfect symmetry.

We find similarly harmonious asymmetry in the syntactic relation between the two independent clauses in quatrain 1 and the first two in quatrain 2. Whereas each syntactic unit in the first quatrain occupies two lines of verse, the format in the second is reduced to a norm of one complete unit per verse-line in each of lines 5 and 6, then expanded back to one unit per two verse-lines in lines 7-8. The *And*-plus-[now] implied construction that connects the parallel syntactic units completed in line 2 and line 4 is thus matched by a corresponding *And*-plus-[let now] implied construction joining two other parallel syntactic units each completed within the smaller compasses of line 5 and line 6. The relation of syntactic units to verse-line units in the poem's first two quatrains is therefore: *Now* (lines 1-2), *And* [now] (lines 3-4), *Let now* (line 5), *And* [let now] (line 6), *Let* [now] (lines 7-8); it may be described numerically as 2, 2, 1, 1, 2; or 2 *And* 2, 1 *And* 1, 2.

The most immediate ideational connection between quatrains 1 and 2 lies in the juxtaposition of *towres* and *chimneys,* both phallic structures. The combination of *chimneys blaze* in line 5 is interesting. *Chimneys* comes first and parallels *towres;* with it—amplifying the phallic image—*blaze* suggests fire roaring from the top of a chimney. Then, as one goes on to the blaze-plus-wine party, the blaze becomes a fire at warm, snug, mulled ground level. One comes to think not of towering rooftop chimneys but of the hearth itself, the hollow place where fire burns. This indoor scene is warm and snug but not dry: the *cups o'erflow with wine.* The pattern of a logical opposition between the verbs *blaze* and *o'erflow* in this pair of one-line syntactic units repeats and intensifies the pattern of opposition between the verbs *enlarge* and *discharge* and *o'erflow, stormes* and *wine:* two kinds of vessels spilling two kinds of liquids. Everything agrees here except the location and relative desirability of the different elements involved: the outdoor, chilling and hostile dissolution of clouds results in the inclemencies of bad weather; the indoor, warming and convivial drinking of wine takes away its sting, makes us feel good inside. The contraction of focus in the progression of subjects in these six lines—a logical and spacial narrowing in the movement from *winter nights* to *clouds* to *chimneys* to *cups*—corresponds to the poem's movement from outside to in, from visibly expanding night to a snug, fire-lit room. What we hear in that room—*well-tun'd words*—is singing, voices intoning so beautifully that their *harmonie* seems, like the music of the spheres, *divine*. What we hear, ultimately, is a song like "Now winter nights enlarge"—its multiple harmonies a warm, dizzying fusion of patterns and details conspiring to *amaze* us, drive us to wonder.

Like the first, the third quatrain is divided into two corresponding independent clauses of two lines each:

> Now yellow waxen lights
> Shall waite on hunny Love,
> While youthfull Revels, Masks, and Courtly sights,
> Sleepes leaden spels remove.

Its initial temporal adverb, *Now,* completes a pattern of rhyme-like syntactic identity parallel to the opening logical and phonetic identities of the poem's first three quatrains: *Now, Let now, Now.* Notice also that the pattern of *Let* in lines 7-8 followed by *Now* in lines 9-10 is an expansion of *Let now* in line 5. These patterns of initial syntactic likeness in the three major formal units of stanza 1 in turn compliment a range of syntactic patterns that operate in the four lines of this quatrain and reflect upon the chain of syntactic events in the preceding eight lines. This final stage in a progression of verbs that runs from present indicative in the first quatrain to imperative in the second to future indicative in the third is remarkable. *Shall*—explicit and implied—in quatrain 3 in effect fuses the indicative and imperative moods of quatrains 1 and 2 because "shall" and "will" have always been as interchangeable as grammarians say they are not:[5] given the three commands of quatrain 2 preceded by the two declarative statements of quatrain 1, the force of both apparently indicative verbs in quatrain 3 manages to be simultaneously indicative (*Shall waite,* [Shall] *remove*) and imperative ("must" *waite,* ["must"] *remove*). Moreover, though "shall" is understood with *remove,* it is not there; the superficially apparent present indicative construction of the last two lines of stanza 1 thus fuses present with future and testifies to the length of winter nights, the length of the season, and the dream-like sameness of a seemingly endless succession of winter evenings.

Like the stanza's previous run-on lines (1-2, 3-4, 7-8), the verse structure of lines 9-10 imitates their continuing syntax. But though the first clause in quatrain 3 extends for two lines, its versification has been subtly varied from the pattern in the poem's previous two-line clauses because the verb *Shall waite*, rather than concluding the first line of the pair (as did *enlarge, discharge* and *amaze*), has been delayed until the beginning of the second line. This variation is itself varied in the quatrain's second clause: upsetting normal English word order, the verb *remove* comes after its object, is in fact delayed until the end of both clause and stanza; thus the relation between syntax and formal rhyme pattern is also different in quatrain 3. For example, with one exception (*wine/divine*), the members in each of the two pairs of formal rhyme words in quatrains 1 and 2 also rhyme gramatically: the "a" rhymes in quatrain 1 (*enlarge* and *discharge*) are both verbs, the "b" rhymes (*houres* and *towres*) nouns; in quatrain 2, the "a" rhymes (*blaze* and *amaze*) are again verbs (and both conclude lines that begin with another, non-formally rhyming pair of verbs—the imperative *Let* and *Let*). This pattern of different kinds of rhyme-like effects is continued with variation in the "a" rhymes of quatrain 3 (*lights* and *sights* both function as nouns), but the two verbs in that quatrain do not make up a formal rhyme pair. *Remove,* however, is a formal rhyme word, the second half of the "b" rhyme pair *Love/remove;* because it is not part of any formal rhyme pair, *Shall waite* is like the verb *o'erflow* in the corresponding line of quatrain 2. The formal rhyming of a noun with a verb in lines 10 and 12 therefore maintains with variation the pattern of grammatically dissimilar "b" rhyme words begun in the exception mentioned above, the *wine/divine* pairing of a noun with an adjective.[8]

The third quatrain continues to amplify the indoor scene first presented in quatrain 2. It also continues to make vague and distant sexual references like those suggested by the phallic imagery of towers and blazing chimneys, the vaginal imagery of cups and the fireplace, and the orgasmic imagery of spilling liquids in the verbs *discharge* and *o'erflow*. In pointing out these references I do not mean to imply that "Now winter nights enlarge" is an elaborately disguised dirty joke.[9] The poem has clear simple content—it is about what it says it is about: the pleasure of civilized conviviality on long winter evenings. (In its paraphrasable substance, "Now winter nights enlarge" has a strong kinship with Horace's Soracte Ode–I.9, *"Vides ut alta stet nive candidum"*–upon which Campion himself wrote a Latin variation–*Epigrammatum Liber Secundus,* 40.) What I am saying is that "Now winter nights enlarge" is informed by a multitude of intrinsic patterning elements that do not in any way compete or even interfere with the primary syntactic and substantive structure of its sentences–patterning in this case established by a density of sexually suggestive language that is not essential to and does not alter the meaning of the particular statements in which it occurs but that is related essentially to the poem's topic. This network of patterning undoubtedly impinges even less on a reader's experience of the poem than patterns of rhythm or non-formal phonetic rhyme. Nevertheless, the poem offers throughout a substratum of incidental sexual suggestions which in effect expand the scope of its topic–love–and its general assertion that long winter evenings can be fun. In talking about these suggestions I do not presume to offer an alternative reading to the one the surface invites; I am merely pointing to a common denominator in them that relates them to the avowed substance of both stanzas. The key here is not the unrealized potential of any one word but the conglomerate effect of so many words with unrealized sexual potential at once.

There is a pulsating logic–a contracting and expanding of ideas–in lines 9 and 10. An initial sharpening of focus upon a concrete subject, *yellow waxen lights,* widens to a general object, *Love,* whose possible senses in this context actually range from the most abstract ("Love" as a principle or quality) to the most concrete ("love" as sexual copulation). The clause supports this range of meanings–particularly the physical–in several different ways. For one thing, the word *Love* suggests personification, not only as a goddess or god[10] but as a real beloved person, one's "sweetheart," especially female. For another, these lights are obviously candles and, therefore, like the towers and similarly blazing chimneys in lines 4 and 5, are also phallic. There is, moreover, vague and distant suggestiveness inherent in the juxtaposition of *yellow waxen lights* and *hunny:* one erect and burning, the other sweet, sticky and traditionally associated with vaginal secretion.[11] At the same time, in context of such imagery, obscure but related innuendoes may also be suggested in the verb *waite,* which plays between "to wait" meaning "to serve," "to wait on," and "to wait" meaning "to remain in readiness for," "to expect with desire," "to await."[12] Given this substratum of potentially inherent meanings, the subject and object of the clause in lines 9-10 are thus connected not only in a syntactic relationship but as the parts by which men and women couple sexually: what these *lights* wait on—servant-like and with desire—is that which receives them, their female counterpart, where *Love* takes place.[13] Copulation, the rhyme-like coupling of men and women, becomes a metaphor not only for the coupling of Campion's words and notes but for the multiplicity of relationships that unify and divide like and unlike identities throughout "Now winter nights enlarge." It is at once the song's implicit subject and the means by which it is conveyed.

A dynamic ideational polarity balances the subject and object of the stanza's final clause. The nouns in the three-part subject in line 11 are all related technically as words pertaining to the lavish domestic theatricals of the early seventeenth century—*Masks*—which included music, singing and dancing, pageantry and ingenious stage-display.[14] *Revels* were, specifically, the central dance in these formal entertainments-as-play, members of whose audience actually joined the revels.[15] Moreover, the most notable feature of Renaissance masques was their *sights*[16]—the spectacular scenic effects created by a prodigiously expensive theatrical mechanics. The words in the direct object of line 12 are also connected logically, but by a very different thread. Immediately opposed to *sights,* the unconsciousness of sleep (death's *leaden* counterfeit) is presented here as antithetical to all the life-celebrating activities in the preceding line and is analogous to the poem's opening season, *winter,* the dead time of the year. Lead, used for coffins and traditionally attributed to sleep and its powers, is also sacred to Saturn, a sluggish and winter-related god. The word *spels* denotes enchantment, incantation, charms[17]—all words that suggest singing. Thus, while the subject and object of this clause are strongly and deeply opposed to one another, and though a potential effect of the festivities in line 11 is literally to *remove* sleep's dullness, the separateness between them is vaguely counteracted by an implicit thematic idea—singing, songs—common to both.[18] The stanza closes as it began and has continued, with things pulling simultaneously together and apart, with rhyme-like unity in division.

The first stanza in "Now winter nights enlarge" is composed of seven syntactically complete clauses whose relation to the stanza's twelve-line verse structure may be described numerically as 2, 2, 1, 1, 2, 2, 2–two lines each for the clauses on *nights* and *clouds* (lines 1-4), one each for those on *chimneys* and *cups* (5-6) and two each for the clauses on *words, lights* and the *Revels-Masks-sights* trio (7-12). In contrast, the syntax of the poem's second stanza is more abrupt; into its twelve lines are compressed eleven different syntactically complete clauses; their relation to verse structure expressed numerically is 2, 1, 1, 1, 1, 1, 1, 1, 1, 1, 1–one unit each for *time, speech, beauty, All, Some, Some, Some, Summer, Winter, Love and all his pleasures,* and *They.* Less expansive than the clauses of the first stanza, these one-line units tell us much in little. Moreover, the different syntactic character of each stanza in "Now winter nights enlarge" corresponds to their different ideational focus. In stanza 1, concrete nouns and adjectives, together with verbs denoting specific actions, are ordered by a restrained but straining syntax that spills over from one line to the next, then stops, then spills again. The poem's setting having been established, its second stanza backs off, gradually moves away from the specificity of objects in a fire-lit room toward more abstract and aphoristic perceptions and assertions. Since part of the intention of this stanza is to comment upon the situation presented in the first, to comprehend and evaluate it,[19] the syntax here is accordingly sharper, more "energetic," more able to contain statements of epigrammatic brevity and compression. It is, in a sense, an onomatopoetic syntax–its terseness imitative of the abbreviated substance which it contains and delivers: what matters here is the sprightliness and sense of content and of confident freedom that inheres in the series of line-long alternatives.

The first clause in stanza 2 is summary as well as progressive; it looks forward by looking back:

> This time doth well dispence
> With lovers long discourse.

For one thing, the unfinished subject-verb word order in line 13 duplicates the same syntax in lines 1, 5 and 7 above, and the prepositional phrase in line 14 vaguely resembles the *With* phrase in line 8. More importantly, this opening clause in stanza 2 returns us to the beginning of the entire poem, not only because it is set to the same music as the opening of the first stanza but because its subject, *This time,* is a logically equivalent specification of that stanza's first word, *Now.*[20] For this same reason, the beginning of quatrain 4 is also linked to the beginnings of quatrain 2 (*Let now*) and 3 (*Now*). Still, however much their initial indications of present tense pull the poem's first four quatrains together in one way, the fourth pulls apart from the first three in another; for though *This time* and *Now* are logically the same, their syntactic functions within their respective clauses are radically different: one is a noun subject, the other three are temporal adverbs.

The meaning of the verb *dispence* in line 13 is "to deal out," "to distribute";[21] it appears to be a transitive verb which will act upon some direct object, for example the luxuries in stanza 1. I say "appears" because, while the phrase *lovers long discourse* in line 14 is a true direct object, the verb *dispence* followed by the preposition *With* forms a distinct verbal combination, "dispense with," which in fact carries two additional self-negating meanings. It means "allow" (Davis' gloss of *dispence/With*), "condone," "put up with"[22] (as it does in *Measure for Measure* III.i.136-37: "Nature dispenses with the deed so far/That it becomes a virtue"); and it also means what it still means (and means in *Love's Labors Lost* I.i.148: "We must of force dispense with this decree"): "do away with," "do without."[23] Lines 13-14 provide a context congenial to both senses, and one in which both senses let the line suggest that this is a good time for amatory activity: "There is plenty of time for courting and flirting" (the stronger sense) and—on suggestions also inherent in the next clause—"On long winter nights long conversation is beside the point; couples can skip over the courtly foreplay and get right to bed." Both readings are correct; in fact, separated formally by the division between lines but at the same time unified by sense, *dispense/With* operates in three ways. When we first read or hear *dispence* at the end of line 13 we understand "distribute," and therefore assume that what follows will be a direct object, that which is well-distributed, well-spent. (That direct object never quite materializes in the complete sentence.) As we then read or hear the preposition *With* at the beginning of the next line, however, we must immediately readjust our understanding of *dispence* to include the two additional ideationally opposite meanings: "to do with" and "to do without."[24] The space across which the enjambment leaps both on the page and in the air is a pregnant one; in order to accommodate the dynamics of all three meanings we must change our sense of what is being said even as it is being said. (Note, in contrast, the relatively simple logical parallelism in the juncture of lines 14 and 15: *long discourse;/Much speech.*)

The multiple meanings of lines 13-14, focused in the enjambment *dispence/With*, are played out in the following two lines:

> Much speech hath some defence,
> Though beauty no remorse.

Notice the interlocking contexts coupled by *defence*. In line 15 *hath some defence* means "can in a pinch be justified"; line 16 focuses on unassailably chaste beloved ladies; the simple, physical sense of *defence* (from which derives its abstract use to mean justification) cooperates with the substance asserted in line 16 to give that line the metaphoric support of the whole tradition by which remorseless beloveds are likened to military opponents (and, in particular, beseiged castles, defending against the verbal assaults of desperate lovers). If the balanced declarative concision of line 15—subject and object surrounding the verb, the ideational rhyming of two logically related but opposed adjectives—makes it sound like an epigrammatically definitive statement condoning long conversation on winter evenings, notice also that Campion effectively undercuts the virtue of "Much" *speech* by according it only "some" *defence*. This casual suggestion is made explicit in the next line: though it may be justifiable, long-windedness is ultimately beside the point when it comes to love; *beauty*—abstract quality or personification—has no pity for idle courtship: it/she wants action.

The syntactic and logical patterns in quatrain 5 reflect what it is about—distinctions in unified groups:

> All doe not all things well:
>   Some measures comely tread,
> Some knotted Ridles tell,
>   Some Poems smoothly read.

To begin with, the group defined by the pronomial use of the adjective *All* in line 17 (we understand "All people"[25]) is divided into three smaller groups in lines 18-20 by the anaphora in *Some*.[26] Similarly, the general verbal action in line 17 (which is again a kind of ellipsis: we understand "do not do") is particularized in the verbs of the next three lines—*tred, tell* and *read,* as is the general direct object, *things,* in the objects *measures, Ridles* and *Poems.* In the same way, the adverb of general excellence in line 17, *well,* has as its counterparts the words *comely* (an adverb modifying *tread* and/or an adjective modifying *measures*), *knotted* (an adjective modifying *Ridles*) and *smoothly* (an adverb modifying *read*)—all words denoting specific excellence in the action or thing they describe. Thus the quatrain is divided differently by three different systems: the abab rhyme pattern, the pattern of four one-line syntactic units, and the 1, 3 pattern of its logic. Moreover, the parallelism of lines 18-20 as supporting evidence for line 17 is divided not only by syntax and the formal rhyme scheme but by a syntactic patterning factor that distinguishes two of the three *Some* clauses from the third: *comely* before *tread* and *smoothly* before *read* link the same two lines that the rhyme scheme links but do so in the modifiers that precede the rhyme words and do so in a way that distinguishes lines 18 and 20 from line 19 (the other *Some* clause) but not from line 17 (which is distinguished from lines 18 and 20 by its rhyme and from 18, 19 and 20 by its substance—it talks about *All* rather than *Some.* Finally, the unity of the three lines by their logical function in the argument, and their simultaneous division as distinct particulars nonetheless coupled by the formal and syntactic pairing of lines 18 and 20, is further complicated by the logical parallelism of lines 19 and 20—both of which mention activities involving words, language.

Despite its multitude of internal coherences, there seems to be a logical black hole between quatrain 5 and what precedes it. The poem has been talking about indoor activities on long winter evenings—amatory activities in particular—and it suddenly breaks away with a sententious-sounding statement about human limits followed by examples *things* that people *doe . . . well.* These activities could of course all take place inside on winter evenings; moreover, telling riddles and reading poems share an important similarity that invites us to think again of *speech* (line 15), *discourse* (14) and even *words* (7). Be that as it may, the middle quatrain in stanza 2 seems oddly divorced from the previous four quatrains; what is going on? In proposing an answer to that question, I should say again that what follows is in no way meant to exclude, reinterpret or strain the obvious reading of lines 17-20. These lines mean what they say: everyone does not excel in everything but different people do excel in different things—for example dancing, telling riddles, reading poems. But aside from Campion's personal literary bias toward reading poems "smoothly," there is a more pointed underlying rationale for his choosing the evidence of these particular activities to support the statement *All doe not all things well.*

Quatrain 5 is itself made somewhat riddle-like by its concentration of sexually suggestive language—language whose subsurface, non-essential but nonetheless potential meaning corresponds to the explicit substance of the preceding quatrain and to the orgasmic suggestions in stanza 1. A pertinent context for this language is established by what the negative aphorism *All doe not all things well* seems to imply: that there is one thing that everyone does well. Given the larger context of this poem, the sexual meaning of "do" (to copulate—implied elsewhere in Campion in *A Booke of Ayres*, XIX: *You may doe in the darke/What the day doth forbid*[27]) seems, though mistakable, both likely and relevant to what the poem has been talking about. Bawdy overtones have already been at least indirectly suggested by the phrase *lovers long discourse* in line 14, since even as neutral a word as "conversation" could in the seventeenth century refer to sexual intercourse.[28] Moreover, while *doe* as an intransitive verb meaning "to copulate" is made improbably inaudible by the direct object, *things,* that word has itself always been a euphemism for both the male and female genitals.[29] Similarly, the word *All* might (I repeat, *might*) also have had a bawdy sense, as it seems to have at the end of Ben Jonson's *A Celebration of Charis,* 10:

> All I wish is understood.
> What you please you parts may call,
> 'Tis one good part I'ld lie withall.[30]

I do not take this reference and the references in note 30 as instances of "all" *meaning* genitalia or as proof that such meanings existed; I am merely pointing out that Campion's readers *might* have been accustomed to hearing the male or female sex organ called an "all";

the bawdy sense of *all things* would thereby become doubly potent. There may also be a bawdy pun on *well* as "vagina."[31]

The possibility of these sexual overtones in line 17 becomes increasingly more probable given the following two lines. Although to "tread a measure" was a familiar Renaissance expression for dancing, *tread* in the seventeenth century could also mean to engender, beget and, in reference to birds, copulate.[32] Furthermore, in the context of so many words with free-floating sexual potential, the word *comely* may also be potentially loaded. Compare the innuendoes suggested by *come* and *comfort* in the refrain of *A Booke of Ayres*, III:

> I care not for these Ladies
> That must be woode and praide,
> Give me kind Amarillis
> The wanton countrey maide;
> Nature art disdaineth,
> Her beautie is her owne;
> > Her when we court and kisse,
> > She cries, forsooth, let go:
> > But when we come where comfort is,
> > She never will say no.

In his footnote to the word *countrey* in line 4 of "I care not for these Ladies," Davis calls attention to "the common obscene pun (see *Hamlet* III.ii.123 ['country matters'], a pun reinforced by the alliteration on *c* and the assonance of words in 1.9." Campion uses the word *come* with probable sexual intent in a number of other songs.[33] At the same time, there appear to be sexual overtones in *knotted Ridles*, which suggests both "love knot"[34] and, with physically much stronger sexual meaning, "virgin-knot"—as in *The Tempest* IV.i.15: "If thou does break her virgin-knot" and *Pericles* IV.ii.161: "Untied I still my virgin knot will keep."[35] Moreover, the "knot" by itself is a particularly graphic word for copulation, as in *Othello* IV.ii.59-62 (the passage on Desdemona as fountain and cistern, i.e. "well"):

> The fountain from the which my current runs
> Or else dries up; to be discarded thence!
> Or keep it as a cistern for foul toads
> To knot and gender in.

Similarly, the word also has potential meaning as "vulva," as in *A Celebration of Charis*, 9.50 (the description of her ideal man): "Nor tie knots, nor unweave." In this light, consider also the *knot/not* pun in quatrain 5 of "Now winter nights enlarge"–the same pun that occurs in *All's Well That Ends Well* III.ii.20-22: "She hath recovered the king and undone me. I have wedded her, not bedded her; and sworn to make the 'not' eternal." In fact, it seems likely that any kind of negative–"nothing," "naught," "none," "not," "no"–was available as a slang word for the female genitals (compare the shape of a zero);[36] this would presumably sharpen the numerous potential double edges in line 17: *not all, not . . . things, not . . . well.*

The probability of an implicit and merely potential subsurface of sexual meaning in quatrain 5 is neatly confirmed in John Stevens' summary of the courtly conventions involved in dancing, telling riddles and reading poems:[37] dancing was,

> the very embodiment of the courtly way of life–'curtesy' in action . . . the perfect symbol then, as in all ages, of male-and-female, of sex–even if not always signifying 'matrimonie.' The dance also 'betokeneth concord,' social solidarity, and youthful gaiety . . . . Moreover, these associations are what gives the use of the same symbol in the Dance of Death its macabre relevance and potency: death is everything that love is not–the extinction of all 'kindly' impulses and social joys. (pp. 167, 169)

In turn, telling riddles was a common form of "love-talking" used to entangle questioner and answerer in a literal love knot:

> Analogous to the riddle, on this side, is the *double entendre*. I do not mean, particularly, the 'dirty joke' hidden behind the apparently harmless riddle, of which there were certainly plenty, but the speech or poem of syntactic double meaning. (p. 162)

Reading poetry, a social rather than solitary recreation in the sixteenth century, was another form of "love-talking" which,

> in the right company gives the courtier an opportunity to display the finesse of his approach [cf. *smoothly*] to the opposite sex and the delicacy of his understanding. There was perhaps a general expectation of 'dalliance' before, after, and perhaps even during, a reading of a love poem. (p. 163)

These comments are clearly relevant as background to "Now winter nights enlarge," whose imperatives set a warm, fire-lit room filled with "'kindly' impulses and social joys" not only in opposition to the long cold nights of winter–the dead time of year–but as a necessary means of warding off death-like *Sleepes leaden spels.* They indicate that the three activities mentioned in lines 18-20 are in their "double meaning" equivalent as means of seduction; and thus that in addition to supplying evidence of different people excelling in different pursuits (as suggested by the syntax of *All/Some, Some, Some*) these three lines also develop the antithesis of *all things* by presenting different people "doing" in different ways the same thing.

The syntax in the first two lines of the poem's final quatrain is nearly identical:

> The Summer hath his joyes,
> And Winter his delights.

The rhyme-like syntactic pairing of these lines corresponds to their rhyme-like logic: *joyes* and *delights* are substantially the same, are in fact synonymous; *Summer* and *Winter,* though opposites, are also generically the same–both are seasons. Furthermore, because of the synonymous nature of *joyes* and *delights,* lines 21-22 suggest that *Summer* and *Winter* are also the same–not merely because they are seasons but because they have the same virtues. In this regard, lines 21-22 operate as an ideational counterpart to the three preceding lines, which presented examples of different people doing things well. Since joys and delights are both good "things," to have them must also be good, must therefore be analogous to people treading comely measures, telling knotted riddles and reading poems smoothly. Moreover, because these three pursuits all seem to have double meaning in the context of this poem, the *joyes* and *delights* of *Summer* and *Winter* must by the same analogy be those of love. But despite the apparent personification of *his/his,*[38] *Summer* and *Winter* are not people but seasons–seasons that return us to the idea of season at the beginning of the poem. At the same time, since *Summer* in line 21 stands in generic opposition to the season depicted in quatrain 1, it is itself comparable to the ensuing indoor scene in which conviviality–depicted in the fire's *blaze, cups* spilling with *wine, words, harmonie, lights* and *love*–staves off the cold realities of winter night and leaden sleep.

The progression from *Summer* in line 21 to *Winter* in line 22 thus reduces and reverses the pattern of the progression from the opening outdoor winter scene to the warmth and light of the following indoor scene: the poem presents winter nights as artificially created summer days. As a result, when line 22 tells us that *Winter* [also hath] *his delights*—the delights of being inside a warm fire-lit room, the delights of singing and dancing, telling riddles and reading poems, the delights of "dalliance" and, ultimately, sexual coupling—it tells us something we already know, have already seen in action in the multiplicity of artistic couplings and uncouplings manifest throughout lines 1-22.

There is a pattern of circular tautology that informs the poem's final two lines:

> Though Love and all his pleasures are but toyes,
> They shorten tedious nights.

The second part of the two-part subject in line 23, *pleasures,* is a synonym for the synonymous direct objects in lines 21 and 22, *joyes* and *delights* (note the recurrence of the personal pronoun, *his*); at the same time, since these were by implication amatory joys and delights, there is already a strong underlying connection between them and the first part of the subject in line 23, *Love.* Furthermore, the word "pleasure" was also used specifically to mean sexual orgasm;[39] thus, both halves of the subject in line 23 are also urgently connected. That subject is itself logically equal to the pronoun subject of line 24, *They;* it is also coupled by means of the copula *are* to the object of line 23, *toyes,* a word that connotes things of little or no value, things that do not last long (particularly since the brevity of sexual pleasure is proverbial). Since *toyes* was also used to mean "amorous sport," "dallying,"[40] line 23 is itself a tautological equation in which the two parts of its subject and its object are united by both syntax and idea. Moreover, the wise disillusionment suggested in line 23 has been initially undercut by that line's opening conjunction, *Though,* which alerts us to the possibility that while the concession that follows is admittedly true, it will itself be followed by another statement of fact, another truth: though the fleeting pleasures of love are indeed but *toyes/They shorten tedious nights.*[41] That assertion here becomes a mind-scrambling paradox. The last two clauses are perfectly reasonable and prose simple (*Love*['s] *pleasures* pass the time), but the connotations that arise from the conjunction of *Love*['s] *pleasures* and *toyes* in a context that opened with the increasing length of winter nights make line 24 paradoxical as well as straightforward. Like the circular closure initiated in this quatrain by the words *Summer* and *Winter* (words that return us to the poem's opening idea of season[42]), the poem's conclusion again returns us to line 1, the circle is again closed. Only this time it is not so much circle as moebius strip, for when we come back to the assertion in line 1 we arrive from the far side of "Now winter nights enlarge"—in whose dream-like array of framed harmonies *winter nights* have already become dawn.

Thus manifesting its subject—harmony—in the means by which it is conveyed, "Now winter nights enlarge is a self-reflexive whole whose primary artistic message is, quite literally, its medium: a structure of intricately related structures designed to massage its audience, to "amaze" the mind of anyone fortunate enough to experience the full complexity of its *well-tun'd words*. Ironically enough, it is because of this very excellence that Campion will necessarily remain a minor poet. For though he has and uses the resources of a tamer of ideational lions, he uses them to master pussycats. He meets greater challenges that he sets himself because his range of conventional topics and assertions are for the most part trivial, merely *"toyes."* His resources are sufficient for him to have captured agonies; instead he makes empty cages. They give us a sense of mastery but not of mastery *of* anything except, finally, themselves. Still, since this is what we have traditionally required of art—that it tame its materials, that against the infinite randomness and diversity of the real world it create coherence and order—we will continue to value Campion's art and value it highly: for in its controlled display of multiple harmonies we find the world "framed," and so find ourselves able to read and comprehend the dynamics of an amazingly more complex and elusive book, nature.

Chapter 3

"*Eare-Pleasing Rimes*": Phonetic Structure

The habits of literary critics have generated habits in their readers—notably the habit of assuming that an effect must be unusual to be. In the analysis that follows I will talk about many, many minimally assertive sound patterns in two short simple stanzas. The effects I will describe occur all the time in all language. Reminded of the vaguely familiar story of the famous composer who remarked that he and "X"—another master—had only eight notes between them, my reader may be tempted toward parody—tempted to point out that the kind of "patterns" I fuss about in "Now winter nights enlarge" are present in his own prose or mine even at their most pedestrian (e.g. "tempted toward parody," "tempted to point," "patterns," "present," "prose," "pedestrian"). Succumbing to that temptation would, I think, be altogether salutory—if the parodist pursued his analysis as far as I pursue mine. My point is to exclaim not upon the presence of the phonetic links and patterns in this song—and in other Campion songs for which "Now winter nights enlarge" here stands as a typical example—but upon their density and imbrication. A parodist mocking the solemnity with which I label grains of sand would, I believe, exhaust his illustrative sample many (probably tedious) pages before he would exhaust a Campion song. I know because I have tried it on my own prose and on texts as apparently unimpressive—as unflashy—as Campion's verse, texts that lack the unexplained appeal that gives Campion so many pages in general anthologies. Parodists will, if they have the patience, generate the convincingly ingenuous and thus persuasive "control" experiments that, for obvious practical reasons, I cannot present here; experiments that will demonstrate that what may seem wanton and silly ingenuousness in my descriptions has something to reveal beyond the critic's patience and his dogged indifference to the law of diminishing returns.

In this chapter, then, I plan to analyze rather closely the phonetic structure of "Now winter nights enlarge." While it is clear that each of the poem's different ordering systems is phonetically informed (we *hear* the iambic pattern of the first line, we *hear* the syntactic parallelism between lines 5 and 7), I mean here to concentrate upon those patterns of sound texture that have an identity independent of patterns of meter, syntax, ideas, and so on. I will talk about these non-referential phonetic patterns by isolating sounds and combinations of sounds that recur throughout the poem and by describing the correspondences (whether by exact, near-exact, or more distant echo) among them. My descriptions will be painstakingly thorough–not because I wish to exhaust the reader with an exhaustive account of the phonetic coherence of "Now winter nights enlarge" but because a demonstration of its phonetic organization will add necessary support to my thesis that a Campion song is organized and coherent in many different systems simultaneously. The principle that governs these phonetic correspondences–rhyme–is manifest throughout the song in rhyme-like relationships among elements in every kind of structure: sounds that are alike pull together, sounds that are at once alike and different pull simultaneously together and apart; so do like and unlike patterns of syntax, substance, rhythm and so on. Moreover, because phonetic patterns determine merely one of several ways in which any song is organized, I mean to insist at the outset that I do not suggest the phonetic relations I point out in this chapter carry a greater weight of importance than other kinds of structural patterns. The point I want to make is simply that these patterns exist–and, therefore, that in combination with other separate but coincident patterns they contribute to the complex unity of "Now winter nights enlarge."

Before I begin I should warn the reader that the following analysis–an analysis of noises in a little poem–will be difficult. It will probably confuse and frustrate the reader, make him feel that the phonetic connections I point out are far too numerous and various ever to be consciously perceived in any single reading of the poem. And they are. That is the point: the phonetic coherence of "Now winter nights enlarge" is extremely complicated; at the same time, it is all but unnoticeable. When I say "unnoticeable" I do not mean to imply that the patterns of sound texture I isolate here—patterns that for the most part call little or no attention to themselves—are aesthetically inefficacious. On the contrary, as I said in the Preface, unnoticed effects are generally more effective than noticed ones. Consider the warp and woof of a bright tapestry. When we view it we do not try to distinguish between the separate red and yellow and green strands, we simply step back and watch the scene shine. Similarly, if Campion has always been praised for the "music" of his verse, his *"eare-pleasing rimes,"* I submit that what people have liked is that in the closely knit, multi-cohesive phonetic systems of his poems each and every thread is connected to so many others in so many ways. Campion's poems sound good because they are made, like this one, with everything in them sounding its own identity *and* like something else. The overall effect is literally symphonic. Moreover, while no one of these patterns distinguishes itself individually and while no reader, even one primed on the following anatomization, could possibly apprehend all of them in any single reading, the fact of their demonstrably harmonious presence suggests the reason why Campion's most admired songs sound so inevitably right. They sound right because everything in them fits together in a multitude of different, simultaneous and urgently unobtrusive relationships. Indeed, one indication of Campion's artistic brilliance is the degree to which the genuine complexity of his songs appears to be genuine simplicity. This song in particular seems to be simple because its assertions are for the most part just cliché evocations of cliché emblems of winter pleasures. Furthermore, because there is nothing in the song that is not in some way related to what has come before, everything that is said sounds—literally *sounds*—familiar. And yet, even without its music, "Now winter nights enlarge" persuades one of its coherence and that what it said—what it had to tell us—was worth hearing.

The simplest and most efficient way of demonstrating the overall phonetic coherence of "Now winter nights enlarge" will be to list—*exhaustively*—and describe patterns of words linked in different ways by their different phonetic similarities. There are two advantages to this dry and admittedly inhumane method: first, it allows me to point out the poem's most important recurring sound patterns quickly and with a minimum of verbal clutter; second, it will allow the reader to skip ahead once he has my point. Here then, again, are the words of *The Third Booke of Ayres,* XII:

> Now winter nights enlarge
>   The number of their houres,
> And clouds their stormes discharge
>   Upon the ayrie towres;
> Let now the chimneys blaze
>   And cups o'erflow with wine,
> Let well-tun'd words amaze
>   With harmonie divine.
> Now yellow waxen lights
>   Shall waite on hunny Love,
> While youthfull Revels, Masks, and Courtly sights,
>   Sleepes leaden spels remove.
>
> This time doth well dispence
>   With lovers long discourse;
> Much speech hath some defence,
>   Though beauty no remorse.
> All doe not all things well:
>   Some measures comely tread,
> Some knotted Ridles tell,
>   Some Poems smoothly read.
> The Summer hath his joyes,
>   And Winter his delights;
> Though Love and all his pleasures are but toyes,
>   They shorten tedious nights.

Several sounds repeat over the whole poem: the *au* diphthong in *Now* (line 1), *houres* (2), *clouds* (3), *towres* (4), *now* (5), and *Now* (9);

short vowel-plus-m/n in *winter* (1), *enlarge* (1), *number* (2), *And* (3), *Upon* (4), *And* (6), *amaze* (7), *harmonie* (8), *waxen* (9), *on* (10), *hunny* (10), *and* (11), *leaden* (12), *dispence* (13), *some* (15), *defence* (15), *Some* (18), *comely* (18), *Some* (19), *Some* (20), *Poems* (20), *Summer* (21), *Winter* (22), *and* (23), and *shorten* (24);

vowel-plus-*r* in *winter* (1), *enlarge* (1), *number* (2), *their* (2), *houres* (2), *their* (3), *stormes* (3), *discharge* (3), *ayrie* (4), *towres* (4), *o'erflow* (6), *harmonie* (8), *Courtly* (11), *lovers* (14), *discourse* (14), *remorse* (16), *measures* (18), *Summer* (21), *Winter* (22), *pleasures* (23), *are* (23), and *shorten* (24);

short *e* in *enlarge* (1), *Let* (5), *Let* (7), *well-* (7), *yellow* (9), *waxen* (9), *Revels* (11), *leaden* (12), *spels* (12), *well* (13), *dispence* (13), *defence* (15), *well* (17), *measures* (18), *tread* (18), *tell* (19), *Poems* (20), *pleasures* (23), and *shorten* (24);

long *e* in *ayrie* (4), *chimneys* (5), *harmonie* (8), *divine* (8), *hunny* (10), *Courtly* (11), *Sleepes* (12), *remove* (12), *speech* (15), *defence* (15), *beauty* (16), *remorse* (16), *comely* (18), *smoothly* (20), *read* (20), *delights* (22), and *tedious* (24); [1]

long *i* in *nights* (1), *wine* (6), *divine* (8), *lights* (9), *While* (11), *sights* (11), *time* (13), *delights* (22), and *nights* (24);

long *u* in *-tun'd* (7), *youthfull* (11), *remove* (12), *beauty* (16), *doe* (17), and *smoothly* (20);

short *u*—the "schwa" sound—in *The* (2), *number* (2), *of* (2), *Upon* (4), *the* (4), *the* (5), *cups* (6), *amaze* (7), *hunny* (10), *Love* (10), *youthfull* (11), *Revels* (11), *lovers* (14), *Much* (15), *some* (15), *Some* (18), *comely* (18), *Some* (19), *Some* (20), *Summer* (21), *Love* (23), and *but* (23);

various kinds of hard and soft *ch* sounds (I am assuming here that *ch*, soft *g*, *sh* and *s-zh* will sound recognizably similar) in *enlarge* (1), *discharge* (3), *chimneys* (5), *Shall* (10), *Much* (15), *speech* (15), *measures* (18), *joyes* (21), *pleasures* (23), and *shorten* (24);

various combinations of liquids in *enlarge* (1), *clouds* (3), *Let* (5), *blaze* (5), *o'erflow* (6), *Let* (7), *well-* (7), *yellow* (9), *lights* (9), *Shall* (10), *Love* (10), *While* (11), *youthfull* (11), *Revels* (11), *Courtly* (11), *Sleepes* (12), *leaden* (12), *spels* (12), *well* (13), *lovers* (14), *long* (14), *All* (17), *all* (17), *well* (17), *comely* (18), *Ridles* (19), *tell* (19), *smoothly* (20), *delights* (22), *Love* (23), *all* (23), and *pleasures* (24);

various kinds of the nasals *m* and *n* in *Now* (1), *winter* (1), *nights* (1), *enlarge* (1), *number* (2), *And* (3), *stormes* (3), *Upon*

(4), *now* (5), *chimneys* (5), *And* (6), *wine* (6), *amaze* (7), *harmonie* (8), *divine* (8), *Now* (9), *waxen* (9), *on* (10), *hunny* (10), *and* (11), *leaden* (12), *remove* (12), *time* (13), *dispence* (13), *Much* (15), *some* (15), *defence* (15), *no* (16), *remorse* (16), *not* (17), *Some* (18), *measures* (18), *comely* (18), *Some* (19), *knotted* (19), *Some* (20), *Poems* (20), *smoothly* (20), *Summer* (21), *Winter* (22), *and* (23), *shorten* (24), and *nights* (24);

various combinations of the dentals *t* and *d* in *Winter* (1), *nights* (1), *clouds* (3), *stormes* (3), *discharge* (3), *towres* (4), *Let* (5), *And* (6), *Let* (7), *-tun'd* (7), *words* (7), *divine* (8), *lights* (9), *waite* (10), *Courtly* (11), *leaden* (12), *time* (13), *doth* (13), *dispence* (13), *discourse* (14), *defence* (15), *beauty* (16), *doe* (17), *not* (17), *tread* (18), *knotted* (19), *Ridles* (19), *tell* (19), *read* (20), *Winter* (22), *delights* (22), *but* (23), *toyes* (23), *shorten* (24), *tedious* (24), and *nights* (24);

a terminal *d/t*-plus-*s* (voiced or unvoiced) in *nights* (1), *clouds* (3), *words* (7), *lights* (9), *sights* (11), *delights* (22), and *nights* (24);

voiced *s* in *houres* (2), *clouds* (3), *stormes* (3), *towres* (4), *chimneys* (5), *blaze* (5), *words* (7), *amaze* (7), *Revels* (11), *spels* (12), *lovers* (14), *things* (17), *measures* (18), *Ridles* (19), *Poems* (20), *his* (21), *joyes* (21), *his* (22), *his* (23), *pleasures* (23), and *toyes* (23);

and unvoiced *s* in *nights* (1), *discharge* (3), *cups* (6), *lights* (9), *Masks* (11), *sights* (11), *Sleepes* (12), *This* (13), *dispence* (13), *discourse* (14), *some* (15), *remorse* (16), *Some* (18), *Some* (19), *Some* (20), *smoothly* (20), *Summer* (21), *delights* (22), *tedious* (24), and *nights* (24).

Moreover, many of the patterning sounds recur in the same metrical positions in their lines. Notice, for example, the roughly similar voiced and unvoiced *s* sounds in *houres, towres, blaze, amaze, lights, sights, dispence, discourse, defence, remorse, joyes, delights, toyes* and *nights* at the ends of lines 2, 4, 5, 7, 9, 11, 13, 14, 15, 16, 21, 22, 23 and 24; the long *i* sound of *wine, divine, lights, sights, delights* and *nights* at the ends of lines 6, 8, 9, 11, 22 and 24; the short *e* sound of *dispence, defence, well, tread* and (perhaps) *read* at the ends of lines 13, 14, 17, 18, 19 and 20; and, though the sounds of vowels preceding *r* are always doubtful, the roughly similar vowel-plus-*r* pattern in *enlarge, houres, discharge* and *towres* at the end of lines 1, 2, 3 and 4.

The presence of so many non-symmetrically patterned phonetic links reaching across the poem's most clearly audible set of phonetic patterns—those determined by its formal rhyme structure—deserves some consideration. The formal rhyme scheme—ababcdcdefef, etc.—divides "Now winter nights enlarge" into six four-line units, in each of which pairs of rhyme words pull together lines that are systematically separated. Coincident with the pairing of alternate lines within quatrains, however, the informal patterns in voiced and unvoiced *s*, long *i*, short *e* and vowel-plus-*r* that occur in the rhyme syllables manifest phonetic unities not implicit in the formal rhyme scheme. As a result, they establish subtle but insistently persuasive connections between lines that do not formally rhyme, and thereby counteract not only the poem's division into separate quatrains but the separation of alternating pairs of rhyme words within those quatrains. For example, while *dispence* in line 13 and *defence* in line 15 are paired by one complex common sound, and *discourse* in line 14 and *remorse* in line 16 by another, all four words are related by their shared final sibilant. Similarly, in the fourth quatrain the abab pairing of alternate rhyme words is counteracted by the sequential aabb pairing of their first syllables by assonance (short *i*, short *i*, long *e*, long *e*). At the same time, the aaab alliterative pattern in the penultimate syllables of lines 13-16 (*d, d, d, r*) establishes yet another pattern of coherence. The entire quatrain is thus held together by a network of terminal correspondences, each system coincident with but opposing three others.[2]

The entire poem is knit together by a number of similarly incidental phonetic patterns which counteract its formal division into quatrains of alternately paired lines, and which are, if anything, even less clearly audible than the patterns listed in the paragraph above. These patterns are as follows: the long *e* sound in *ayrie, chimneys, divine, hunny, Courtly, remove, defense, remorse, comely, smoothly* and *delights* in the penultimate syllables of lines 4, 5, 8, 10, 11, 12, 15, 16, 18, 20 and 22; the voiced or unvoiced *s* sounds in *discharge, chimneys, words, dispence, discourse, things, Ridles, his* and *tedious* in the penultimate syllables of lines 3, 5, 7,

13, 14, 17, 19, 21 and 24; the vowel-plus-*r* sounds in *winter,*
number, their, o'erflow, lovers, measures, Summer and *Winter* in
the third syllables of lines 1, 2, 3, 6, 14, 18, 21 and 22 (notice also
the same sound in *ayrie* in the fourth position of line 4 and in
harmonie in the second position of line 8); the roughly similar
schwa sounds in *The, Upon, Much, Some, Some, Some* and *The* in
the first syllables of lines 2, 4, 15, 18, 19, 20 and 21; and the
roughly similar voiced or unvoiced *th* sounds in *The, With, This,*
With, Though, The, Though and *They* in the first syllables of lines
2, 8, 13, 14, 17, 21, 23 and 24.

The existence of these patterns also deserves some comment. As I
said, the informal phonetic connections here are for the most part
less noticeable than the ones that establish connections among
rhyme words that do not formally rhyme. They are less noticeable
for the simple reason that they do not involve rhyme words.[3] A
reader is not keyed to the possibility that the first or second or even
penultimate syllables in different verse-lines will exhibit any kind
of unifying phonetic likeness similar to the one he expects and
listens for in final syllables. Since he does not expect such a
possibility, he is not likely to notice a random accumulation of
initial *th* or schwa sounds even when he hears them. Since such
patterns are themselves almost entirely self-effacing, they hardly
begin to threaten the primacy of the other patterns that simultaneously compete for our conscious attention—patterns of syntax,
substance, formal rhyme, meter and so on. Consequently, they
hardly begin to interfere with a reader's comprehension of the
poem as he reads it even if he knows for a fact that they are there.
Still, it is the unnoted presence and interrelatedness of incidental
patterns like these that accounts for the aesthetic appeal of this
poem, this song, and the other Campion songs for which it stands.
Once it becomes clear that everything—every syllable—participates
in a multitude of variously overlapping phonetic patterns, nothing
in "Now winter nights enlarge" can sound *merely* incidental. Each
of these patterns is to be sure incidental; furthermore, none of them
conveys substantive meaning. Nevertheless, the collective presence
of so many separate but coincident patterns—patterns that link
words and parts of words simultaneously linked in different ways
by different patterns—is aesthetically awesome: it demonstrates the
physics and bewildering effect of what the song calls *harmonie*—in
this case a music-like phonetic harmony made for the sake of

harmony—*divine*. The paragraphs that follow outline the terms of that demonstration.

In seven of the twelve possible instances, there is a pattern of rhyme-like relationship between the beginnings of formally end-rhymed lines. In lines 1 and 3, *Now* and *clouds* are linked by assonance; in lines 2 and 4, *The number* and *Upon the* exhibit a chiasmic pairing of the two definite articles surrounding two disyllables, each of which contains a combination of *n*, schwa and plosive *p/b* sounds; *Let* and *Let* in lines 5 and 7 are identical in every way; in lines 9 and 11, although the first pair of syllables in *Now yellow* and *While youthfull* are not related phonetically, the vowel-plus *l* pattern in *yellow* is echoed in *While* and the second syllable of *youthfull*, and the second two words alliterate in *y*; *Some measures* and *Some poems* in lines 18 and 20 are connected by an anaphora-like repetition in two non-consecutive lines similar to the one in *Let* and *Let*, and the sound of *m*-plus-short *e* in *measures* is reversed and repeated in *Poems* (both words also end in voiced *s*); in lines 21 and 23, *The Summer* and *Though Love* are linked by their initial alliteration in *th* and by the recurrence of schwa in the second two words; finally, in lines 22 and 24, *And Winter* and *They shorten* again have no phonetic relation between their first syllables but their second and third syllables are related by a chiasmus in which the sounds of vowel-plus-*n* and vowel-plus-*r* in *Winter* are reversed and repeated in *shorten*[4].

At the same time, there is a persistence of rhyme-like relationships at the beginnings of lines that do not formally rhyme. In lines 1 and 2, the opening monosyllables are not linked phonetically but the following words both end in *er* and both share a pattern of vowel-plus-*m/n* whose consonant sound is itself echoed in the poem's first word (*Now winter, The number*); the utterly commonplace recurrence of the definite article—a recurrence necessitated by English syntax—makes it just short of ridiculous to point to *the* and *the* preceded by different *n* sounds in line 4 and 5 (*Upon the, Let now the*); the second word in line 7 alliterates with the first word in line 8 (*Let well, With*); the vowel-plus-*l* sound in the second syllable of line 9 is echoed in the first syllable of line 10 (*Now yellow, Shall*); in lines 10 and 11, *Shall* and *While* manifest a kind of phonetic anaphora in the repetition of vowel-plus-*l*; in lines 13 and 14, *This* and *With* manifest another anaphora-like pattern in the repetition of short *i*: there is perfect anaphora in lines 18 and

19 (*Some, Some*) and lines 19 and 20 (*Some, Some*) that is echoed, at least phonetically, in lines 20 and 21 (*Some, The Summer*); in lines 21 and 22, *The Summer* and *And Winter* are paired by a variety of phonetic as well as ideational correspondences; *Though* and *They* in lines 23 and 24 alliterate in *th*.[5]

There are also other more complex kinds of phonetic linkage among words, most of them also extremely unobtrusive. For example, ten times in twenty-four lines there is a pattern of phonetic anadisplosis, in which the final word of one line is echoed in the opening syllables of the next: *houres,/And clouds* (2-3), *towres;/Let now* (4-5), *blaze/And cups* (5-6: a recurrence of voiced and unvoiced *s*), *wine,/Let well* (6-7: alliteration in *w*), *divine/Now* (8-9: long vowel-plus-*n* reversed to *n*-plus-diphthong), *lights/Shall* (9-10), *Love,/While* (10-11), *sights,/Sleepes* (11-12), *well:/Some measures* (17-18), and *delights;/Though Love* (22-23).[6]

A less frequent pattern of phonetic epanilepsis links the beginning and end of a single verse-line by the repetition of a sound in the first word in the last word: the most clearly audible examples of this pattern occur in line 10 (*Shall . . . Love:* alliteration in *l*), line 11 (*While . . . sights*), line 13 (*This . . . dispence*) and line 17 (*All . . . well*).[7]

Finally, the manifestation of rhyme-like unity and division among elements in every system of order is also manifest on a very small scale in the contracting and expanding of different sounds in combination with one another. In these patterns of "pulsating" alliteration, a pair of sounds will occur either in one order or in the reverse order, and either together or spread apart by other intervening sounds. One such pattern involves different combinations of the dentals *t* or *d* with the nasals *m* or *n*. In line 1 the two sounds are juxtaposed in *winter*, reversed and spread apart in *winter nights*, and expanded in *nights*. In line 3 they appear contracted in *And*, reversed and expanded in *stormes*, then again expanded in *stormes discharge*. In line 4, *Upon the ayrie towres, n* and *t* are separated by three syllables and three word divisions; in the next line the same sounds in reverse order are separated only by a word division (*Let now*). Nasal and dental are contracted in *And* (6), separated by a line division and the length of one syllable in *wine,/Let* (6-7), contracted in *tun'd* (7), and reversed and expanded in *words amaze* (7). They are divided by two syllables in *divine* (8), reversed and divided by word division and the length of one syllable in *waxen lights* (9), then reversed again and brought closer together in *waite on* (10); they are reversed and contracted in *and* in line 11, and in the next line are reversed again and pulled slightly apart in *leaden*. The sounds of dental followed by nasal recur in the beginning of stanza 2 in *time* and are immediately reversed in *time doth,* where they are separated by word division but no intervening syllables. They appear again in the same order at the end of line 13, in *dispence,* and in a similar way in *defence* at the end of line 15, which reverses and expands the immediately preceding pattern of *some defence*. In line 16 *t* is divided from *n* by the length of a vowel sound and a word break in *beauty no*. The pattern occurs chiasmically in the next line, once in the phrase *doe not* and once in reverse order in the word *not*. The word *tread* in line 18 also figures in two chiasmic patterns: *comely tread,* in which *m* precedes *t* by the length of a syllable and word break, and *tread,/Some,* in which *d* precedes *m* by a line division and the length of one syllable. Similarly, the *d* in *read* (20) is first preceded by the *m* of *smoothly* and then followed in the next line by the *m* of *Summer*. *N* appears contracted with *d/t* three times in the next two lines—in *And, Winter* and again *and*. In the poem's final line the two sounds appear in a number of interlocking patterns: once split apart in *shorten,* then reversed and separated only by word division in *shorten tedious,* then reversed again and expanded in *tedious nights,* and finally reversed and pulled slightly closer together in *nights*.

At the same time, and often involving the same words as the pattern in *d/t* and *m/n,* a similar pattern recurs throughout the poem in the pulsating unification and division of *d* or *t* and voiced or unvoiced *s*. Dentals and sibilants are heard together in the examples of terminal *d/t*-plus-*s*: *nights* (1), *clouds* (3), *words* (7), *lights* (9), *sights* (11), *delights* (22) and *nights* (24). In *discharge* (3), they are separated by the sound of short *i*; the separation is more pronounced in *towres* (4), where the *s* is voiced. The two sounds appear again in *And cups* (6), separated by a word break and the length of one syllable, and again in *Courtly sights* (11), separated by one syllable and a word division. They are separated by two syllables in *defence* (15), four syllables and two word

divisions in *beauty no remorse* (16), two syllables and two word
divisions in *not all things* (17), and by only a line division in
tread,/Some (19-20). See also *dispence* (13), *discourse* (14), *Ridles*
(19), *tell,/Some* (19-20), *read./The Summer* (20-21), *Winter his*
(22), *toyes* (23), and *tedious* (24). Expanded patterns of a sibilant
preceding a dental occur in *stormes discharge* (3), where the voiced
s is separated from *t* by a word division and one syllable; *blaze/And*
(5-6), where voiced *s* is separated from *d* by a line division and one
syllable; and *Masks, and Courtly* (11), where unvoiced *s* is
separated from *t* by two syllables and two word divisions. See also
sights (11), *This time* (13), *lovers long discourse* (14), *some
defence* (15), *remorse./All doe* (16-17), *measures comely tread*
(18), *Some knotted* (19), *Ridles tell* (19), *smoothly read* (20),
joyes,/And (21-22), *his delights* (22), *pleasures are but* (23), and
tedious nights (24).

A different pattern of pulsating alliteration links words containing sibilants and liquids. The sound of *l* immediately precedes
the sound of voiced *s* in *Revels* (11), *spels* (12), and *Ridles* (19);
and *l* is divided from unvoiced *s* by only the silence of a line break in
well:/ Some (17-18), and *tell,/ Some* (19-20). An *l* sound
immediately follows the voiced *s* in *Sleepes* (12), whose final *s* is in
turn followed by *l* at the beginning of the next word, *leaden;*
similarly, voiced *s* is divided from *l* by a line break in *towres;/ Let*
(4-5), and by a word break in *lovers long* (14). Expanded patterns
of *l* preceding voiced or unvoiced *s* appear in *nights enlarge* (1),
clouds (3), *yellow waxen* (9–I am assuming here that *x* will be
pronounced as the sound of hard *c* plus barely voiced *s:*
"waksen"), *lights* (9), *Courtly sights* (11), *well dispence* (13),
lovers (14), *all things* (17), *delights* (22), *all his* (23), and *pleasures*
(24). Spread apart combinations of voiced or unvoiced *s*-plus-*l*
occur in *chimneys blaze* (5), *cups o'erflow* (6), *waxen lights* (9),
lights/ Shall (9-10), *things well* (17), *measures comely* (18),
smoothly (20, *his delights* (22), and *his pleasures* (23).

Liquids also figure in combination with the fricatives *f/v* in a
pattern which, though it appears less frequently than the pattern in
s and *l*, is nevertheless important because five of its ten occurrences
involve words that are thematically crucial. In *Love* (10), the
sounds of *l* and *v* are separated only by the vowel; the same pattern
is repeated in *lovers* (14) and *Love* (23); the order of the two

sounds is reversed and their separation increased in the phrases *lovers long* (14) and *Love and all* (23). The two sounds are contracted in *o'erflow* (6), pulled slightly apart in *youthfull* (11), reversed and separated by word break and the length of a syllable in *youthfull Revels*—where the *f* sound is voiced (*v*), reversed again and pulled closer in *Revels*, and finally again reversed and split apart in *spels remove* (12). Voiced and unvoiced fricatives appear in combination with various *r* sounds in a pattern that involves some of the same words: *number of* (2), *youthfull Revels* (11), *Revels, remove* (12), and *lovers* (14).

Different *r* sounds also appear in pulsating combinations with *l*, *m/n* and *d/t*, again often in words that figure in the patterns I have already mentioned. Separated only by a short vowel sound, *r* follows *l* in *enlarge;* the sounds are divided by two full syllables in *clouds their*, and by voiced *s* and a word break in *spels remove*. They appear in similar combinations in words that echo one another in several different ways: *lovers* in line 14 and *pleasures* in line 23; and their separation in the inexact trisyllabic rhyme pair *comely tread* and *smoothly read* is identical except for the intervening *t* of *tread*. *R* precedes *l* in *towres;/ Let, o'erflow, Revels* (echoed in *Ridles*), *Courtly, lovers long* (where the order of the two sounds reverses their order in *lovers* by itself), *measures comely* and *Winter his delights*.

Combinations of *m/n* and *r* occur more frequently. In lines 1-2 the pattern of nasal followed by *r* in *winter* is echoed closely in *number* and less closely in *enlarge*. The order of the sounds is reversed and the distance between them expanded in *houres,/ and;* they come together in *stormes*, pull apart across two syllables and a line break in *discharge/ Upon*, and then are reversed in *Upon the ayrie*. They are expanded twice in line 6, in *And cups o'erflow* and, in the reverse order, in *o'erflow with wine;* in the next clause they reappear twice in the same order, expanded in *words amaze* and contracted in the thematically crucial word *harmonie*. They also recur in the same order but with varying degrees of separation in *Revels, Masks, remove* (echoed in *remorse*) and *shorten;* they appear expanded in the reverse order in *Masks and Courtly, leaden spels remove, measures, comely tread* and its trisyllabic echo *smoothly read, knotted Ridles, Summer* and its echo *Winter*.

The pattern in *d/t* and *r* includes many of these same words. The two sounds are all but contracted in *winter* and *Winter* in lines 1 and 22, and are in fact contracted in *tread;* they come together in the reverse order in *words, Courtly* and *shorten.* Combinations of dental preceding *r* appear in *clouds their, stormes, towres, leaden spels remove, discourse, beauty no remorse* and *read./ The Summer;* reverse combinations occur in *stormes discharge, ayrie towres* and *towres;/ Let* (each of which stands in chiasmic relation to the pattern of *t*-plus-*r* in *towres* by itself), *harmonie divine, lovers long discourse* (which also reverses the pattern in *discourse* by itself), *tread* (again), *Ridles, read* and *are but.*

As well as expanding and contracting in combination with *m/n, s* and *r* sounds, the dentals *d* and *t* also figure in a pulsating pattern with one another. The pattern appears twice in line 3, the two sounds first spread widely apart in *clouds their stormes,* then reversed and brought closer in *stormes discharge.* It reappears in this order but with the sounds pulled closer together in *tun'd* in line 8, and recurs in a similar combination across a word division in *time doth* in line 13. The two sounds are reversed in *doe not* and reversed again in *tread,* which is echoed in *knotted;* they follow immediately in the opposite order in *Ridles tell.* The pattern appears once in the phrase *Winter his delights* and once in the reverse order in the word *delights* by itself; it also appears chiasmically in line 24, first pulled almost together in *tedious* and then pulled apart in the phrase *tedious nights.*

In the same way, the nasals *m* and *n* also come together and split apart throughout the poem. They first appear in line 2 in *number,* with the two sounds separated only by a short vowel. In *chimneys* (5) they are next to each other but reversed; they appear again in the same order, again separated only by a short vowel, in *harmonie* (8). They reappear in this order but more distantly spread apart in *Masks, and* (11), *some defence* (15), and *Some knotted* (19). The pattern appears in the reverse order in the phrase *no remorse* (16).[8]

The preceding analysis does not exhaust this song but it does illustrate the conclusions I have reached by analyzing more Campion songs than a reader will tolerate hearing me describe. The reader may test the validity of these conclusions against the evidence compiled in Notes 4-12 of the Appendix. What the analysis demonstrates is that a Campion song—typified in "Now winter nights enlarge"—is organized by a multitude of informal phonetic patterns operating within the parameter of its formal rhyme structure. Though each pattern has a distinct identity, no pattern is heard distinctly because the complex of sounds in any given syllable may cause it to participate in any number of different, simultaneous and equally distinct relationships. As a result, words that sound different in one frame of reference (*well*, and *tread, his* and *tedious*) may sound alike in another: pulling together and pulling apart, they are attracted and opposed at the same time. When one hears the song one shifts continually from one frame of reference to another, but there are so many different overlapping frames and, consequently, such an amazing number of shifts to be made that it becomes virtually impossible to focus upon any single pattern. While the frames can in fact be distinguished separately, as I have done, the intellectual effort required to apprehend the simultaneity of these controlled aesthetic relationships is like the effort one makes to apprehend unstructured relationships in everyday reality. The other chapters in this study, which demonstrate the presence and similar effect of simultaneous unity and division among elements in a variety of different ordering systems, indicate that the same mental agility is required throughout one's experience of "Now winter nights enlarge."

In the remainder of this chapter I will talk at some length about the song's line-by-line continuity. I want to show that each of the twenty-four verse-lines in "Now winter nights enlarge" has its own phonetic identity—even if it is only the one legislated by the placement of lines on the page and even though elements in it may simultaneously figure in various larger patterns of phonetic coherence. The point of the analysis is to demonstrate that, while a Campion line may—like any line of verse—answer the demands of several different systems of order simultaneously, a Campion line is almost invariably knit together by some identifying or identity-making cluster or clusters of sound, some thread of phonetic theme and variation of its own. The evidence I describe in the following pages in support of this assertion again comes from only one song, but I invite the reader to test its validity against the evidence of other Campion songs.[9]

Line 1, *Now winter nights enlarge*, contains a repetition of vowel-plus-*n* in *winter* and *enlarge;* coupled with the alliteration of *n* in *Now* and *nights,* the alternating pattern of *n*-plus-vowel and vowel-plus-*n* in the first and third and second and fourth words of the line establishes a kind of abab structure that ties the whole line together. This chain of paired sounds is given further cohesiveness by the fact that *n* recurs in each of its elements. But while *Now* is related to *nights* and *winter* to *enlarge* because of certain phonetic similarities, *winter* and *nights* are themselves related by a different likeness: the pattern of *nt* in *winter* repeated with variation in the spread-apart pattern of *n*-vowel-*t* in *nights*.

In line 2, *The number of their houres,* the near triplication of the short *u* sound—the schwa— in *The, num-* and *of* (the first, second and fourth syllables) gives a slight but discernible weight to the opening of the line, an effect that is itself outweighed by the even heavier concentration of vowel-plus-*r* combinations in *-ber, their* and *houres.* Thus, while the line's end obviously receives more stress than its beginning for a variety of reasons, it is nonetheless built around a kind of asymmetrical balance of sounds. The pattern of schwa in the first two syllables stands against the pattern of vowel-plus-*r* in the last two; but, since the middle two syllables (*-ber of*) reverse the alignment, the two pairs of sound clusters are also interconnected, yoked together in a way that forcibly prevents the line from splitting apart into two equal halves. Still, it is clear that the two phonetic halves of the line are not equal, nor were ever meant to be heard as evenly balanced counterparts to one another. The first of three vowel-plus-*r* units occurs in the metrically unaccented second syllable of *number* (we heard it in the same metrical position in line 1: *winter*); vowel-plus-*r* occurs again in *their,* a monosyllable which, though also metrically unaccented, is both quantitatively longer than *-ber* and rhetorically more emphatic; and it recurs once more in *houres,* the metrically accented rhyme word whose vowel is in fact a diphthong and quantitatively even longer than the vowel in *their.* This progressive lengthening of similar vowel sounds preceding *r* functions in two important ways. First, supplanting the schwa pattern in *The, num-* and *of* at the beginning of the line, its massing of sound slows the line down and so helps to bring it to an audibly satisfying close, one that is itself given further support by the completion at this point of both the syntactic unit begun in line 1 and the musical phrase to which these two lines are set. (Notice that this slowing effect is supported by the

rhythm of the line's music: ♪ ♩ ♫ ♫ ♩ ♩ .) Second,

The num-ber   of   their houres.

the progressive lengthening of vowel sounds preceding *r* suggests the substance of lines 1 and 2: the increasing number of winter night hours is manifest in the increasing duration of the words used to describe it.

Line 3, *And clouds their stormes discharge*, repeats some of the sounds that have occurred in the preceding two lines: *clouds* echoes *Now* in line 1, *their* duplicates *their* in line 2 and more distantly echoes the sounds of vowel-plus-*r* in *winter, enlarge, number* and *discharge*. The echo of *Now* in *clouds* is the poem's first instance of an informal phonetic connection at the beginning of end-rhymed lines. It parallels the formal rhyme pairing of *enlarge* and *discharge*, and one of its effects is to suggest the missing but implied syntax of line 3 (*And* [now] *clouds*). Notice that the phonetic likeness and difference of *Now* and *clouds* is also echoed musically: *Now* is set to the root, G, and *clouds* to the fourth, C. This kind of coincidence of harmonies in different systems of organization gives a sense of the song's overall coherence, a sense of balance and symmetry that is confirmed by what we hear in line 3 by itself. In line 3 the second and penultimate syllables are drawn together by the *ds* sound in *clouds* repeated in the expanded combination of *d*-vowel-*s* in *discharge*. Standing between *clouds* and *discharge*, the two middle syllables of line 3, *their stormes*, are connected both syntactically and by a shared pattern of vowel-plus-*r*, a phonetic unity whose repetition with variation in *-charge* works to integrate the end of the line with its center. (Notice that the descending scale of vowel sounds preceding *r* in *their, stormes* and *discharge*[10] are themselves set to a descending melodic progression:

And while the line's second syllable, *clouds,* is related to its second to last, *dis-*, by the pulsating repetition of *d* and *s* sounds, *clouds* and *stormes* are themselves related not only by syntax and logic but by their terminal voiced *s* sounds and by a reordering of the dental-plus-*s* conjunction at the end of *clouds* in the initial *s*-plus dental conjunction in *stormes*. Similarly, *stormes* and *discharge* are identified both by their vowel-plus-*r* patterns and by a suggestion of the initial *s*-dental consonance in *stormes* at the juncture of syllables in *discharge*. Finally, these several instances of phonetic relationships between syllables at different points in the line—relationships that in effect span the distance between those syllables and so tie the line together in several ways at once—are given a final barely audible variation in the phonetic unity and division of *-charge*, whose initial *ch* sound is distantly echoed in its final soft *g*.

The last syllable in line 3 slides easily into the opening of the next line, *Upon the ayrie towres:* in the enjambment *-charge/ Up-* one hears the complex sound of "charge" first by itself and then elided with the following syllable—"jup." A similar elision immediately recurs between the two syllables of *Upon:* the word is naturally divided into *Up-* and *-on,* but the plosive *p* is in effect proclitic, so that what one actually hears is "U-pon." This detail would not be worth mentioning were it not that the sound of *U-* by itself is so closely followed by and parallel to the sound of the line's second word, *the.* Since schwa is the commonest sound in the language and since the definite article is the commonest word, let me assure the reader that in pointing out this effect I do not mean to confuse what *is* with what is *unusual.* The force of *Up-* or *the* taken separately is negligible on every count, but their proximity and phonetic likeness is another subtle instance of the way Campion couples similar sounds. Moreover, since this particular coupling occurs at the beginning of the line and since its schwa is the same sound that appeared in *The, num-* and *of* in line 2, this effect, however slight, becomes remarkable: the unification of line 1 with line 3 and line 2 with line 4 by a formal end-rhyme pairing of *enlarge/ discharge* and *houres/towres* is matched and reiterated by the informal congruences of *Now/clouds* and *The, num-, of/Up-, the* at the beginnings of these lines. A similar but more clearly audible phonetic coupling takes place in *ayrie* and *towres,* whose vowel-plus-*r* sounds continue the pattern in vowel-plus-*r* that has already occurred at least twice in each of lines 1-3. Furthermore, the probably exact rhyming of *their, their* and *ayre-* in lines 2, 3 and 4 pulls the middle of those three lines together the way other phonetic likenesses pair the beginnings and ends of lines 1 and 3 and lines 2 and 4. At the same time, the repetition of the assonance in *Now, houres* and *clouds* in *towres* not only completes the formal b rhyme of lines 2 and 4 but laces the whole quatrain together with what in visual terms appears as a kind of zigzag stitch that runs from the beginning of line 1 to the end of line 2 to the beginning of line 3 to the end of line 4.

Line 5, *Let now the chimneys blaze,* is sung to the same music as line 1; it also repeats certain key sounds from the first quatrain. It therefore demonstrates the operation of several separate but coincident systems of coherence: *Let* (line 5) is like *Now (1)* because it is set to the same note; *now* (5) is identical to *Now* (1);

now (5) is set to the same note, B, on which musical section A concluded; *now* (5) echoes the vowel sound of *towres*, the last word in quatrain 1; *Let now* (5) follows *towres* in the same way that *And clouds* (3) followed *houres*. Thus, though one has not heard line 5 before, the sound of the word *now*, its setting and the word itself are in several ways familiar. If somewhat less resonant, the phonetic parallelisms between *the chimneys* and *the ayrie* in the same metrical position of line 4 is equally effective in giving a sense of the poem's overall coherence. (Notice that the multiple similarities between these two pairs of words is counteracted by their grammatical difference: *ayrie* is an adjective, *chimneys* a noun.) There is a similar sense of unity in the verb *blaze* at the end of line 5, which repeats the voiced *s* sound of *houres, clouds, stormes, towres* and *chimneys* (all nouns). Finally, matching the rhyme-like relation of vowel-plus-*n* patterns in the second and penultimate syllables of line 1 (*win-* and *en-*), *now* and *-neys* relate to one another contrapuntally: *now* is stressed by verse meter and *-neys* is not, but while the musical duration of *now* (set to a dotted quarter-note) is longer than that of *-neys* (set to two eighths), the natural speech duration of *-neys* is longer than that of *now*.

In line 6, *And cups o'erflow with wine*, *And cups* (*And c–s*) echoes *And clouds* (*And c–s*) at the beginning of line 3. Its unvoiced *s* also echoes the voiced *s* in *blaze* at the end of line 5, thus providing phonetic linkage between lines. Notice that *cups* and the metrically and melodically corresponding syllable in line 2, *num-*, are also coupled by assonance. Similar but more striking congruences are heard in *o'erflow*, whose first syllable picks up the vowel-plus-*r* pattern running through the first stanza (it matches the *or* sound in *stormes* exactly) and whose two syllables are set to a descending series of eighth-notes-high G, F sharp, E, D–which audibly represent the meaning of "overflow." This four-note series first occurred as the setting of *-ber of* in line 2, the first syllable of which shares the vowel-plus-*r* sound of *o'er-* and the second of which shares the *f/v* sound of *-flow*. In the same way, and equally unnoticed, the alliteration in *with wine* at the end of line 6 corresponds both to the repetition of *r* sounds at the end of line 2 (*their houres*, also set to the same notes) and to the repetition of terminal voiced *s* sounds at the end of line 5 (*-neys blaze*). While none of these three lines rhyme formally, they are thus related by the different harmonies between the final two syllables in each.

In line 7, *Let well-tun'd words amaze,* there are further examples of multiple phonetic linking. Because *Let* is also the first word of line 5, the formal *blaze/amaze* pairing at the end of the two lines is again reinforced by anaphora. The identity of *Let* and *Let,* contrasting with the initial off-rhyme pairing of lines 1 with 3 and lines 2 with 4, makes this third consecutive instance of informal rhyme at the beginnings of lines that also rhyme formally even more remarkable. The second syllable of line 7 is a phonetic variant of the first (*l*-plus-short *e* in *Let* reverses the sound in *well*[11]); notice also that the first letter of the following syllable, *-tun'd,* creates for an instant an *elt* sound that is itself a phonetic anagram of *Let.* Moreover, because *well-* picks up the alliteration of *with wine* at the end of line 6, and because the alliterative pairing of those two words is itself like the assonant pairing of *Let well-,* the juncture of lines 6-7 manifests another complex instance of phonetic ana-diplosis. The beginning and end of line 7 are also linked phonetically, not only because the pattern of dental-plus-*w* in *Let well-* is reversed to *w*-plus-dental in *words* but because the pattern of voiced *s* repeated in *words amaze* parallels the pattern of repeated assonance in *Let well-.* (I do not mean to say that the vowel sounds in *Let well-* and the consonant sounds in *words amaze* sound alike; I am merely pointing out that the patterns of repeated sounds are analogous—that the alliterations themselves alliterate.) In the same way, the alliteration of *with wine* in line 6 matches the terminal consonance of *words amaze*—again making an effective but altogether unobtrusive rhyme pair out of two lines which do not formally rhyme; similarly, since the voiced *s* consonance in *-neys blaze* duplicates that in *words amaze,* the ends of lines 5 and 7, which do rhyme formally, are doubly connected.

The last line of the quatrain, *With harmonie divine,* begins with a word that continues the alliteration in *w* that has run through the previous two lines. Following so soon after *words, With* completes yet another pattern of phonetic anadiplosis. In each of its different occurrences (lines 2-3, 4-5, 6-7 and 7-8), this pattern has had the same effect: sounds at the end of one line repeated at the beginning of the next break down the formal and syntactic boundaries between lines; as such, the pattern is a sort of phonetic syntax that works to insure the poem's line-by-line continuity. Alliteration or assonance that takes place more locally across the division not of lines but words within lines (as in *Let well, with wine, chimneys blaze, their houres* and so on) has the same common denominator in its effects: phonetic cohesion among otherwise disparate materials, unity in spite of disunity. The effect occurs in line 8 in *harmonie divine*, where long *e* in the last syllable of the first word is sounded again in the first syllable of the next.

Line 9, *Now yellow waxen lights,* begins a quatrain in which nearly all of the stanza's previous phonetic patterns are repeated in some way or another. The line opens by re-introducing sounds that began quatrains 1 and 2: *Now* duplicates the *Now* of line 1 (they are set a fifth apart, to G and D, and are accompanied by two different roots in the bass); *Now yel-* duplicates in reverse the assonance and some of the consonance of *Let now* in line 5. Because line 9 starts with the same *n* sound that closed the preceding line (*divine./Now*), it completes another pattern of phonetic anadiplosis—this time across the division not only of lines but of quatrains. The *el* pattern in the first syllable of *yellow* matches the one in *well-* in the same position of line 7; similarly, the enjambment across word division of *en*-plus-*l* in *waxen lights* at the end of the line duplicates the same pattern in the same position of line 1 in a single word, *enlarge*. Moreover, the unvoiced *s* consonance at the end of the first syllable in *waxen* and in *lights* echoes the voiced *s* consonance in *words amaze* in the same position of line 7. Finally, creating phonetic balance within the line itself, the *el* conjunction in the line's second syllable, *yel-*, recurs in the expanded *e(n)l* conjunction across word division in its last two syllables, *-en lights.*

The second line of quatrain 3, *Shall waite on hunny Love,* is balanced in two distinct ways: by the incidental repetition of *l* in its first and last syllables (notice that we also do not notice the similar epanilepsis in line 5: *Let . . . blaze*); and by the repetition of vowel-plus-*n* in its two middle syllables. Since the vowel precedes *l* in *Shall* and follows it in *Love*, a further rhyme-like symmetry informs the line. Echoing sounds from the preceding line, the pattern of *w*-plus-*h* in *waite on hunny* expands the same pattern in *with harmonie* (however, the aspirate "h" in *hunny* and *harmonie* might not have been heard in seventeenth-century pronunciation) and the thematically important phrase *hunny Love* recalls the thematically crucial phrase *harmonie divine* in several ways at once: the combination of *h*, *n* and long *e* in *hunny* condenses the same sounds spread out across *harmonie;* long *e* in the penultimate syllable of line 9, in *hunny,* repeats long *e* in the same position of line 8, in *divine;* and the vowel-plus-*v* pattern in *Love* reverses the same pattern in the second syllable of *divine.*

The aesthetic effect of line 11, *While youthfull Revels, Masks, and Courtly sights,* is extraordinarily important: with ten syllables instead of the usual six, it does not fit the trimeter pattern of the preceding ten lines. At the same time, despite its metrical irregularity, line 11 also fits; in fact, its pertinence and impertinence are both exaggerated. Though the line is recognizably pentameter, recognizably longer than any line thus far, it is integrated into the stanza because (a) it repeats sounds from the previous ten lines, (b) it suggests the expected termination after its sixth syllable, and (c) it cushions the surprise of the final four syllables by echoing sounds from its own preceding six syllables and from syllables at the ends of preceding lines. Like other lines in the stanza, line 11 is phonetically balanced in itself—primarily by the liquids in its first, third, fifth and ninth syllables, by the differing final *s* sounds in its substantively related third, fourth and last words, and by the recurrence of long *i* in *While* and *sights.* It also continues several sound patterns we have already heard. The vowel-plus-*l* in *While* both matches one in *Shall* in the same position of line 10 (giving the unity of consonance to the beginnings of lines 10 and 11) and is a chiasmic echo of *l*-plus-vowel in *Love* at the end of line 10, again providing phonetic linkage between lines. Furthermore, *While* continues an alliterative thread in *w* that has at this point run through six consecutive lines. Other sounds from the preceding lines are contracted and expanded in the next three words— *youthfull, Revels* and *Masks.* [12] As I have suggested, the special aesthetic value of line 11 is that it both fits the poem *and* does not. *Masks* would have been the final word in a normal six-syllable line, but, even for a listener without the printed text before him, it obviously is not the last syllable in this line. It does not sound like the end of the line because it does not rhyme formally with the last word in line 9, *lights.* [13] But though the lack of formal rhyme closure in *Masks* may come as a surprise, the line's syntax is at this point also incomplete (so is its music). A listener is therefore compelled forward by the as yet unsatisfied demands of closure in several different systems simultaneously. The phrase *and Courtly sights* answers the demands both of syntax (*and* indicates that the next item will be the final one in the list) and of sound (the rhyming—ideational as well as phonetic—of *sights* with *lights*). Furthermore, as well as supplying a needed phonetic link to line 9, the phrase *and Courtly sights* is itself linked phonetically to the rest of line 11: the assonance in *Masks, and* provides continuity between the line's first six syllables and its last four; that bond is asserted again in the repetition in *Courtly* of the *l* sounds in *youthfull* and *Revels;* it is reasserted in a repetition of the line's initial vowel sound in *sights,* which, also echoing the *s* in *Masks* echoes a host of other *s* sounds at the ends of previous formal rhyme words. At the same time, with no clear and independent phonetic identity of its own, there is nothing in the phrase *and Courtly sights* to cause it to split apart phonetically from the preceding six syllables of line 11. The line thus persuades us that it belongs with lines 1 through 10 even though it clearly does not.

Line 11 is also strongly tied to the sounds of the next line, *Sleepes leaden spels remove.* The ideational opposition between *Sleepes* and *sights* is counteracted phonetically because both words begin and end with unvoiced *s;* the pattern of *l*-plus-long *e* in *Sleepes* duplicates the same pattern in *Courtly;*[14] the initial *sl* in Sleepes contracts and reverses the order of the same two sounds split apart in *Coutly sights* and in *lights.* But the single most obvious phonetic correlation between lines 11 and 12 is a repetition of the *els* sound of *Revels* in *spels,* which, since it is metrically stressed, again intensifies the rhyme. This correlation also partakes of several others: *spels* by itself echoes the vowel-plus-*l* patterns of *While* and *youthfull* in line 11; *leaden spels,* which connotes a kind of drugged unconsciousness, is identified by its recurrence of short *e* sounds with *Revels,* with opposite connotations of light-hearted festivity (notice that it also spreads out the *le-el* pattern in *Let well-*); at the same time, *leaden* by itself reverses the *el* sound in *Revels.* The *r-m* sequence in *Revels, Masks* is in turn contracted in the next word of line 12, *remove,* in which the *v* of *Revels* also recurs. The imperfect—at least for a modern reader—rhyming of *remove* with *Love* in line 10 is made more sufficient because long *e* in the penultimate syllable of line 10 (*hunny Love*) is echoed in the first syllable of *remove* (making the rhyme disyllabic); in the second syllable of *remove* we also hear the long *u* sound of *youthfull.* Furthermore, as the preceding line was knit together by the repetition of four different *l* sounds, *l* also occurs in a variety of related combinations in the first three words of line 12. The conjunction of *ls* in *spels* recurs chiasmically in the *sl* of *Sleepes* and occurs again in elongated form in the *l* of *sl* and the final *s* of *Sleepes;* the *sl* combination in *Sleepes* is in turn repeated, stretched across word division in *Sleepes leaden,* and then is further expanded in *spels.* The phonetic relations between *Sleepes* and *spels*—words also identified by substance—are thus numerous and highly complex: both words begin and end with *s; sl* at the beginning of one opposes *ls* at the end of the other; *l*-vowel-*p* in the middle of *Sleepes* inverts *p*-vowel-*l* in *spels; ps* at the end of *Sleepes* simultaneously stands against the initial *sp* of *spels* (which itself joins the first *s*-plus-*p* of *Sleepes*) and pulls together its final *p-el-s.* In effect, concentrating patterns that have recurred in nearly every line thus far, the harmonious interrelation of *s, p, l* and *e* sounds in line 12 summarizes the phonetic whole of the first stanza, brings it to an audibly resonant and recognizable close.

The first line of stanza 2, *This time doth well dispence,* is knit together by four different phonetic pairings: short *i*-plus-*s* in *This* and *dis-, th* in *This* and *doth, d* at the beginning of *doth* and *dispense,* and short *e* in *well* and *dispence.* Unlike eight of the preceding twelve lines, it is not tied phonetically to the end of the line before it. While the lack of immediate phonetic continuity is appropriate to the division between stanzas, line 13 nonetheless echoes line 12 in many ways. In fact, the phonetic connection between these two lines is vigorous—primarily because of the recurrence of *s, p, e, l* and *n* sounds in the phrases *leaden spels* and *well dispence.* Various short *e* sounds occur five times in these six syllables. Furthermore, the *el* in *well* reproduces the one in *spels* and inverts the same pattern in *leaden.* At the same time, *dispence* echoes the *en* in *leaden,* and its *s-p-s* sequence echoes the similar but differently proportioned *s-p-s* sequence in both *Sleeps* and *spels.* Finally, both phrases juxtapose *en* and *sp* sounds, but the arrangement of those sounds in *leaden spels* is reversed and contracted in *dispence.* Matched only by the song's mirror-like musical settings of lines 12 and 13, the number and variety of phonetic correspondences between these two small groups of words acts as a kind of acoustic cement by which the poem's two stanzas are set firmly together.

Line 14, *With lovers long discourse,* is linked to the preceding line by its penultimate syllable and by its final *s* sound. More noticeable than anything like it thus far, the attraction of *dispence* and *discourse* across the pattern set up by an alternating rhyme scheme is made considerably stronger by other informal phonetic relations between the two lines. For one thing, the pattern of short *i*-plus-*th* in *With* occurs chiasmically in *this*—the first word in line 13; the echo is underscored musically because both words are set to high G. *With* is also connected by alliteration to *well*, by its short *i* to *dispence*, and by its final *th* to *doth*. The *w-l* sequence that occurs across a word division in *With lovers* is an expansion of the same sequence in *well;* the next word in line 14, *long*, is also linked to *well*—by the chiasmic pairing of their *l*-plus-vowel/vowel-plus-*l* sounds and by the fact that both words are set to high B. These chiasmic relations between the two lines would be less remarkable were it not for the fact that the most obvious phonetic pattern by which line 14 is itself unified is another chiasmus: the assonant coupling of *With* and *dis-* surrounds the alliterative coupling of *lovers* and *long*. Less obviously, but of equal importance in giving the line phonetic identity, the opening and closing sounds of *lovers* repeat after an appropriately elongated interval in the next phrase, *long discourse.* (Compare the *th* and *is* sounds in the preceding line—first joined together in *This*, then split apart in *doth well dispence*.)

The tongue-twisting required to enunciate the clogged sounds of line 15, *Much speech hath some defence*, suggests the "much speech" it talks about. The line's phonetic identity is complex. Two ideationally related but opposed adjectives are linked by the chiasmic pattern of their *m*-plus-schwa and schwa-plus-*m* sounds. This pattern encloses a pair of terminal *ch* sounds in *Much* and *speech* (contrast the pair of initial *l* sounds in the preceding line: *lovers long*) and the combination of sounds in *Much* is at the same time reversed and spread apart in *speech hath some*. Ordering the line in a different way, the *m, ch, ch, m* chiasmic sequence in these four words is overlayed by the alternating sequence of *s, e, s, e* in *speech hath some defence*. Since the line also echoes a variety of earlier *m, sp, th* and schwa sounds, it is at once whole and wholly implicated in the phonetic network that precedes it.

Line 16, *Though beauty no remorse*, is unified by a different sequence of alternating sounds: the pattern in long *o, e, o, e*. It is also tied to the preceding line by the assonance of its penultimate syllable and its final voiced *s*, thus repeating the pattern of the informal rhyming of lines 13 and 14 (*dis-/dis-, de-/re-*). Although

long *e* has already occurred in the penultimate syllables of seven
lines, two of those instances are especially relevant here: *remorse*
duplicates exactly the *re-m* conjunction across syllabic boundary in
remove in line 12; and, set to exactly the same notes, it also pulls
apart the pattern of long *e*-plus-*s* (voiced rather than unvoiced) in
ayrie towres in line 4. In contrast to this parallel ordering of like
sounds, one of the numerous vowel-plus-*r* patterns which *remorse*
echoes occurs in *Courtly,* where a pattern of vowel preceding *r* in
one syllable followed by long *e* in the next (again penultimate)
exactly reverses the arrangement of the vowel sounds in *remorse*.
Similarly, in *beauty* the syllabification of long *u* followed by long *e*
inverts the pattern of long *e* and a different but very similar *u* sound
in *remove*—which thus participates in two separate complex
phonetic relationships with line 16. The long *u* in *beauty* also
underscores important ideational connections between that word
and *youthfull* and *well-tun'd*.

The first line of the next quatrain, *All doe not all things well,* is
punctuated with vowel-plus-*l* combinations, and that punctuation
insists that the line has independent phonetic identity. Though they
clearly echo sounds from previous lines, the *l* sounds in its first and
last syllables enclose the line and work to isolate it, make it a kind
of island cut off from the sounds which precede and follow it. This
phonetic isolation corresponds to the syntactic and ideational
separateness of line 17: beginning a new quatrain, it also opens a
new and general train of thought. If the triplication of *l* in *All, all*
and *well* is the poem's most clearly audible example of one sound
permeating and unifying an entire line, it still resembles the less
exact recurrence of three vowel-plus-*l* combinations in line 11
(*While youthfull Revels*) and three vowel-plus-*r* combinations in
line 2 (*number of their houres*). The difference between those lines
and line 17 in this regard is that their subtlety depended upon a
dissimilarity of similar elements within the unifying pattern,
whereas in line 17 those elements are almost identical. Almost but
not quite, since the variation from *All, all* to *well* in the end gives the
line just enough phonetic asymmetry to keep the pattern from
becoming merely perfect. Instead, its harmonious mixture of
agreement and disagreement offers as clear and simple an il-
lustration of the rhyme principle and its physics as one could ask:
All and *well* are alike; they are also different; pulling together and
pulling apart, they are attracted and opposed at the same time. The

strong but strongly imperfect identity of *All/all* and *well* gives to
line 17 a pleasing and dynamic proportion—one that in fact
complements the physics of the distinction expressed in a substance
in which *All* is set against *not all*. At the same time, the vowel
sequence in the words *All, not* and *all* orders the line's sounds in a
different way—one that conflicts with and disrupts the more
noticeable pattern of liquids in *All, all, well*. Since *all* sounds in one
way as much like *not* as in another like *well*, it actually participates
in two sets of similar relations, neither of which may be said to take
precedence over the other. The emphasis of formal rhyme given to
the *All, all, well* triplet is counteracted both by the symmetry of *all,
not, all* and by the fact that this triplet is the first to be completed:
again we have a line whose simple sound patterns are, quite simply,
complex. Notice also that the disruption of perfect symmetry in the
sequence *All, all, well* has as its counterpart the now completed
triplication of *well, well* and *well* in lines 7, 13 and 17. (Though the
identity of this sequence is not as urgently insistent as the less exact
identity of the other, it is more important thematically: "Now
winter nights enlarge" is, after all, about doing things "well"
—about suiting one's thought and action to the occasion, that
present here and *Now . . . now . . . Now* set down in its first three
quatrains.

A grosser triplication is begun and completed in the anaphora in
Some in the next three lines:

> Some measures comely tread,
> Some knotted Ridles tell,
> Some Poems smoothly read.

I talked in the last chapter about how lines 18-20 stand together as
a complex ideational and syntactic unit following from but coupled
to the general statement of line 17. This unity in several other of the
poem's orders is further complicated by the multiplicity of informal
relations among the rhyme words in lines 17-20. For one thing, the
assonance in *well, tread* and *tell* counteracts the abab division of
the rhyme scheme; so does the initial *t* in *tread* and *tell*. The inexact
rhyming of *tread* and *read* is on the other hand counteracted by the
recurrence of *r* and *d* at similar points in both words; at the same
time, it is underscored by the fact that *tread* begins with a dental
and *read* does not. Since *tell*, the second "a" rhyme word, begins
with the same dental, there is at least one good reason to make

another sub-grouping of the lines–*tread/tell/read*–which corresponds exactly to their grouping by the repetition of *Some/Some/Some*. There are two other reasons for including *tell* in the *tread/read* group: all three are verbs, and *tell* and *read* are themselves ideational rhymes, both referring to verbal communication. And yet, despite the imperfection of the "b" rhyme, the formal unification of *well* with *tell* and *tread* with *read* effectively counteracts any informal unification of the quatrain's final three lines; the point, again, is that "Now winter nights enlarge" is structured by a multitude of conflicting and/or congruent phonetic relationships, the physics of whose interaction is highly complex.

Other patterns of phonetic coherence identify lines 18, 19 and 20 individually. Like the line that precedes it, *Some measures comely tread* is knit together by a triplication of one consonant sound–in this case *m*–which conflicts with other simultaneous patterns in the line. The unification of *Some measures comely* by a shared *m* consonance coincides with the separate pairings of *Some* and *comely* by assonance in schwa, *measures* and *tread* by a similar short *e*, and *Some* and *measures* by their *s*-vowel-*m*/*m*-vowel-*s* chiasmus. This last grouping extends further, since the final *s* in *measures* is itself joined across word division and an initial *c* to the vowel-plus-*m* sound in *comely*. The *s*-schwa-*m* pattern in *Some* is therefore matched by similar vowel and *s* sounds pulled apart and repeated in *measures comely*, as is the initial *s, m, m, s* sequence in *Some measures* by the *m, s, s, m* sequence in *measures comely*. Again, this phonetic network involves numerous sounds from previous lines. For example, the short *e* in *measures* echoes the one in *well* in line 17, thus providing phonetic linkage between lines; the vowel-plus-*rs* pattern in the same word echoes similar patterns in the rhyme words in lines 14 and 16 (*discourse, remorse*); *Some* duplicates *some* in line 15, reverses the *m*-plus-schwa pattern in *much* in the same line, and recalls all of the sounds already echoed by those two words.

The knotted alliterations in line 19, *Some knotted Ridles tell*, suggest the line's substance. Vowel-plus-*d* in *knotted* is immediately followed by the same pattern in *Ridles; te* in *knotted* recurs in *tell; el* in *tell* inverts the pattern in the syllable that precedes it. Thus a unification of *-ted* and *tell* surrounds the separate pairings of both *-ted/Rid-* and *-les/tell*. Preceding this tight complex of sounds, *Some* and *knot-* are linked by the chiasmic patterning of a pair of similar vowel sounds enclosing a pair of nasals. *Knot-* and *not* in line 17 are in fact homonyms, and their phonetic identity (underscored musically because both are set to high C) reasserts the pun already latent in line 17: *All* "knot"–with strongly physical implications.

In the final line of the quatrain, *Some Poems smoothly read,* there is again a concentration of *s* and *m* sound. As in line 18, the basic *sm* conjunction occurs three times: once broken apart in *Some,* then contracted and reversed in *Poems,* and then contracted in *smoothly.* The *s, m, m, s, s, m* sequence thus duplicates the sequence in *Some measures comely* above. (Granting that all of these patterns are very small in their effects, as well as being unnoticed as effective or as there at all, the evidence of patterning in *s* and *m* in lines 18 and 20 should convert any reader who has not already walked out on this analysis.) In contrast to the pattern in line 19 of a separate unification of the first two and last four syllables, the grouping of *Some Poems smooth-* around the recurrence of *s, m,* and a range of *o* sounds is balanced in this line against the repetition of long *e* in *-ly read.* The phonetic unification of syllables in lines 19 and 20 are thus exactly opposite in one respect: the 2, 4 division of the first line is reversed to 4, 2 in the second. The recurrence in *read* of the vowel-plus-*d* pattern in *knotted Ridles* creates a further unity between these lines. Finally, as I suggested earlier, the identity of the penultimate syllables (*-ly*) in lines 18 and 20–an echo made even stronger by the recurrence of *m* and, less exactly, *o* in each of the preceding syllables–establishes a bond that counteracts the imperfect likeness of "tred" and "reed" by making the rhyme in these two lines trisyllabic rather than monosyllabic.

The opening of line 21, *The Summer hath his joyes,* is almost identical to the opening of lines 18, 19, and 20; almost, but not quite. In fact, *The Sum-* simultaneously asserts and denies the break in anaphora in *Some, Some, Some* and the break between quatrains. (*Summer* by itself ought to finish off the last honest sceptic who still doubts the existence of patterning in *s* and *m.*) The line has several different unities: *th* and the beginning of *The* stands against a different *th* at the end of *hath;* the schwa assonance in *The Sum-* parallels the alliterative coupling of *hath his;* that coupling in turn parallels the coupling of *his joyes* by terminal voiced *s.*

Line 21 is also pulled by an anaphora-like connection to line 22,

And Winter his delights. Winter and Summer–ideational
rhymes–are paired phonetically as well, by patterns of vowel-plus-
m/*n* in their first syllables and *er* in their last syllables. (It is curious
that the word *when*–probably pronounced "win"–does not
appear in a poem about time and winter that exploits the phonetic
likeness of *Some* and *Summer*.) In the same way, the ideational
unity but formal division of *joyes* and *delights* is also stressed
phonetically, by the fact that each is preceded by an aspirate *is* and
concludes with a similar but different *s* sound. Notice that the
internal phonetic order of line 22, while it calls little or no attention
to itself, is as variously complex as that of any line in the poem; it is
built upon the repetition of five different kinds of sound: vowel-
plus-*n* in *And* and *Winter,* short *i* in *Winter* and *his*, *s* in *his* and
delights, *t* in *Winter* and *delights*, and *d* in *And*[15] and *delights*.

Line 23, *Though Love and all his pleasure are but toyes*, is linked
formally, musically, substantively and phonetically to the penultimate line in the first stanza. Like that line, its first six syllables are
also pulled together by a series of *l* sounds: *l*-plus-vowel in *Love*, a
similar vowel-plus-*l* in *all*, *l*-plus-vowel in *plea-*. At this point,
having already heard the precedent of line 11, and with its syntax
clearly incomplete and the "a" rhyme (*joyes*) clearly unanswered, a
listener knows that line 23 will continue. And it is for this
reason–because the demands of several different systems of
organization have led us to expect the pentameter line at this point
in the stanza–that the rhyme-like identities of *his pleasures* with the
conclusions of lines 21 and 22 (*his joyes, his delights*) is so brilliant.
Contrary to everything we know to be true, this subtle but vigorous
suggestion of closure–ideational, syntactic, phonetic–momentarily persuades us that line 23 has also closed. Of course it has not,
nor are we in any way surprised to hear the next three words. In fact
they sound inevitably familiar: *are* echoes the immediately
preceding vowel-plus-*r* in *pleasures;* the *b* in *but* echoes the *p* in
pleasures (voiced and unvoiced forms of the same sound), its schwa
echoes *Love* and its *t* slides (almost before we hear it) into the *t* of
toyes; toyes in turn echoes the final voiced *s* sounds in *his pleasures*
(to which it is also coupled by syntax and substance) and delivers,
finally, the expected rhyme (*joyes*/*toyes*–itself complexly
ideational).

The *t-s* pattern in *toyes* reasserts itself throughout the poem's
final line, *They shorten tedious nights*. The *s* in *shorten* is purely

visual; coupled with *h* it sounds less a sibilant than an aspirate variation of the first *s* in *pleasures*. We first hear *t*–dwarfed by a preceding *r*–in *shorten*, then hear it again more assertively in *tedious* (compare the similarly different forms of the *t* sounds in *but toyes*). The pattern of *t* and *s* sounds enclosing a monosyllable in *toyes* is expanded in *tedious*, whose potential three syllables were probably meant to be heard as two ("teed-jus") rather than "teed-ee-us").[16] The complex of sound in the middle of *tedious* therefore echoes–faintly–the *sh* of *shorten* and the sound of the first *s* in *pleasures*; it also echoes–almost exactly–the initial consonant in *joyes*, whose connotations (as well as those of *pleasures*) are directly opposite to those of *tedious*. Finally, the division of *t-s* in *toyes* and *tedious* is contracted at the end of the poem's last word, *nights*, whose effect in duplicating the long *i*-plus-*ts* sound of its rhyme syllable is to contradict the ideational polarity of *-lights* and *nights*. (Compare the corresponding *t, s, t, s* sequences in *Winter his delights* and *tedious nights*.) These same three words are also laced together by similar pulsations in *n* and *s*–divided as the final sounds in *shorten tedious*, reversed and contracted across the word division in *tedious nights*, reversed again and separated in *nights*; and *t* and *n*–all but contracted in *shorten* (compare the pattern of dental-plus-*n* in *leaden*: same sound, same note, same point in the last line of stanza 1), reversed and contracted across the word division in *shorten tedious*, again reversed and divided in *nights*.

The tight triplex of *n, t* and *s* sounds in line 24 is matched in the poem only by the permutations in line 12 of *s, l* and *n*, whose function was to bring stanza 1 to an audibly recognizable and satisfying close. The task here is similar but more demanding. Although we can guess from the poem's substance, without the text in front of us we do not know for sure at this point that there will not be a third stanza. The cadenza-like flourish in line 24 tells us that there is not a third stanza because it tells us that not only the second stanza but the entire poem has come to an end. It does so by closing the poem's phonetic circle, by reaching back–all the way back–almost to where the poem began. The obvious sameness and difference of *shorten* and *enlarge* is underscored by the subtlety of their phonetic coupling: the initial *sh* sound in *shorten* echoes faintly the terminal consonant in *enlarge*; the vowel-plus-*r* in the first syllable of *shorten* is like a different vowel-plus-*r* in the last of *enlarge*; the identity of *-en* and *en-* is modulated phonetically by the fact that one follows and one precedes the other two patterns, and musically by the fact that one is set to the fourth and the other to the root. At the same time (their more insistent identity again modulated musically by the fact that one is set to the root and one to the fifth), *nights* duplicates *nights*. Thus, with its circle of resonant phonetic harmonies truly unbroken, "Now winter nights enlarge" sounds in conclusion as it has sounded throughout—constantly fluent, symphonic, bewildering, and right.

This chapter has been long and tedious. It is longer by far than the two stanzas that are its subject and, unfortunately, far more tedious than the pleasurable winter nights those stanzas talk about. I do not apologize for the fact that the analysis is long, however, because in order to demonstrate fully the existence and effects of the network of interrelated sound patterns in "Now winter nights enlarge" it could not have been shorter. Nor do I apologize for its tedium. As I said in the Preface, if this kind of analysis—the analysis of noises in a little poem—is to be useful and efficient it cannot at the same time be humane. I have therefore consciously and purposefully avoided the convenience of those genteel amenities that seem to characterize the more popular sorts of literary criticism. The reader who has had the patience and stamina to stay with me will have seen that, while the phonetic coherence of "Now winter nights enlarge" is exceeding complex, the principle behind it—the rhyme principle—is simple: corresponding parts in any aesthetically appealing whole are *very* likely to be at once similar and different, attracted and opposed. Despite the rigors of the analysis, my one claim for the patterns I have described is also simple: they exist. Substantively meaningless, their meaning is entirely aesthetic, entirely a matter of how a dizzying, always shifting multiplicity of sound patterns linked in different but seemingly always familiar syllabic combinations with one another conspires to bewilder—literally *amaze*—the mind of any listener who hears them. The chapter that follows—a logical counterpart to this one and just as rigorous—will take up the equally bewildering sound patterns of the notes to which we hear the well-tuned syllables in "Now winter nights enlarge" sung.

Chapter 4

"Motions of the Spheares": Music

The fact that Campion wrote songs—music as well as words—continues to pose an embarassing problem for modern readers and critics of his words only. We have known when we read Campion's words on the page that behind them lies a whole other set of ordering principles the operation of which we do not know; indeed, as I suggested in Chapter 1, the fact that Campion's music has remained "silent" has probably had something to do with the admiration his words alone have received since Bullen first printed them in *Lyrics from the Song-Books of the Elizabethan Age* in 1887. Though that admiration is deserved, the fact of our ignorance does not change the fact that Campion intended his words to be sung and heard together wth his music. In the following two chapters I plan to confront the problem directly—by focusing upon the interrelation of words and music in one Campion song, "Now winter nights enlarge," and upon a listener's experience of that interrelation.

I set out in the last chapter to dissect the verbal "music" of "Now winter nights enlarge," the music-like harmonies of syllables sounding together in a multiplicity of different but coincident phonetic relationships. In the chapter that follows I will talk about the song's music per se. I will argue what is obvious: that the notes Campion composed with and for the words of "Now winter nights enlarge"—notes according to whose direction the words were meant to be sung and heard—are, like the words, ordered and coherent in several different structures simultaneously. Specifically, I will argue that the mutually interdependent metrical, rhythmic, melodic and harmonic structures which organize the raw materials of the song's music (notes) determine a unified and whole identity that is at once genuinely simple and genuinely complex.

My purpose will be to demonstrate that a listener perceives the music as well as the words of "Now winter nights enlarge" as a multi-faceted identity of parts and patterns whose individual identities not only overlap but are literally in a constant state of flux. My general purpose will be to suggest again that the rhyme-like interaction of harmoniously fixed but (for a listener) fleeting patterns of order in Campion's music, Campion's words, and Campion's words and music together, imitates the physics of harmony and flux in the natural universe; and to suggest, consequently, how and why Campion's music is itself like the music that, in *The Fourth Booke of Ayres,* VIII, Campion attributes to Apollo—*God of Musicke*—who sings with his lute,

the motions of the Spheares,
The wondrous order of the Stars, whose course divides the yeares,
And all the Mysteries above.

Before I begin I should outline my method of procedure. In order to describe as closely as possible what a listener actually hears when he hears the words of "Now winter nights enlarge" sung, I will talk first about the overall identity of the song's music (a whole that is itself a part: it repeats for the second stanza); then about the identity of each of the two "sections" which simultaneously divide and unify the entire music (section A, the setting of quatrains 1, 2, 4 and 5; and section B, the setting of quatrains 3 and 6); then about the identities of the musical "phrases" that comprise the two sections (phrase I, the setting of lines 1-2, 5-6, 13-14 and 17-18; phrase II, the setting of lines 3-4, 7-8, 15-16 and 19-20; phrase III, the setting of lines 9-10 and 21-22; phrase IV, the setting of lines 11 and 23; and phrase V, the setting of lines 12 and 24); and finally about the interrelated identities of a network of small-scale rhythmic and melodic patterns (each consisting of only a few notes). I should also repeat and clarify what I said in the Preface about the way I treat this material. I am not a musicologist, nor do I imagine an audience of musicologists for this book. I have therefore restricted my analysis of the song's music to an analysis of the *"Cantus"* and *"Bassus"*—the voice and bass parts—first because I lack the technical competence to deal with the lute part, second out of charity—because doing so would multiply a reader's tedium in an already demanding analysis, and third because the hard-won conclusions of an analysis of the relations of the voice, bass and lute parts can be stated without an all out analysis: the interaction of the lute part with the voice and bass parts adds one more dimension to the operation of the rhyme principle in the song.

A text—modernized for purposes of analysis—of the voice and base parts of *The Third Booke of Ayres,* XII, together with the words of the first stanza, appears below.

Now win - ter nights en - large The num - ber of their
Let now the chim - neys blaze, And cups o'er - flow with

houres, And clouds their stormes dis - charge Up - on their
wine, Let well - tun'd words a - maze With har - mo -

ayr - ie towres; Now yel - low wax - en lights Shall
nie di - vine.

waite on hun - ny Love, While youth - ful Rev - els,

Masks, and Court - ly sights, Sleepes lead - en spels re - move.

Let me begin by pointing out what is obvious: that the song's entire music is repeated for the second stanza. The convention here of inserting the words of a first stanza into a musical score and of printing subsequent stanzas *en masse* below the entire score indicates clearly enough the normal practice of "strophic" setting, i.e., that each stanza be sung to the same music. But while the settings of ballads, folk songs and other forms of vocal music are invariably strophic, strophic setting as practiced by Campion and others has special historic importance: it was one of the features that distinguished the English air from the Italian and English madrigal. High-style madrigal settings always consisted either of a single stanza "through set" from beginning to end or of a single stanza divided and set as two separate madrigals;[1] air settings were, in contrast, made to serve each of a poem's several stanzas. Thus, the music for every stanza in a Campion song—whether it has two, three, four or five stanzas—is the same.[2]

The practice of using the same music for the different stanzas of a song points to an important principle of all songs of two or more stanzas. Namely, though the two stanzas of "Now winter nights enlarge" are clearly different, they are set to and accompanied by the same piece of music, and so they are also similar: unified by imperfect likeness, they "rhyme." As a result, when a listener hears the first stanza sung to a piece of music and then hears the second stanza sung to the same music repeated exactly, he will be persuaded to put the two stanzas together, to connect them and also at once to contrast them. For example, when the words *This time doth well dispence* are sung to the same notes as the words *Now winter nights enlarge,* a listener will experience their simultaneous sameness and difference: the music,

is the same, the words are different. And yet they are not, or at least not entirely. *Time* is a generalized restatement of the specification (*winter nights*) in line 1; the adverb and adjective that begin each line and qualify the circumstances described therein (*Now* and *This*) are sung to the same two notes (G and A) and are logically analogous; furthermore, the penultimate syllables in each line (*en-* and *dis-*), though sung to the same two eighth-notes (G and F), are contrasted by their nearly opposite sense—the first meaning "to bring into a certain condition" and the second "to turn out . . . to undo or reverse."[3]

The obvious similarities between rhythmic, syntactic ideational structures of the two lines suggest an important qualification to the principle that song stanzas set to the same piece of music will be paired by their non-verbal likeness: they must be paired to begin with. Suppose, for instance, that one were to ask a composer to write a setting for the words of a single stanza; he would be able to allow his music to proceed more or less as he wished, embellishing and turning it back upon itself, following only the particular suggestions of verbal sound and sense at any one point; when he came to the end of the stanza his task would be done. But if the same hypothetical composer were asked to write a strophic setting for a poem of several stanzas, he would have to couple his music not only to the formal and syntactic and ideational structures of the first stanza but to those of each stanza thereafter. Faced with such a problem, he would have to decide whether or not the given poem was in fact "settable," whether its different stanzas were similar enough to be framed by a single piece of music. (Most of the "songs" in Donne's *Songs & Sonets* were, as far as we know, never set, nor could they be with any margin of success: the structural variations from one stanza to the next are simply too great.)

Of course the perfect harmony of an exactly duplicated identity—the pairing of middle C and middle C for example—is no harmony at all. Rather, as a landscape viewed from the perspective of one eye shows no depth of field, this kind of one-dimensional congruence excludes the possibility of perceiving the tension of difference in similarity—discord in concord—that is crucial to harmony. In the same way, the correspondence between a pair of too distantly related identities—the E above middle C and the D below it, stanzas from two different poems—may not permit one to apprehend the equally important but opposite tension of similarity in difference. As Leonard B. Meyer has written:

> One of the absolute and necessary conditions for the apprehension of shape, for the perception of any relationships at all, no matter what the style, is the existence of both similarities and differences among the several stimuli which constitute the series under consideration.
> If the stimuli comprising the series cannot be

perceived as being similar in any respect whatsoever, then they will fail to cohere, to form a group or unit, and will be perceived as separate, isolated, and discrete sounds, "signifying nothing." Since contrast and comparison can exist only where there is similarity or equality of some sort, the mental impression created by such a series will be one of dispersion, not disparity; of diffusion, not divergence; of novelty, not variety.

Complete similarity, proximity, and equality of stimulation, on the other hand, will create an undifferentiated homogeniety out of which no relationships can arise because there are no separable, individual identities to be contrasted, compared, or otherwise related. There will be coexistence and constancy but not connection; uniformity and union but not unity. In short, both total segregation and total uniformity will produce sensation, but neither will be apprehended as pattern or shape.[4]

Though Meyer's statement is useful, it needs to be qualified. It would seem, for instance, that entirely "undifferentiated homogeneity" can never actually arise in any work of art—temporal or spacial—for the simple reason that no two otherwise identical elements can occur in exactly the same place at exactly the same time. Consider any song with a refrain:[5] the only distinction between lines that are systematically repeated (they occur at different temporal points in the song) is an essential and aesthetically meaningful distinction. As a phonetic rhyme pair asserts the likeness of its two different syllables *and* their unlikeness, the exact replication of a refrain works to contradict *and* accentuate a song's formal division into stanzas. The same holds true for any song with a strophic setting, any song like "Now winter nights enlarge," in which both the unities and disunities of related but manifestly separate stanzas are underscored by the fact that one hears them sung to the same identical music.

If the musical setting of "Now winter nights enlarge" is a single whole identity that repeats for the second stanza, it is at the same time composed of two smaller identities—the musical sections—both of which also repeat. Lines 1-4 of the first stanza are set to section A (bars 1-7), which is then repeated as the setting of lines 5-8; lines 9-12 are set to section B (bars 8-16), which is then repeated together with lines 9-12. This pattern is duplicated for the

second stanza. The relation of formal verse and music structures
may be diagrammed as follows:

Quatrain	Musical Section
1	A
2	A
3	B
3	B
4	A
5	A
6	B
6	B

The diagram makes certain aesthetic implications clear. To begin
with, the coincidence of divisions between musical sections and
verse quatrains asserts the formal unity of each quatrain and each
section. Furthermore, though there is a major verbal and musical
pause after line 4 and after bar 7, and though the song continues
beyond this point, its music moves forward only by repeating itself,
by moving back. As a result, though quatrains 1 and 2 are clearly
different, they will also be at least partially the same for a listener
who hears them sung to identical music. (Notice that to a listener
who has heard only quatrains 1 and 2, "Now winter nights
enlarge" sounds *like* a song organized in four-line stanzas, each
rhyming abab and each set to a single unit of music.)[6] Similarly,
quatrains 4 and 5—sung to the same by now familiar music—will be
connected not only to each other but to the first two quatrains in the
first stanza. The effect of repeating musical section A to quatrains
1, 2, 4 and 5 is therefore analogous to the effect of repeating the
song's entire music to stanzas 1 and 2: the disunity of separate but
related verbal identities is at once asserted and denied by the fact
that they are each coupled to a single musical identity. At the same
time, the reverse is also true: the setting of two different verbal
identities to the song's entire music and the setting of four different
verbal identities to musical section A at once proves and disproves
the identity of each musical unit.

The last quatrain in each stanza presents a slightly but sig-
nificantly different case. Consider quatrain 3. Whereas a listener
hears the A section once for quatrain 1 and then again with the new

words of quatrain 2, he will hear the B section once with quatrain 3 and then once again, again with the words of quatrain 3. The effect of surprise and non-surprise in the difference between setting quatrains 1 and 2 to section A and quatrain 3 twice to section B is rhyme-like: the A and B musical sections are similar in that both recur twice in each stanza; they are also different in that in each stanza the A section repeats with new words and the B section repeats with the same words. But the repetition of the poem's third and sixth quatrains to the B section has an even more important aesthetic effect: it signals closure. Different lines set to the same repeated piece of music will tend to be unified within the whole framework of a song (as different areas of a painting are related by the colors they share); in contrast, lines and groups of lines that are themselves repeated when their music repeats will be given an emphatic, refrain-like quality that will tend both to isolate them from non-repeating lines and, crucially, to interrupt the forward progress of the stanza in which they occur. When a listener hears the music *and* the words of the third and sixth quatrains in "Now winter nights enlarge" not once but twice, he will feel a sense of inevitable finality—a sense appropriate to the end both of each stanza and of the song.

The repetition of a song's words and music together is by no means unusual. Nearly all songs (including madrigals) repeat the stanza's final couplet or quatrain together with its music.[7] However, it should be noted that Campion repeats the same music for *different* lines in his stanzas considerably more often than any of the other Elizabethan composers. In a recent article addressed to the problem of Campion's music,[8] David Greer has calculated that Campion uses the first musical section for new words in the stanza in 49 percent of the 119 songs Greer examines,[9] as compared to Dowland, Campion's closest rival, who uses the first section twice in only 22 percent of his 88 songs. But Greer's conclusion ("the overall impression one receives is that [Campion's musical repetition] is due mainly to his desire for musical simplicity and economy"), though it confirms the opinion shared by most musicologists that Campion's music is not particularly interesting or sophisticated, is typically mis-directed toward the cause rather than its aesthetic effects. Like his verse, Campion's music *is* simple and economical; within a limited framework it is also, like his verse, exceedingly complex. Moreover, the fact that musicologists have been generally indifferent toward Campion's music says something important about that music: never intended to stand by itself as a separate dimension, purely as music, it asserts its identity as part of another whole identity—the song—one whose complexity is greater by far than that of either of its parts by themselves.

If the song's entire music (which recurs twice) is divided into two musical sections (each of which recurs four times), it is also at the same time divided into five distinct musical phrases, each of which also recurs four times. These phrases are roughly analogous to prose sentences. Like sentences, they are determined by syntax—in this case a musical "syntax" of rhythm, note pitch and supporting harmony; also like sentences, they indicate divisions within the larger framework of the paragraph-like sections in which they stand. In Chapter 5 I talk in detail about the rhythmic character of these divisions; for now, suffice it to say that their aesthetic effect is remarkable: a listener hears the rhythm of "Now winter nights enlarge"—the rhythm of its music *and* the rhythm of its words—defined primarily in increments of the musical phrase.

Though the term musical "phrase" cannot be used with much exactitude, the phrases in "Now winter nights enlarge" are clearly defined. Each one is separated from the phrase that precedes and/or follows it by a quarter-note rest, and each one but the last concludes with a partial but imperfect harmonic resolution. The relation of the five phrases to quatrains, line structure and musical sections is as follows (in the interest of clarity, the diagram describes only the first stanza; the pattern of units within units in stanza 2 is the same):

Quatrain	Verse-Line	Phrase	Section
1	1-2	I	A
	3-4	II	
2	5-6	I	A
	7-8	II	
3	9-10	III	B
	11	IV	
	12	V	
3	9-10	III	B
	11	IV	
	12	V	

The diagram again makes certain aesthetic implications clear. For one thing, as the poem's two stanzas are united by their identical music and as the first two quatrains in each stanza are in turn united by their identical music, in each stanza the repetition of musical phrases I and II will unite the first and third pairs of lines and the second and fourth pairs of lines. For another, the musically-dictated repeat of the third quatrain in each stanza actually involves the repetition of three distinct musical units, one of which (phrase III) unifies the first pair of lines in each quatrain and the other two of which (phrases IV and V) divide the second pair of lines. This relation of phrase and verse-line structure indicates that, while the two musical sections assert the formal unity of the poem's individual quatrains and vice versa, each of the phrases counteracts the formal unity of the quatrain it partially sets by dividing it in ways that are at once congruent and in conflict with its division in other systems of order. The remainder of this chapter will, among other things, outline some of these effects.

Having defined the major musical identities in "Now winter nights enlarge"—the whole music (itself a part because it recurs twice), the two sections, the five phrases—and having sketched out some of the ways in which they simultaneously divide and unify the song, I want now to focus on the musical unity and division produced in "Now winter nights enlarge" on the smallest scale by the operation of a limited variety of recurring rhythmic and melodic patterns. For clarity and convenience, I will discuss these patterns of rhythm and melody in context of the song's musical phrases and the words they set. (I will comment parenthetically upon a variety of remarkable—and remarkably unobtrusive—correspondences between certain words and their notes.) I want to show both that every phrase has its own "atomic" unity, and that the entire music is unified by the network of related rhythmic and melodic patterns recurring throughout it.

Before I begin I should comment generally upon the special nature of these small-scale rhythmic and melodic patterns. Since the duration of a note of music can no more exist without its pitch than the horizontal dimension of a painting without the vertical, every note has two simultaneous identities—rhythmic and melodic. This is obvious: the first eighth-note of *Now* in line 1 is also G, the second eighth-note is A, the half-note of *houres* at the end of line 2 is D, and so on. Consequently, like the sap and bark of a tree or two sides of the same coin, the rhythmic and melodic patterns of any series of notes are isochronic and mutually dependent parts of the same thing: an organization of precisely determinable frequencies, each lasting for a certain proportionately fixed length of time. As acoustic phenomena responsible for the creation of sound texture, these atomic musical patterns are analogous to the phonetic patterns of a poem's words. Moreover, like phonetically related words or syllables, any two series of notes that share a rhythmic and/or melodic likeness may in several different ways be simultaneously attracted and opposed. For example, the opening rhythmic pattern in phrase I (♫ ♩. —the setting of the first foot[10] in lines 1, 5, 13 and 17: *Now win-, Let now,* etc.) is identical to the ♫ ♩. pattern in the middle of bar 2 (the setting of the last foot in those four lines: *enlarge, -neys blaze,* etc.), whose descending melodic pattern (G-F-E) inverts and raises the pitch of the ascending pattern in the first three notes (G-A-B). Similarly, the rhythmic pattern at the beginning of phrase II (♫ ♩ —the setting of the first foot in lines 3, 7, 15 and 19: *And clouds, And cups,* etc.) repeats, with the variation of a quarter-note for a dotted quarter, the opening pattern in phrase I, and is itself duplicated exactly in the opening rhythmic pattern of phrase IV (the setting of the first foot in lines 11 and 23: *While youth-, Though Love*), whose melodic pattern (C-D-E) exactly inverts the melody at the beginning of phrase II (E-D-C). Finally, as a patterning of elements in one system of order may assert or contradict a coexistent patterning of identical elements in a different system (*nights* in line 1 and *-lights* in line 10 sound alike but are ideationally opposed), a musical pattern may or may not harmonize with —i.e., amplify —patterns of sound and/or sense in its syllables and words. For example, there is a special appropriateness in the root-fifth melodic kinship in the setting of *Now* (the temporal adverb) and *nights* (the temporal noun) in line 1; similarly, as I mentioned in the last chapter, there is a special appropriateness in setting *o'erflow* in line 6 to a progression of descending eighth-notes (G-F sharp-E-D) which represent musically the meaning of "overflow"; on the other hand, there is a special, though purely incidental, *in*appropriateness in setting the second syllable of *yellow* in line 9 (*-low*) to the highest note in phrase IV and the next syllable (*wax-,* suggesting increase) to the lowest note in the phrase.[11]

The music of "Now winter nights enlarge" is laced together by an interlocking network of patterns like these, patterns whose basic rhythmic and melodic formulae recur again and again either exactly or with variations of note quantity and/or note pitch. In its own way, this maze of atomic musical relationships is as complex as the poem's maze of phonetic relationships. I therefore insist at the outset that my analysis of the structure of rhythm and melody in "Now winter nights enlarge" means no more to suggest that a listener will consciously apprehend each and every musical connection on his first, second or *n*th hearing of the song than my analysis of the poem's sound patterns meant to imply that a reader is conscious of the multiplicity of its ear-pleasing phonetic rhymes in any given reading of the poem. In fact, I again make no other claim for these rhythmic and melodic patterns except that they exist—and, therefore, that they operate whenever a listener hears the song whether he knows it or not. I must also insist that the intricate complexities of the two separate but coincident sound textures that I describe in this and the preceding chapter is not unusual. All music, all verse and all songs exhibit this *kind* of complexity. At the same time, because Campion's songs exhibit a particularly large amount of it, this kind of complexity—a quilt-like complexity of surface rather than depth, form rather than content, shape and pattern and design rather than abstract meaning; a music-like complexity about which literary critics and musicologists alike have had little or nothing to say—is one of the distinguishing features of Campion's art.

Phrase I—the setting of lines 1-2, 5-6, 13-14 and 17-18—is three and one-half bars long:

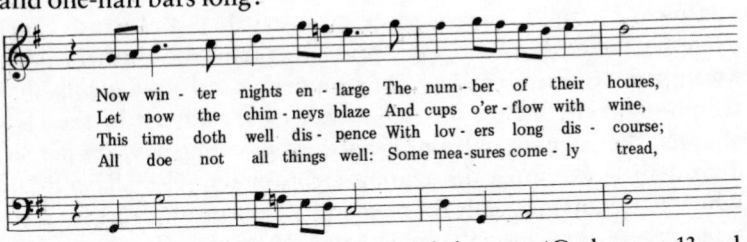

The voice part begins with a pair of eighth-notes (G, the root,[12] and A: the setting of *Now, Let, This* and *All*) and ends on a half-note (D, the fifth: the setting of *houres, wine, -course* and *tread*); the bass part, two octaves lower, also begins on G and ends on D. The partial but not final harmonic resolution on the dominant cadence here coincides with other kinds of temporary closure reached at the ends of lines 2, 6, 14 and 18. For example, the end of the phrase marks the end of one-half of a four-line formal rhyme unit; it also marks the end of the two-line syntactic unit completed in lines 2, 6 and 14; notice, however, that the unity of the phrase contradicts the syntactic independence of lines 17 and 18.

Like the lines of verse that it sets, phrase I is also unified internally. I have already pointed out how its opening rhythmic pattern in the setting of *Now win-*, etc. ♩♩ ♩. recurs exactly in the setting of *enlarge,* etc., whose descending melodic pattern inverts the ascending pattern of *Now win-*. The rhyme-like unity of these two equal but opposite patterns at the beginning and end of lines 1, 5, 13 and 17 makes the musical setting of those lines into a kind of balanced and momentarily isolated whole. This unity is complicated by the fact that the rising melody of foot 1 of the first line in each pair (G-A-B) continues to rise by whole steps in foot 2 (C-D); moreover, the melodic integrity of the initial five-note ascent from root to fifth in the voice part is itself underscored by the fact that all four syllables in *Now winter nights,* etc. are in various ways accompanied by a root in the bass. Notice that while the resonance established here by an ascending fifth in the voice and a tonic concentration in the bass is especially appropriate to the syntax of line 1 (*Now winter nights* presents the clause's subject) and to the phonetic patterning in line 17 (the identity and non-identity of *All* and *all* is variously emphasized by their root-fifth melodic settings with G and G an octave higher in the bass), it does not particularly complement the declamation of line 5 or line 13. However, the incongruence of music and verse structures in lines 5 and 13 must not be taken as a contradiction of the existence and efficiency of the congruences manifest in lines 1 and 17: a coincidence of musical energy and phonetic, syntactic and/or semantic energy can be justly said to be effective if it *is* effective; the fact that nothing special happens when *Let now the chim-* and *This time doth well* are set to the same music that underscores the syntactic unity of *Now winter nights* and the phonetic unity of *All doe not all* no more undermines the truth of my assertions about lines 1 and 17 than—say—the absence of onomatopoeia in some lines of iambic pentameter can be taken to discredit an assertion of its presence and effectiveness in other iambic pentameter lines in the same poem.[13]

Although the subdominant cadence in bar 2 (on C) is a genuine half-close, a point of momentary rest that in effect separates the first of each pair of lines set to musical phrase I from the second, other factors in the phrase work to pull both lines of each pair together. The lack of melodic resolution in the voice part (-*large*, *blaze,* etc. are set to E) drives the end of the first line onward into the beginning of the next. This coupling is made more explicit by the fact that the setting of foot 1 in the second line echoes melodically the setting of foot 3 in the first line:

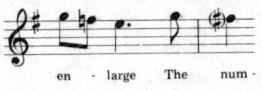

en - large   The   num -

(The melodic linkage that in effect couples the end of one verse-line to the beginning of the next—a kind of musical anadiplosis—underscores the assonance in short *i* that links lines 13-14: *dispence/With.*) Foot 1 of the second line and foot 2 of the first line are also connected musically: by their identical rhythmic patterns (♪ ♩) and related melodic patterns (the half-step descent from G to F sharp inverts and decreases the whole step ascent from C to D). Melodic continuity is maintained through foot 2 of the second line as well. The pair of eighth-notes that set the first syllable in foot 2 (G and F sharp, the G intensified by a G in the bass) duplicates the melodic pattern in foot 1, and the first three notes to which foot 2 is set (G-F sharp-E) all but duplicate the G-F-E setting of foot 3 in the first line. And, whereas that previous three-note pattern avoided harmonic closure by ending on the unstable sixth, the full setting of foot 2 in the second line descends clear to the fifth:

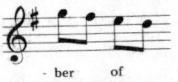

- ber   of

Nevertheless, the stability of the melodic progression here from root to fifth is contradicted rhythmically by the pattern of four eighth-notes, whose insistent instability and lack of closure again drives the music forward. I have commented on how this descending series of eighth-notes amplifies the meaning of the verb *o'erflow* in line 6; similarly, notice how the vowel-plus-*r* pattern in -*ber* (line 2), *o'er-* (6), -*ers* (14) and -*sures* (18) is subtly underscored by the identical setting of these syllables, as is the schwa pattern in *num-, cups* and *love-* in the preceding foot—all set to F sharp. Finally, the melodic pattern in foot 3 of the second line (E-D) duplicates the melody of the second syllable in foot 2, an echo that is emphasized rhythmically not only because the second E is held twice as long as the first and the second D three times as long as the first but because each foot is accompanied by a full half-note in the bass. In effect, this musical unity subtly yokes together the last three syllables in lines 2, 6, 14 and 18 (notice that the linkage is especially appropriate to the syntax and substance of -flow with wine, long discourse and comely tread), and in so doing helps to underscore the various sorts of poetic closure reached at these points.

Phrase II—the setting of lines 3-4, 7-8, 15-16 and 19-20—is also three and one-half bars long:

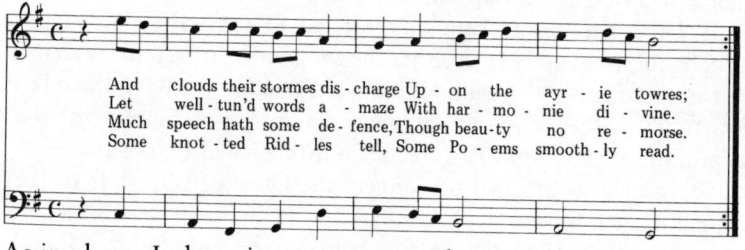

As in phrase I, the voice part opens with a pair of eighth-notes (E falling to D inverts the pattern at the start of phrase I and duplicates the pattern at the end of the phrase—thus providing melodic linkage between phrases); the bass again opens with a single quarter-note and closes with a half-note (the root). This root in the bass completes a five-note descent from the fifth: D-C-B-A-G— emphasized rhythmically by the slowing effect of B, A and G (all half-notes); the cadence underscores not only the formal verse-line unity of Upon the ayrie towres, etc. but the formal completion at this point of quatrains 1, 2, 4 and 5 and the syntactic completion of three two-line units and one one-line unit. At the same time, notice that closure in these several systems is counteracted by the melodically unresolved conclusion (on B) of the voice part—the part to which the song's words are actually sung. This incongruence of an open-ended melody and words that reach temporary, but only temporary, formal and syntactic closure is of course appropriate: the song does not stop after bar 7 but continues, its music either returning to bar 1 to begin the setting of the first half of quatrains 2 and 5, or moving on to bar 8.

The lack of melodic resolution at the end of the voice part in phrase II is structurally and aesthetically efficient in its own right. To a listener who hears the first two notes of the triad (D and B) but not the third note (G), the close of the voice part will seem urgently inconclusive. And yet, almost simultaneously, as the A section starts to repeat after lines 4 and 16, it will also seem complete: in the opening notes of phrase I we hear, however briefly, not only the root we did not hear at the end of the voice part in phrase II—the "missing" root we did hear in the final half-note in the bass—but the entire triad repeated:

The effect of this overlapping of structures is all but unnoticeable. Still, since the completion of the triad in the voice part is not synchronized exactly with either the completion of sound and sense in the quatrain or the completion of the triad in the bass, there is a knitting together of the end of one verbal and musical unit with the beginning of the next. As a result, a listener will be persuaded to divide and also at once to connect the close of phrase II to the reopening of phrase I. A similar but melodically less insistent musical link overlaps the division between the end of phrase II and the opening of phrase III, which, instead of returning to the root, outlines the elements of a triad anchored on high G:

(This connection is supported in the bass by the fact that phrase II ends on the root and phrase III begins on the root an octave higher.)

In the same way, the simultaneous unity and division of the two verse-lines in each pair of lines set by phrase II is underscored musically by the fact that phrase II is itself unified and divided by a pair of inverted triads anchored on the same G:

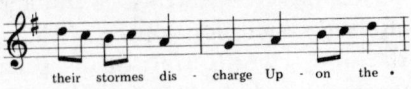

A listener hears the gradually falling triad D-B-G in the setting of the last four syllables of one line—notice that the sense of finality manifest in a perfect cadence in the voice part is counteracted by a fifth-sixth progression in the bass—and immediately hears it again in the setting of the last syllable of the first line plus the first three syllables of the second line. Like the overlapping of musical structures between the end of section A and the beginning of section A repeated, the end of one triad here is simultaneously the start of the same triad inverted, a triad whose presence and effectiveness is made all the more insistent by the fact that its melodic progression (G-A-B-C-D) duplicates the initial progression in section A.

While the unity manifest in these instances of interlocking melodic patterns is structurally and aesthetically remarkable, I should point out that the dynamics of what I am describing here are actually quite simple. What a listener hears when he hears the words *their stormes discharge Upon the* sung is a moment-by-moment intonation of syllables and parts of syllables. Like those syllables, every musical note is physically contiguous to two others—the one that precedes it and the one that follows it. Moreover, because the song's music exists in time as well as space, the temporal division between any two notes and any two rhythmic or melodic patterns is not fixed but moves as the song moves. A listener hears one note and then he hears another. He hears one pattern begin and then hears another beginning even before the first has ended. He identifies the close of one pattern only to find that it marks the opening of the next. Like a turning wheel, the end of one musical cycle becomes the beginning of the same cycle over again—and so on through the entire song, every pattern constantly changing into or growing out of some other pattern. At the same time, because these rhythmic and melodic patterns are themselves composed of a limited number of raw materials—notes of certain durations and certain pitches—the number of their potential combinations is comparatively small. Thus, inevitably, we hear versions of the same patterns used over and over again. This harmonization of musical sameness and variety corresponds to the harmonization of like and unlike patterns I describe in other of the song's organizing systems; its effect here and elsewhere is the same: though one's sense of the coherence and order of individual patterns is continually shifting, one's sense of the coherence and order of "Now winter nights enlarge" is very strong.

Like phrase I, phrase II is unified internally by a number of incidental patterning factors. The proportions of the three-note melodic descent in foot 1 of the first line (E-D-C) recur in the first three-notes of foot 2 (D-C-B); this melodic pattern is repeated exactly in the last three notes of the phrase.[14] Similarly, the rhythmic pattern in foot 1 of the first line (♫ ♩) is repeated in the

setting of foot 2-3 (♫ ♩ , ♫ ♩ , etc.); this pattern

stormes dis -   words a -

appears again in the setting of foot 1-2 in the second
line (♪♪ ♩, ♪♪ ♩ , etc.), and is repeated with variation (a half-

- on the   har - mo -

note instead of the quarter) at the end of the phrase. The quarter-
note rhythm *and* proportions of the melody in the setting of foot 3
of the first line (*discharge,* etc.) and foot 2 of the second line (*the
ayr-,* etc.) are identical. Finally, that setting of foot 2 is itself part of
the larger conclusion of phrase II—which balances a pair of rhyme-
like rhythmic and melodic progressions (B-C-D and D-C-B) around
a center point, high C:

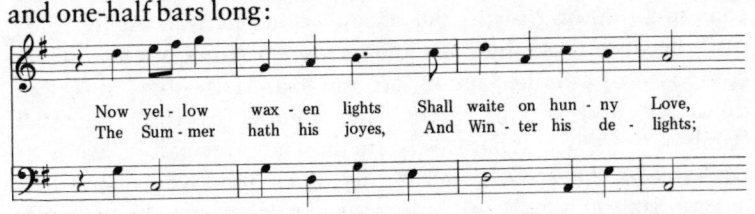

I remarked in the last chapter on how this setting encourages us to
hear long *e* in the first syllable of *divine* in line 8; at the same time,
its melodic and rhythmic unity helps to underscore the syntactic
and logical unity of the thematically important phrase *harmonie
divine;* it also complements the declamation of *beauty no remorse*
in line 16 and *Poems smoothly read* in line 20.

   Phrase III—the setting of lines 9-10 and 21-22—is once again three
and one-half bars long:

Now yel - low   wax - en   lights   Shall waite on   hun - ny   Love,
The Sum - mer   hath his   joyes,   And   Win - ter his   de - lights;

The phrase is different from phrases I and II in several important
ways. For one thing, it sets two rather than four distinct pairs of
lines; as a result, though a listener will actually hear phrase III
repeated as many times as either phrase I or phrase II, two of those
times will be accompanied by a repetition of words he has already
heard: twice sung to words that are familiar, the phrase itself will
sound doubly familiar. For another, its voice and bass parts both
conclude on the second (A) rather than on a note of the triad
(phrase I ends on the fifth in both parts, phrase II on the third in the
voice and the root in the bass); the sudden shift in harmony here
drives the music forward into the next phrase.[15] Finally, the voice
part in phrase III opens with a single quarter-note (D) instead of
two eighths. This small but compelling difference is worth some
attention.

   The initial rhythmic pattern of the notes in phrase I(♪♪ ♩.)and phrase II (♪♪ ♩) underscores in two ways the initial iambic rhythm of the lines set by those notes: first, because the rhythmic and melodic instability of the opening pair of eighth-notes in each phrase plus the rhythmic stability of the following dotted quarter-note in phrase I and the following quarter-note in phrase II emphasizes the fact that the first syllable in lines 1, 3, 5, 7, 13, 15, 17 and 19 is metrically unstressed and the second syllable is metrically stressed; second, because the accent of the musical downbeat coincides with the strong syllable of the metrical foot and the non-accent of the musical upbeat coincides with the weak syllable of the metrical foot.[16] A strictly congruent patterning of verse and musical meter here is no accident. Campion has limited himself in this song to an overall framework in which the metrical foot of the verse is, on average, covered by two beats in the music. And he does so on the simplest possible level, allowing only a short rest between pairs of lines and only the most minimal decoration, rhythmic or melodic, in the form of eighth-note groups or the dotted quarter and eighth pattern. As a result, syllables accented by verse meter are *always* set to notes that are themselves accented as either the first or the third downbeat of a four-beat measure; conversely, metrically unaccented syllables are *always* set on the unaccented second or fourth upbeats. Thus the metrical feet of the pairs of lines set by phrase I, for example, are represented musically by an alternation of ♪♪ ♩. with ♪ ♩ , until the cadence reverses the anacrustic pattern by introducing a pair of eighth-notes on the second strong beat of bar 3 followed by a steady quarter-note upbeat to give a sense of temporary conclusion:

-ber   of   their   houres.

The conformity of iambic stress patterns in two independent metrical systems insures that a listener will hear the iambic rhythm of "Now winter nights enlarge" in two ways simultaneously—once in its music and once in its words. (The effect of the imposition of a song's musical rhythm is such that if a song's music is iambic a listener will inevitably hear an iambic rhythm when he hears the song even if that rhythm is not present and clearly audible in the song's words without their music.)[17]

I have suggested that the rhythmic opening of phrase III is noticeably different from the openings of phrases I and II because it begins with a quarter-note followed by two eighths rather than the other way around (♩ ♫ rather than ♫ ♩. or ♫ ♩). The musical meter in bar 8 is still weak-strong, but it is deemphasized by a combination of factors: a steady tonic chord on the initial quarter-note upbeat; the instability of the two passing eighth-notes on the downbeat; the fact that these eighth-notes are followed by G, the highest note in the phrase, which occurs on a weak beat. These gestures are effective for several reasons. The rhythmic and melodic emphasis given to *Now* at the start of quatrain 3 helps to underscore the opening syntactic parallelism and non-parallelism of that quatrain with quatrain 1 (*Now*) and quatrain 2 (*Let now*); the unity and division of *Now, now* and *Now* is made even more pronounced by the fact that the notes to which they are set (G, B and D) form a perfect triad; the rhyming of *Now* in line 1 and *Now* in line 9 is further remarked by the fact that each is accompanied in the bass by a quarter-note G. Similarly, the melodic emphasis given to the first syllable of *Summer*[18] underscores the fact that the anaphora of *Some, Some, Some* in lines 18, 19 and 20 has been at once interrupted and not interrupted in line 21.

Something else is happening here. *Waxen lights Shall waite* in lines 9-10 and *hath his joyes, And Win-* in lines 21-22 are set to a G-A-B-C-D melodic progression identical to the one that in phrase I set *Now winter nights,*[19] etc. and also identical to the one that in the middle of phrase II set *-charge Upon the,* etc. The progression in phrase III and the one in phrase II have a particular kinship: both come in the middle of the phrase and—as identifiable units in themselves—both in effect counteract the formal division between the words in the first and second lines of each pair they set.[20] At the same time, the likeness *and* the unlikeness of all three progressions is asserted by their separate rhythms, which are both similar and recognizably distinct. The rhythmic pattern of the ascent in phrase III (♩ ♩ ♩. ♪ ♩) varies the pattern of the ascent in phrase I (♫ ♩. ♪ ♩) by substituting two quarter-notes for the initial pair of eighths and a downbeat on the first note for an upbeat; similarly, the pattern in phrase III varies the pattern in phrase II (♩ ♩ ♫ ♩) by substituting a dotted quarter for an eighth-note and a downbeat on the last note for an upbeat. Still, despite the variousness of these rhythms, because all three progressions impose the acoustics of an identical melody upon the different words they set—and because by the time a listener hears the repetition of phrase III in the second stanza he will have heard one version or another of the progression no less than ten times—the musical and, consequently, verbal identity manifest in the insistent recurrence of the G-A-B-C-D thematic thread weaves a subtle but inevitably effective pattern into the sound fabric of "Now winter nights enlarge."

Phrase IV—the setting of lines 11 and 23—is only three bars long:

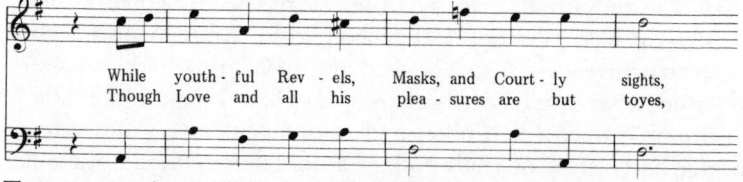

Two counts shorter than any phrase thus far and in each occurrence setting a single verse-line instead of two, the truncated formal incongruity of phrase IV corresponds in reverse to the elongated formal incongruity of the penultimate lines in each stanza. Moreover, the rhyme-like aesthetics of lines 11 and 23 without their music—they both do and do not fit the poem—are underscored by the aesthetics of their music.

The series of eight consecutive quarter-notes in bars 12 and 13 is quite unlike anything else in the song. In effect, its absolute rhythmic regularity emhasizes the formal incongruity both of phrase IV and of the lines it sets. By previous indication, these lines should stop after their sixth syllables (*Masks* and *plea-*) and phrase IV should continue for another two counts after *sights* and *toyes*. Urged to expect verbal closure, we are denied it; urged to expect musical continuation, we are brought up short by the premature closure on D. At the same time, while the conclusion of phrase IV on the D of *sights* is surprising in context of phrases I-III,[21] it is not surprising in context of the internal melodic patterning of phrase IV—primarily because in both the voice and bass parts the tonal center of phrase IV is the fifth, D. A listener hears D in both parts on *Masks* and *plea-*, syllables that would normally have ended the first verse-line of a two-line pair; moreover, because D in the bass is a half-note, there is actually a stronger sense of closure here than at the mid-point of either phrase II or III. When the fifth is repeated in both parts on *sights* and *toyes*—completing circular patterns of D-F-E-E-D in the voice and D-A-A-D in the bass—the conclusion sounds, at least temporarily, right. (Notice that the conclusion of phrase IV on this relatively stable dominant cadence at once asserts and denies the syntactic and logical incompleteness of lines 11 and 23.)

Despite its formal non-conformity, phrase IV is linked in various rhyme-like relationships to phrases I, II and III. As in phrase I, the voice part in phrase IV begins with a pair of rising eighth-notes (C and D instead of G and A—one note of the triad sounded in each case) and ends on the fifth, a half-note, preceded by a quarter-note E; like the bass in phrase I, the bass part in phrase IV also begins with an octave leap (A to A instead of G to G), also marks the sixth syllable (what would have been the end of lines 11 and 23 were they "normal") with a half-note, and also concludes on the fifth (a dotted half instead of a half-note.) The initial rhythmic and melodic patterns in the voice part of phrase IV (♪♪ ♩ , C-D-E) are, respectively, identical and opposite to those in phrase II (♪♪ ♩ , E-D-C), whose penultimate note in the bass is also A (a half-note that falls to the root instead of a quarter-note that rises to the fifth). Finally, phrase IV is linked by a sort of anadiplosis to phrase III: the quarter-note A that begins its bass part repeats with variation the A that concludes the bass in phrase III (a half-note).

Phrase V—the setting of lines 12 and 24—is two counts shorter than phrase IV, is in fact nearly half the length of phrases I, II and III:

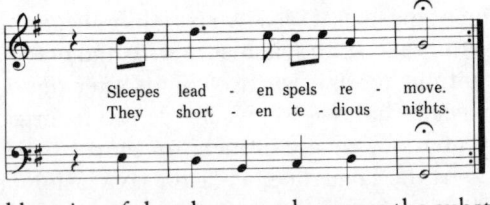

The spirited brevity of the phrase underscores the substance of the lines it sets. At the same time, the phrase reasserts the musical character of phrases I and II, and provides a handsome resolution to the tension produced by a relatively stable dominant cadence at the end of phrase IV in conjunction with the urgent lack of syntactic and logical closure at the end of lines 11 and 23[22].

As in phrase I, the voice part in phrase V begins with a pair of rising eighth-notes followed by a dotted quarter-note, the fifth; returning so quickly to D, the phrase is yoked to the dominant cadence at the end of phrase IV, to which it is bonded as well by the

fact that in the bass there is no intervening rest between the final D
of phrase IV and the opening C of phrase V. This fusion of phrases
IV and V is aesthetically effective. It carries a listener smoothly not
only from the song's most incongruous phrase to its simplest and
most epigrammatic but from the syntactic and logical units left
dangling at the conclusion of phrase IV to their conclusions at the
end of line 12 and line 24. Everything in phrase V works in unison
to that point. The fifth that sets *lead-* and *short-* (accompanied by a
fifth in the bass) is simultaneously the last note in the phrase's
initial three-note ascent and the beginning of a six-note descent to
the root; the melodic and rhythmic patterning in the first three
notes of the phrase (B-C-D, ♫ ♩.) are inverted and duplicated in
the first three notes of that descent (D-C-B, ♩. ♫); the pair of
eighth-notes that set *Sleepes* and *They* recur identically as the pair
that set *spels* and *te-*; the fifth in the bass that accompanies the
penultimate syllables *re-* and *-dious* at once repeats the one heard
with *lead-* and *short-* and prepares for the tonic close that follows
immediately. Moreover, all of this sounds familiar: the six notes of
the cadence in phrase V (D-C-B-C-A-G) duplicate the melody, but
not rhythm, of the descent from fifth to root in bars 5 and 6. But
whereas that series of notes kept the music going, its final G not
only a conclusion but the beginning of a repetition of the song's
initial ascending fifth, this cadence lands on the tonic, gives
extended intonation to *-move* or *nights,* and stops.

   And yet it does not. Reaching its inevitable final note—G, the
sound with which it began—the music returns to the start of bar 8 to
repeat all of the B section together with the words of quatains 3 and
6. The dynamics of this return are intensified by its melodic design.
The bass part repeats the final G of phrase V an octave higher.
Beginning on D, the voice part immediately completes the same
fifth it has just fallen at the end of phrase V; rising to the root (*-low*
and *-mer*), it completes the octave; falling back to the root (*wax-*
and *hath*), it completes it again; rising in four notes to D (*waite* and
Win-), it completes the fifth again—and so on through to the final
descent to G (*-move* and *nights*). At which point, at least after
-move, the entire music is repeated for stanza 2. And even so radical
a juncture as this—the return from bar 16 to bar 1—has its own
familiar, circular logic. Beginning again on G, the final note in
phrase V, the setting of *This time doth well* inverts the falling fifth
just completed in the setting of *leaden spels remove*. At the same

time, this entire ten-note combination—the end-plus-beginning of the song's music—duplicates exactly the falling and rising melody heard in bars 5 and 6 (the settings of *their stormes discharge Upon the*, etc.). The setting of the juncture of two lines becomes the setting of the larger juncture of two stanzas. Every pattern repeats itself: each time we hear it is different, and also the same.

Like a Chinese ivory globe carved and moving in time rather than space, the music of "Now winter nights enlarge" is a music literally of spheres. The whole piece of music is itself a sphere within a sphere: it occurs once for the first stanza and then again for stanza 2. We hear a part of that whole (the A section) once with quatrain 1 and then three more times, with quatrains 2, 4 and 5; we hear another part (the B section) four more times, twice with quatrain 3 and twice with quatrain 6. Within these sections, we hear the recurrence of five identifiable phrases—phrases whose multiple similarities and dissimilarities function to unify and at the same time divide the whole. Moreover, because this entire musical system has only a limited number of terms—notes of four different durations and ten pitches—the number of possible combinations of its terms is also limited. We therefore hear variations of the same rhythmic and melodic patterns over and over again. Like different stanzas sung to the same whole piece of music and different quatrains sung to the same sections, different words and parts of words sung to these recurring patterns will sound not only different but also the same, will "rhyme." Indeed, a listener who hears the words of lines, quatrains and stanzas set to a piece of music encompassing many smaller pieces of music—atomic parts that appear and reappear in a variety of rhyming mutations—will hear the wondrous order of a highly artificial structure whose fundamental parts—words and notes—reach out to touch one another in conflicting and/or congruent relationships at nearly every point. The untiy of "Now winter nights enlarge" is more than the unity of two stanzas set to the same music or four quatrains set to one part of that music and two quatrains set to another part. It is a unity of anatomically complex and controlled proportions, a unity of multiple harmonies, multiple rhymes.

Chapter 5

"Some Poems Smoothly Read": Prosody

There is a fundamental difference between our experience of these words read aloud, *Now winter nights enlarge The number of their houres,* and these same words sung to these notes:

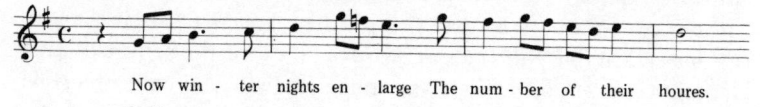

Now win - ter nights en - large The num - ber of their houres.

It is a difference, immediately perceptible to the ear, resulting from the powerfully insistent impact of music upon verse. I say *powerfully insistent* because, while people like Ralph W. Short are absolutely wrong when they claim that "whoever aims at justly appreciating [Campion's] poetry had best forget his music," they are right in feeling that when a Campion poem is sung its music invariably gets in the way of its words. It gets in the way because it imposes a musical rhythm and melody upon the rhythm and "melody" of lines of verse. Indeed, what we hear when we hear a Campion poem sung is no longer a poem but a song–words sounding the air with exactly proportionate time values and frequencies, words being "read"–smoothly read–according to a precise set of instructions composed with and for them. As a result, while a listener will in fact continue to hear the stress patterns, durations and sound textures of Campion's words when they are sung, he will hear them overlayed by, and in terms of, the analogous but urgently separable stress patterns, durations and pitches of a series of abstract notes.[1]

The following chapter is conceived of as an essay on the principles of rhythm in songs, demonstrated in the operation of those principles in "Now winter nights enlarge." I will examine the interrelation of the rhythm-producing factors in what I take to be this representative Campion song, and in so doing hope to give the reader a working understanding of their operation in all songs—an understanding he can himself apply to any song. Specifically, I will attempt to show how and why two distinct and, when taken by themselves, apparently simple rhythmic structures—one in words and one in music—operate concurrently whenever "Now winter nights enlarge" is sung to produce a single rhythm of dynamically complex but unified proportions. And, by focusing in this way upon the multi-faceted character of a Campion song's rhythm—a rhythm composed of the multiple congruences and incongruences of its rhythms, I will also be attempting to account again for how and why his songs sound as good as they do and please us as much as they do.

Though the issue of prosody is basic to the question of what we value in Campion's art, it has never been satisfactorily investigated. The issue turns out to be very complicated. I mean to discuss it with ruthless clarity; I will try to cut through all of the self-insulating jargon of literary specialists and musicologists who have preceded me in attempting to explain the subtleties of Campion's "delightful rhythmic effects" and "golden cadences." Phrases such as these simply do not help us to understand such effects. What is required instead is a doggedly specific analysis of the harmonizing components that together determine the rhythm not only of a Campion song but all songs. This chapter provides such an analysis. It will again be systematically exhaustive, not because I wish to lose whatever readers have had the patience to bear with me thus far but because an account of the interaction of elements that produce the song's rhythmic complexity should enable us to understand the prosody of songs in general and should also add final support to my thesis that the excellence of Campion's simple-seeming songs lies in the similarly complex multiplicity of their many and various orders. I therefore ask the reader to bear with me once again as I lead him through observations which from time to time may appear to be so minute as to be nugatory. I assume that, while some of the patterns and details I point to may well be incidental when taken by themselves, their cumulative effects—together with other equally incidental patterns and details in every system of order—are what have earned Campion's songs their justifiably high reputation.

Before I begin I should differentiate more precisely between the prosodic factors which operate in any song. Rhythm may be defined most simply as a structure of quantitative relations, "a form cut in to TIME."[2] Rhythmic structure is always necessarily complex, however, since it is created or established by relations not only of quantity (temporal duration) but of intensity (accent, stress). In music and in all systems of verse these primary or constitutive elements provide rhythmic structures based upon the time value of notes and syllables on the one hand, and upon the counting of stresses on the other. Furthermore, in making the distinction between rhythm and melody we recognize that pitch, though it is not an essential factor of rhythm in either music or verse, may be used together wth intensity to enforce or even to supplement a stress, and may function similarly with duration. In the same way, when either intensity or duration is the primary factor in creating rhythm, the other may operate simultaneously as an adjunct or secondary principle. (Indeed, since verse, unlike music, is an ordering of speech rather than abstract sound, the non-phonetic elements of syntax and substance may also be used for secondary rhythmic figuration, not only in the balance, parallelism, closure and so on of syntactic and semantic units but in the construction and internal divisions—commonly labelled caesurae—of lines and stanzas.) A listener will therefore apprehend the essential prosodic structure of any song as a coincidence of patterns in four primary elements (verbal stress, verbal quantity, musical stress and musical quantity) and two secondary elements (verbal pitch and musical pitch), each one supporting and/or counteracting the others within a single complex rhythm.

Though the rhythm-producing factors in any song are co-occuring, and will thus be experienced synchronically, they must be separately isolated before their mutual relations and functions can be properly understood. This will enable us to focus upon the simpler rhythmic bases that, in combination with one another, determine the rhythm of any song. In the following pages I will therefore attempt to point out the operation of each of the primary rhythmic factors in "Now winter nights enlarge" and to suggest some of the dynamics of their interaction.

The verbal meter of "Now winter nights enlarge" is so simple and obvious that it would seem to require no special analysis. This will therefore be a good place to begin an investigation of Campion's prosody. For purposes of scansion, the poem's ar-

rangement of metrically unstressed ("x") and stressed("/")
syllables in each unit of measure—or "foot"—can be described as
follows:

```
      x    /    x    /      x  /
   Now win | ter nights | enlarge
       x    /     x   /      x   /
    The num | ber of | their houres
      x    /      x    /       x  /
   And clouds | their stormes | discharge
      x /     x    /    x   /
    Upon | the ayr | ie towres
   x    /      x    /      x       /
   Let now | the chim | neys blaze
      x   /      x    /      x   /
    And cups | o'erflow | with wine
   x    /      x       /     x  /
   Let well | tun'd words | amaze
      x     /     x /      x  /
    With har | monie | divine
   x    /      x    /     x  /
   Now yel | low wax | en lights
       x     /     x   /     x   /
    Shall waite | on hun | ny love
   x      /      x   /    x   /      x    /     x   /
   While youth | ful Rev | els Masks | and Court | ly sights
        x     /     x  /     x   /
     Sleepes lead | en spels | remove

     x  /      x    /     x  /
   This time | doth well | dispense
       x   /     x   /       x   /
     With love | ers long | discourse
     x       /     x   /      x   /
   Much speech | hath some | defense
         x     /     x  /     x  /
      Though beau | ty no | remorse
   x   /      x  /       x   /
   All doe | not all | things well
```

```
      x    /      x    /     x    /
  Some mea  |  sures come  |  ly tread
    x   /      x    /     x   /
  Some knot  |  ted Rid  |  les tell
    x   /      x     /      x   /
  Some Po  |  ems smooth  |  ly read
   x    /      x    /      x   /
  The Sum  |  mer hath  |  his joyes
     x    /      x    /      x /
  And Win  |  ter his  |  delights
    x     /      x   /    x  /     x    /       x  /
  Though Love  |  and all  |  his plea  |  sures are  |  but toyes
     x    /     x /     x    /
  They short  |  en te  |  dious nights
```

This map of the poem's metrical structure reveals that Campion's choice of words and their placement in lines has guaranteed that every line will follow a perfectly regular iambic pattern in which the first syllable in each foot is unstressed and the second syllable stressed. That is, in every foot containing two monosyllables the first word is, for a variety of reasons, less emphatically pronounced than the second: *their houres* (2), *And clouds* (3), *their stormes* (3), *Let now* (5), *And cups* (6), *with wine* (6), *Shall waite* (10), *This time* (13), *doth well* (13), *Much speech* (15), *hath some* (15), *All doe* (17), *not all* (17), *things well* (17), *his joyes* (21), *Though Love* (23), *and all* (23), and *but toyes* (23).[3] At the same time, in every foot in which the first syllable of a disyllabic word is preceded by a monsyllable, that monosyllable is naturally pronounced with less intensity than the syllable which follows it: *Now win-* (1), *The num-* (2), *The ayr-* (4), *The chim-* (5), *Now yel-* (9), *on hun-* (10), *While youth-* (11), *Sleepes lead-* (12), *With lov-* (14), *Though beau-* (16), *Some mea-* (18), *Some knot-* (19), *Some po-* (20), *The Sum-* (21), *And Win-* (22), *his plea-* (23), and *They short-* (24). Also at the same time, in every foot in which the naturally unstressed syllable of a disyllabic word precedes a monosyllable, the monosyllable is more strongly accented: *-ter nights* (1), *-ber of* (2), *-ie towres* (4), *-neys blaze* (5), *-tun'd words* (7), *-en lights* (9), *-ny Love* (10), *-els Masks* (11), *-ly Sights* (11), *-en spels* (12), *-ers long* (14), *-ty no* (16), *-les tell* (19), *-ly read* (20),

-mer hath (21), *-ter his* (22), *-sures are* (23), and *-dious nights* (24).
Again, in every foot containing a disyllabic word by itself, the
disyllable is one whose second syllable is stressed in prose: *enlarge*
(1), *discharge* (3), *Upon* (4), *o'erflow* (6), *amaze* (7), *divine* (8),
remove (12), *dispense* (13), *discourse* (14), *defense* (15), *remorse*
(16), and *delights* (22).[4] Finally, this congruence of metrical and
speech stress in words of one and two syllables is preserved in the
poem's thematically crucial trisyllable, *harmonie* (8), whose
primary speech stress falls in the second position of one foot and
whose unstressed and secondarily stressed syllables comprise the
next foot.

The congruence of metrical and speech stress in these words of
one, two and three syllables is not at all surprising or unusual. A
poem's speech stress, the "natural" reading, always determines its
metrical stress-pattern, the "artificial" reading. In any regular
iambic pattern, therefore, the second word of a pair of monosyllables that fall within the boundaries of a single metrical foot
will have to be naturally pronounced with greater intensity than the
first. Similarly, disyllabic words in which the primary speech stress
falls on the second syllable will have to be contained by foot
boundaries, and those in which the primary stress falls on the first
syllable will have to be divided by foot boundaries. Like bars in
music, these boundaries between metrical feet are of course
artificial; not consciously heard in any reading of the poem, they
merely help us to describe the pattern of relative speech accents
which determines a poem's meter. (If anything is unusual about the
meter of "Now winter nights enlarge," it is that the iambic pattern
of unstress-stress in its verbal meter is so constant *and* so constantly
reinforced by the iambic pattern of upbeat-downbeat in its musical
meter.)

Having introduced the distinction between metrical and speech
stress, I should at this point examine it more closely. Meter, as I
have defined it, is the measurableness of a disposition of
stresses—an arbitrary system of values superimposed on the
syllables of a line of verse. Because the system is binary and
recognizes only relative intensity or non-intensity, any syllable in a
line will either receive an accent or it will not. When actually
spoken, however, the syllables in any line will in fact be pronounced with a variety of natural intensities. For instance, though
the second, fourth and sixth syllables in line 2 of this poem, *The*

number of their houres, are all described as carrying equal metrical stress, it is clear that the fourth, *of,* will receive less emphasis than the sixth, *houres;* similarly, in line 7, *Let well- tun'd words amaze,* the metrically unstressed syllables, *(Let, -tun'd* and *a-)* will also differ greatly in the amount of their speech emphasis—the schwa-sound of the first syllable of *amaze* less weighted than the monosyllable *Let,* and both of these considerably less weighted than *-tun'd* (which could, if the line were in prose instead of verse, carry as much speech emphasis as either of its surrounding metrically accented syllables, *well-* and *words*[5]). To scan any line of verse is thus only to approximate the actual stress profile of its syllables. For this reason, while it is perfectly true that Campion wrote lines 11 and 23 of this poem in "iambic pentameter" and the other lines in "iambic trimeter," by labelling them as such we cannot help but reduce almost to nothing the subtleties of stress variations we hear when we hear the poem read—variations we are aware of because we are aware of the metrical scheme. Thus, while any sensitive reader will, if not consciously, at last unconsciously apprehend these subtleties, to analyze them demands that we put aside the convenience of standard metrical terminology and look to the relative speech values of the syllables which it describes. And this raises the question of quantity.

Campion was himself interested in syllabic quantity. In the concluding chapter of his *Observations in the Art of English Poesie*[6] he sets down two dozen profusely illustrated "rules" governing the length of English syllables. Arguing that "we must esteeme our sillables as we speake, not as we write, for the sound of them in a verse is to be valued, and not their letters," he begins by conceding that the length of any syllable will be measured "chiefly by the accent." He then goes on to assert that *position—*"when a vowell comes before two consonants, either in one or two words"—can nevertheless make a normally short syllable long. For example, "In words of two sillables, if the last have a full and rising accent[7] that sticks long upon the voyce, the first syllable is always short, unlesse position, or the diphthong, doth make it long, as *dĕsire, prĕserve, dĕfine, prŏphane, rĕgard, mănure,* and such like"; and, echoing Gabriel Harvey's remarks on the analogous word *Carpenter,* "though we accent the second of *Trumpington* short, yet it is naturally long, and so of necessity must be held of every *composer.*" (My italics here indicate the crucial point: Campion was a composer—both of words and of music; he was keenly aware that the amount of time required to pronounce the different syllables in a line will necessarily influence our sense of that line's rhythm.)

Though valuable in themselves as a record of how he intended certain syllables to be pronounced,[8] Campion's "rules" are limited because their account of syllabic quantity is based upon the quantity measured by Latin meter, and therefore recognizes only two kinds of syllables, long and short. In fact, as Campion himself must instinctively have realized, there are subtle but significant grades of quantitative difference that distinguish the syllables in any line. The different syllables in a line will be pronounced with a variety of intensities *and* with a variety of durations. In describing these quantitative differences the terms "long" and "short" are thus only as effective as the terms "stressed" and "unstressed were in describing actual speech intensity. Though they may well approximate what we truly hear,[9] the rhythmic subtlety of most of Campion's lines is such that it cannot be described accurately by any binary system of measure. In the following discussion, therefore, I will consider the quantity of a given syllable as a relative value—not absolutely "long" or "short" but merely longer or shorter (i.e. requiring more or less time) than the particular syllables which happen to surround it.

At this point let me take up some of the ways in which the stress and quantity, the relative intensities and temporal durations of syllables in a line, can intersect. To begin with, they can be mutually supportive. In line 3 of "Now winter nights enlarge," for example, *their* will receive less time and less intensity than either *clouds* or *stormes* (both of which will require roughly the same time and same intensity) but more time and intensity than the first syllable of *discharge* (which will itself require less time and less intensity than the second). Similarly, in line 11 *Masks* will receive more time and intensity than the phonetically related following word, *and,* the first syllable of *Courtly* more time and intensity than the second but less than the following word, *sights.* When taken by themselves, there is nothing particularly exciting or unusual about these instances of relative stress and quantitative variation among the syllables in a line. They are standard events of the language. When considered together and in light of the poem's regularly iambic meter, however, their aesthetic implications become remarkable.

Though stress and quantity operate as distinct but simultaneous rhythmic factors in any line, their mutual conformity here reinforces the rhythm established by each one separately. In line 3 emphasis in one system coincides with emphasis in another: *clouds, stormes* and *-charge* are quantitatively demanding and also metrically stressed, *their* and *dis-* are relatively undemanding and also metrically unstressed; similarly, in line 11 *Masks, Court-* and *sights* are all "long" and are also all stressed, *and* and *-ly* are both "short" and unstressed. This congruence of metrical and quantitative patterning again embodies a kind of harmonious unity in division—another kind of "rhyme"; in effect, with two sources of prosodic information delivering the same message, the smoothly iambic rhythm of line 3 and the end of line 11 is unmistakably clear.

As well as reinforcing a line's stress pattern, quantity can also cross or play against it to create an effect of subtle but audibly significant rhythmic "counterpoint." This similarly rhyme-like *in*congruence of metrical and quantitative patterning may be achieved (in ways often imitative of sense) either when a quantitatively long syllable falls in the unstressed position of a foot or when a quantitatively short syllable is stressed; that is, by grouping sounds either "cloggingly" or "trippingly." Take, for example, the fourth line of Shakespeare's Sonnet 73, *Bare ruined choirs, where late the sweet birds sang,* which is effectively slowed by the presence of quantitatively cumbersome syllables in the metrically unaccented position of its first and last feet.[10] A similar but more daring instance of the slowing effect of rhythmic counterpoint takes place in Milton's definitive version of the clogged line—*Rocks, Caves, Lakes, Fens, Bogs, Dens, and shades of death* (*Paradise Lost,* II.621), where the piling up of nine long monosyllables (their quantity emphasized by patterns of assonance, consonance and the recurrence of eight terminally voiced *s* sounds) all but obliterate the poem's five-beat iambic meter. Though rarely as extreme as this example from Milton, metrical variations like these are stock effects in English verse from Wyatt (*When her loose gown from her shoulders did fall*) to Google (*Fair face show friends, when riches do abound*) to Jonson (*Good and great God, can I not think of thee*) and Donne (*for you/ As yet but knock, breathe, shine, and seek to mend*) to Pope (*Fans clap, Silks rustle, and tough Whalebones crack*) to Keats (*neither twist/ Wolf's-bane, tight-rooted, for its poisonous wine*) to Tennyson

(*On the bald street*) to Yeats (*And what rough beast, its hour come round at last*).[11] They are also commonly found in Renaissance songs, where a composer can further emphasize the slowing effect of the variation by setting a long but unstressed syllable to a long note.[12] As all of these examples indicate, this kind of counterpoint is most often the direct result of a piling up of monosyllables, each of which carries a larger weight of consonants than polysyllabic words, and each of which also establishes a separate logical and syntactic identity that invites stress.

Whenever such a piling up occurs its effect upon a reader is always the same: the line slows down. Thus in the last foot in line 2 of "Now winter nights enlarge" the metrically unstressed syllable *their* is quantitatively longer than the stressed syllable that immediately precedes it, *of,* and the recurrence of two relatively (though for different reasons) emphatic syllables at this point in the line works to slow it down in a way that imitates the assertion that winter nights are now growing longer. In the same way, the long *e*-plus-voiced *s* sounds in the second syllable of *chimneys* in line 5 make it quantitatively longer than the accented first syllable, and the recurrence of two relatively long syllables in the line's final foot, |*-neys blaze*|, again works to emphasize, if not imitate, substance by effectively prolonging the verbal events used to disclose it. The same kind of quantitative variation occurs elsewhere, and with similar effect. As I have already noted, in the second foot of line 7, |*tun'd words*|, the combination of a long vowel plus two different consonant sounds in *tun'd* insures that a metrically unstressed but thematically important adjective will take as much time to pronounce as either of the metrically stressed syllables that flank it. In the first foot of line 12, |*Sleepes lead-*|, another combination of a long vowel followed by two different consonants demands that the articulation of *Sleepes* be drawn out in a way that again emphasizes, and perhaps imitates, its sense. In the first foot of line 15, |*Much speech*|, the slightly clumsy tongue-twisting required to articulate a juxtaposition of terminal *ch* in the metrically unstressed syllable and *sp* (plus an eventual repetition of *ch*) in the stressed syllable contributes significantly to our sense of the assertion that long-winded conversation between lovers is a poor substitute for sexual intercourse. While less clearly significant, the time required to pronounce a combination of *th*-vowel-*ngs* sounds in the unstressed syllable in the last foot of line 17, |*things well*|, is equally effective in both emphasizing a metrically unemphatic word and, as a result, again slowing the line. The beginning of the next line is slowed as well, primarily by the juxtaposition of terminal and initial *m* sounds in its first foot, |*Some mea*-| (Compare Shakespeare's *Bare ru*-);[13] comparable effects are achieved by the *m/n* juxtaposition in the first foot in line 19, |*Some knot*-|. Finally, the end of an already long line 23 is further prolonged by a combination of the initial complex *s* sound and the terminal *r*-plus-voiced *s* consonants in the unstressed syllable of the penultimate foot, |-*sures are*|(compare the effect of the same combination in the second foot of line 18, |-*sures come*-|).[14]

As well as physically slowing a line down, instances of non-coincidence between quantitative and stress patterning can also speed a line up, make it go faster. Since polysyllabic words tend to have just one predominant speech accent ("polysyllábic," "predóminant") and since the meaning of a polysyllabic word is only conveyed when its several syllables are run together, we tend to read them more quickly than monosyllables. Thus when we come upon a line like Donne's *From death, you numberless infinities* (Holy Sonnets, 7) or Milton's *Of Sericana, where Chineses drive* (*Paradise Lost*, III.438)–both composed of five perfectly regular iambic feet but only three major speech stresses[15]–we cannot help but experience them in less time than if for *numberless infinities* Donne had instead written "countless and unbounded hoards" or for *Chineses* Milton had written "East Asians." An illusion of similar speed can also be produced by adding extra, quantitatively undemanding syllables to a line, as in twentieth-century American pronunciations of Wyatt's *Busily seeking with a continual change,* Sidney's *Experience which repentence only brings,* Shakespeare's *The multidudinous seas incarnadine,* Donne's *Inconstancy unnaturally hath begot,* Pope's *Our plenteous streams a various Race supply,* Browning's *For the ripple to run over in its mirth* or Steven's *Ambiguous undulations as they sink.* As the examples demonstrate, such "tripping" effects are common in English verse. The sprightliness we sense in these lines is due to the fact that each line contains the sounds of more than ten syllables and that the formally uncounted syllables run quickly together. (Note, however, that the illusion of speed in the examples from the Renaissance is apparent *only* to a modern ear: the distinctions I have indicated between vowel sounds in words like *continual, experience* and *unnaturally* are ones that would *not* have been apparent to Wyatt, Sidney or Donne, who would probably have heard something like "con-tin-yull," "ex-per-yence," "un-na-trull-ly.")[16]

There is only one theoretically extra-metrical syllable in "Now winter nights enlarge," in *tedious* (see Note 8 above); its occurrence in *They shorten tedious nights* is significant because, as we slur together the last two syllables of *tedious,* the rhythm of line 24 picks up speed in such a way that the line itself—as well as its amorous nights—seems shorter. (Compare the effect had Campion instead written *"They shorten* these cold nights.") In addition to the extra-metrical syllable, "Now winter nights enlarge" also has three clear examples of a quantitatively short syllable receiving formal stress: in the second foot of line 2, |*-ber of*|, the second foot of line 8, |*-monie*|, and the second foot of line 16, |*-ty no*|. However slight, the effect of the counterpoint in each of these instances is again the same: we feel the rhythm of lines 2, 8 and 16 suddenly quicken.[17]

In the preceding pages I have pointed out how the congruence or incongruence of a line's stress and quantitative patterning may either confirm or complicate its basic meter. I want now to look briefly at how the rhythmic factors of a song's music (including pitch) can similarly work against and/or with the rhythms of its words—i.e. reaffirm and/or further complicate the rhythms of its words. Consider, for example, how the rhythmic structure of the following lines in "Now winter nights enlarge" is simultaneously supported and not supported by their musical settings:

In the setting of line 2, *The number of their houres,* each syllable that is stressed by verbal meter is also stressed by the musical downbeat:

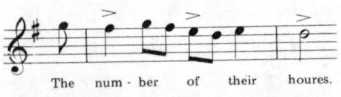

The   num - ber   of   their   houres.

The eighth- and quarter-note setting of *The num-* (followed by the shifting intonation of two eighth-notes on *-ber*) gives quantitative support to the line's iambic metrical pattern, and the half-note setting of *houres* on the fifth gives quantitative and melodic reinforcement to the formal and syntactic closure reached at that point. On the other hand, while it helps to emphasize the relative length of this penultimate syllable, the unstable setting of *of* to two different eighth-note pitches followed by the single quarter-note on *their* works against the line's verbal meter.

Similarly, in the setting of line 3, *And clouds their stormes discharge,* each syllable stressed by verbal meter is again also stressed by the musical downbeat; the shifting intonations of the unstressed   syllables   in   the   first   and   second   feet

(♫ ♩   ♫) again helps to reinforce the line's iambic
And clouds their

pattern; the rhyme syllable, *-charge,* again receives melodic emphasis because it is set to the root:

And   clouds   their   stormes   dis · charge.

At the same time, the fact that each syllable in the line is allotted the same cumulative duration (one quarter-note equals two eighths) overrides the natural quantitative differences between the line's relatively "short" and "long" syllables (compare the cumulatively equal durations of *of* and *their* in line 2); and the shifting intonation of a metrically stressed syllable followed by the more assertive quarter-note setting of a metrically unstressed syllable in

♫ ♩   contradicts the iambic verbal pattern.
stormes dis ·

In the setting of lines 7 and 8, *Let well tun'd words amaze With harmonie divine,* the stress patterns of verbal and musical meter are again congruent; the iambic pattern is again initiated by the instability of two eighth-notes followed by a single quarter-note in the setting of *Let well-;* the conclusion of line 7 is emphasized melodically by the fact that the second syllable of *amaze* is set to G; and the formal rhyme pattern and syntactic closure in line 8 is emphasized quantitatively by the setting of the second syllable of *divine* to a half note:

Let   well · tun'd words a · maze With har · mo · nie   di · vine.

At the same time, the iambic pattern in line 8 is contradicted by the fact that the unstressed syllable of its first foot is set to a single quarter-note and the following stressed syllable to a pair of unstable

eighth-notes   (♩   ♫);[18]   the   quantitative   deemphasis
with har ·

in the second foot of line 8 is countered by the setting of *-monie* to two quarter-notes; and the meter and quantitative pattern at the end of line 7 is countered by the setting of *words* (stressed and "long") to a pair of eighth-notes and *a-* (unstressed and "short") to a single quarter-note.

To take one final example, in the setting of the end of line 11, *Masks, and Courtly sights,* each syllable stressed by verbal meter is again also stressed by the downbeat, the rhyme word is again emphasized by note quantity and pitch (the fifth), and the obvious quantitative differences between the preceding four syllables are again contradicted by the fact that each is set to a quarter-note:

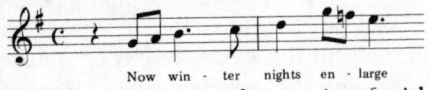

Masks, and   Court · ly   sights.

Having discussed the interaction of the primary rhythmic factors in verse and having noted isolated examples of the interaction of verse rhythm and musical rhythm in "Now winter nights enlarge"—I want now to sketch out the full rhythmic structure produced in "Now winter nights enlarge" by the interaction of verbal stress with verbal quantity and of both with musical stress, musical quantity and musical pitch in "Now winter nights enlarge." For clarity and convenience, I will proceed simply by following a listener's experience of the song's rhythm as it unfolds from one verse-line to the next. This method of procedure is admittedly arbitrary; as I said in the last chapter, a listener will actually hear the rhythm of "Now winter nights enlarge" defined primarily in increments not of its formal verse-line structure but of its five musical phrases. Indeed, the verbal rhythm of a song continues to function in the experience of hearing the song only because that rhythm is the one in which the words have meaning. We do *not* hear it physically, but it registers on the minds of listeners who know the language in which the verse is written. (Consider an extreme example: *The Messiah,* in which verbal rhythms are more twisted than usual because the composer was not a native speaker of English.) When one hears a song one hears the words twice at once—as they sound and as they would "naturally" sound without the independent rhythm imposed by the music. The mind and the ear listen together but to separate sounds of the same thing. (This phenomenon too is rhyme-like in its physics.)

Now win · ter   nights   en · large

Though line 1 is not a complete unit of either syntax or

substance, it defines the poem's rhythmic norm: six syllables in a line disposed in three iambic feet. That basic iambic pattern–x/ x/ x/–is noticeably complicated by grades of stress and quantitative differences among the syllables which it measures. *Now* is unstressed metrically but, as a dipthong, sounds for a longer time than the following stressed syllable, *win-*, which is considerably less time-consuming than the line's second stressed syllable, *nights*, itself intensified both by duration and by the fact that it is monosyllabic, a single unit of sense. Notice, however, that the effect of quantity playing against stress in the first foot is modified musically by the fact that *Now* is set to a pair of eighth-notes and *win-* to a dotted quarter-note, and that the difference in relative duration between *win-* and *nights* is also counteracted since *nights*–set to a single quarter-note–is only two-thirds as long as *win-*. Having climbed to a kind of rhythmic peak on its substantively most important word, *nights*, line 1 closes with a disyllable whose stress and quantitative patterns are perfectly

congruent, $\overset{\text{x } \overline{\text{/}}}{en\text{\textit{large}}}$. This urgently conclusive conclusion of the verse-line is made more insistent by the rhythm of its music, whose pair of eighth-notes falling to a dotted quarter suggest at least temporary closure because they duplicate the rhythm, and echo the melody, of the setting of foot 1. (Notice that the incongruence of a falling melody counterpointing against the rising speech accent of *enlarge* works to forestall a sense of complete rhythmic finality, a sense obviously prohibited at this point in other systems of order.)[19]

The   num - ber   of   their   houres

Line 2 opens, as line 1 did, with an unstressed monosyllable followed by a disyllabic word whose metrically unstressed second syllable, *-ber*, is nearly identical to the corresponding syllable in line 1, *-ter*. Despite the phonetic likeness and the general rhythmic similarity between the openings of the two lines, the next or second stressed syllable in line 2, *of*, is considerably less weighted than *nights*, its counterpart in line 1. Moreover, because of a counterpointing of quantitative shortening on the stressed syllable of its second foot followed by quantitative lengthening on the unstressed syllable of its third foot (*of their*), the verse rhythm in the second half of line 2 is markedly different from that produced by the agreement of stress and quantity in the comparable syllables of line 1 (*nights en-*). At the same time, since each syllable in these two pairs is allotted the same one-beat musical duration and since *num-* and *of* are set to notes accented by the downbeat, their settings again[20] deny the quantitative differences that are clearly audible to a reader of the unaccompanied verse. The effect of this verbal counterpoint in line 2—a speeding up on *of,* a slowing down on *their*—is given additional weight by the line's final word, *houres,* which, as a kind of drawled monosyllable requiring two different articulatory positions ("au-ers") and set to the dominant half-note cadence, is simultaneously emphasized by verbal and musical stress, quantity and pitch. Furthermore, the finality we feel in the rhythmic smoothness of *"their houres"* (followed by a quarter-note rest) is not only pleasing in itself but substantively significant, because the word *houres* concludes not only this line but also completes a two-line unit of sense, the first self-sufficient syntactic whole.

And   clouds   their   stormes dis · charge

The rhythm of line 3 is marked by an exact congruence of patterns in verbal stress and verbal quantity. This congruence is reinforced by the fact that each of its three metrically accented syllables—*clouds, stormes* and *-charge*—invites approximately the same amount of speech intensity and the same duration (note the similarly unifying phonetic patterns of terminal voiced *s* in the first and second of the stressed words and vowel-plus-*r* in the second and third). Still, since the unstressed monosyllable in the second foot (*their*) is more time-consuming than the unstressed syllable in the third foot (*dis-*), the middle of the line is somewhat more rhythmically weighted than the end. Notice, however, that both *their* and *dis-* have the same cumulative musical duration, and that the weighted verbal urgency in the second foot is equalled in other dimensions in the third by the even greater emphasis *discharge* has as formal rhyme word whose second syllable is also set to the root G.

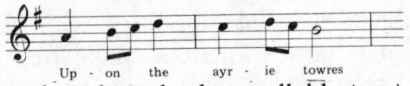

Up · on   the   ayr · ie   towres

The presence of a relatively short syllable (*-on*) in the stressed position of its first foot gets line 4 off to a fast start. This is appropriate: given the precedent of the two-line clause in lines 1-2, the preceding line by itself seems incomplete; we expect the clause to continue. The counterpointing of quantity against stress in the first foot is supported musically: while *-on* is emphasized by the downbeat and by the fact that it is accompanied in the bass by a half-note (shared with *the*), the shifting intonation of its two eighth-notes is relatively unstable compared to the quarter-note setting of *Up-*, *the* and *ayr-*. Leading us quickly through its first three syllables, the line slows for a moment on *ayr-*, which, though it sounds like the substantive independent monosyllable "air," proves to be part of a disyllabic word: because the monosyllable *ayr-* makes sense in this context, it simultaneously asserts its own identity—an assertion underscored rhythmically in the bass part, which gives *ayr(ie)* a full half-note—and presses urgently forward upon the syllable that will complete it. (Notice the play of phonetic similarity and prosodic dissimilarity between *their* in lines 2 and 3 and *ayr-* in line 4: though *ayr-* is metrically stressed and each *their* unstressed, since *their* is an independent monosyllable each is quantitatively longer than its phonetic cousin in line 4.) Since the second syllable of *ayrie* is metrically unstressed, is quantitatively even shorter than its first syllable, is, like *-on,* set to a relatively unstable pair of eighth-notes, and completes an adjective as yet without an object to modify, it too presses forward upon the next word. Thus, aside form the brief emphasis given to the first syllable of *ayrie,* the rapid pace which began line 4 carries us clear through to *towres*—its most emphatic word by virtue of speech stress, quantity, musical duration (made longer by the following quarter-note rest), musical pitch (it is accompanied in the bass by the root), semantic substance, and the fact that it completes both the second formal rhyme pair and the second two-line clause.

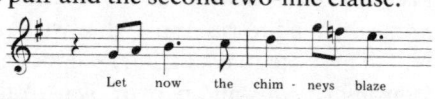

I have already noted the contrapuntal coincidence of two metric identities in the unstressed syllable of the last foot in line 5 (*-neys* is a relatively long syllable in an unstressed position), and how the effect of this incongruence is to draw out the end of the line and thus to slow it down. The rhythmic slowing is particularly apt because it helps to underscore the fact that the end of line 5 also marks the end of a complete independent clause; it is also supported musically by the fact that *-neys blaze* is set to the same three-note cadence we heard at the end of line 1 on *enlarge.* (It is interesting to observe how the music underscores the simultaneous unity and division of *Now* and *now* in lines 1 and 5—each word set to a different tonic chord—and how two similarly accented disyllabic words in the same position of two consecutive lines—*ayrie* and *chimneys*—are made to serve such different rhythmic functions; much of the rhythmic subtlety of so metrically regular a poem as "Now winter nights enlarge" is in fact due to the way that Campion has managed to vary the disposition of one- and two-syllable words in nearly every line.)

Line 6 is also a complete, substantively independent clause. The rhythmic conclusion of its words is not so pronounced as that of the preceding line, but line 6 is considerably slowed by the two alliterating monosyllables that comprise its last foot, *with wine:* each is elongated by a terminal consonant; the first is set to a quarter-note and the second to a half-note fifth followed by a rest (compare *their houres,* set to the same notes at the end of line 2). The effect helps to underscore the completion of the syntax and substance of the clause. At the same time, without the emphasis of its musical setting, the line's final word, *wine,* is less rhythmically prominent than the syntactic subject, *cups,* whose assertive combination of initial hard *c* and terminal plosive-plus-*s* gives it a speech intensity greater than that of either of the other two metrically stressed syllables. Despite this intensity in its first foot, however, the line keeps us moving: while we have to enunciate each of its final two consonants in order to say the word *cups* by itself, the fact that it is followed by a vowel rather than consonant means that one will naturally tend to run it together with the next word: "cu-pso'erflow." (This potential slurring is supported melodically by Campion's setting of *cups* and part of *o'er-* to the same note: F sharp.) From here—since the two syllables of *o'erflow* are themselves set to two pairs of falling eighth-notes (rhythm and melody acting out the word's substance), and since the second ends with an open vowel sound that again leads easily to the next word, *with* (slowed by its quarter-note and by its share of the half-note in the bass)—we are carried smoothly through to the end of the line.

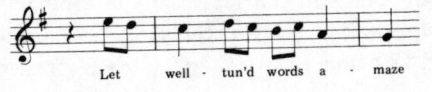

I have already mentioned the counterpointing of quantitative length against metrical deemphasis in the second foot of line 7. Each word in the phrase *well-tun'd words* requires a relatively strong degree of speech stress, and each is also relatively long (notice, though, the slight increase in syllabic duration from *well-* to *-tun'd* to *words*, and, in contrast, the prominence given to *well-* by its setting to a single quarter-note instead of a pair of eighths); the weighted rhythm of the middle of line 7 thus helps underscore the fact that the entire phrase is also a thematically crucial logical unit. Campion gives this unity a melodic emphasis: the high C to which *well-* is set is repeated twice in the setting of *-tun'd words*. Having slowed upon what is probably the poem's heaviest string of monosyllables (compare *clouds their stormes*—set to the same series of notes and in the same position of line 3), line 7 concludes with another disyllabic verb, *amaze*, whose first syllable is the poem's briefest and whose second is emphasized not only because of the elongation of its terminal voiced *s* (compare *words*) but because it is set to the root G and completes a formal rhyme pair.

With har - mo - nie   di - vine

Line 8 completes the clause begun in line 7 and, like line 7, concludes with a disyllable. And yet compare what precedes the disyllable in each of these lines: *well-tun'd words, harmonie.* Indeed, the occurrence here of the poem's first and only metrically and musically acknowledged trisyllable (*-dious* in line 24 functions monosyllabically in the verse meter and is set as a monosyllable) not only stands in direct contrast to the monosyllabic clogging in line 7 but forces us to take the logical unit *harmonie divine* as a single rhythmic unit as well. The unit gets casual musical support from the fact that *harmo-* and *divine* are set to rhythmically similar patterns that are melodic mirror images of one another—patterns anchored around the high C setting of *-nie*.[21] Thus, though lines 7 and 8 stand together syntactically and are set to one complete musical phrase, they are divided by their insistently different verbal rhythms.

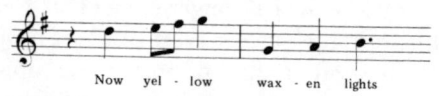

Now yel - low   wax - en   lights

Line 9 is marked by a progressive lengthening of its metrically stressed syllables (*yel-* is shorter than *wax-*, *wax-* shorter than *lights*); these syllables again get casual musical support from the increasing stability and duration of their settings to a pair of eighth-notes, a quarter-note, and a dotted quarter. (Notice again that, while the second syllable of *yellow* is deemphasized by both verse and musical meter, its phonetic identity is asserted—and its logical identity denied—by the fact that *-low* is set to the root G, the highest note in the phrase.) In contrast to this agreement of verbal and musical stress and quantity, the naturally falling speech accents in *yellow* and *waxen*—accents comparable to those of *measures comely, knotted Ridles* and *Poems smoothly* in the same position of lines 18-20, and *shorten tedious* in line 24—are essentially counteracted by their rising melodic settings. Moreover, pitch emphasis in the setting of *-low* is immediately repeated in the setting of *wax-* to a different G (made stronger by G in the bass), and the repetition yokes the syntactically yoked pair of adjectives together musically. As well as playing melody against verbal rhythm, the setting gives an additional contrapuntal emphasis to the unstressed syllables of *yellow* and *waxen*: each is set to a single

quarter-note— ♩ more stable than ♫ , ♩ equally as stable
      -low   yel - -en

as *wax-*. Similarly, because the rhythmic pattern of the setting of *Now yel-* (♩ ♫) inverts the pattern that opens phrase I (♫ ♩.) and phrase II (♫ ♩), it makes a contrapuntal balance between emphasis indicated by verbal and musical stress and emphasis indicated by note duration and (since *Now* is set to a tonic chord) by note pitch—a balance that effectively underscores the syntactic and logical parallelism suggested in the recurrence of *Now* at the beginning of quatrains 1, 2 and 3.

Shall waite on hun - ny Love

Though its verbal and musical stress patterns are congruent, there is a significant rhythmic counterpointing of note duration against syllabic quantity in line 10. Because of its initial and terminal consonant sounds, *Shall,* the unstressed syllable of the first foot, is a relatively long word (longer in fact than the line's second stressed syllable, *on*), but since it is set to a single eighth-note it is sung in a relatively short amount of time. This is appropriate since the auxilliary *Shall* by itself does not specify the verbal action we look forward to after the subject *Yellow waxen lights* in line 9. The rhythmic and melodic emphasis that the music gives to the verb *waite*—longer by half a beat than *Shall* and also set to the fifth—is also appropriate, especially since the setting completes another variation of the five-note melodic figure which initiated musical phrase I and which also overlapped the two halves of musical phrase II. From this point, the line moves on with an even, one-beat-per-syllable regularity that works to emphasize the metrically unemphatic and quantitatively undemanding syllables *on* and *-ny*, and so lead us smoothly to its final word. While *hunny Love* is again set to a version of the falling melodic pattern that previously concluded phrase II, the supertonic cadence at the end of phrase III gives *Love* a melodic identity altogether different from that of the syllables at the end of phrase II (*towres* and *-vine*), which closed on the tonic. At the same time, the melodic asymmetry of the conclusion of phrase III is counteracted by its rhythmic stability (A is a half-note followed by a rest), by the phonetic balance of the words it sets (*Love* sounds like the first syllable in *hunny*), and by the fact that it marks the conclusion of another two-line unit of sense.

While   youth - ful   Rev - els,   Masks, and   Court - ly   sights

I have already remarked upon the smoothly iambic rhythm that we feel in the conclusion of line 11—a rhythm produced in part by the clock-work regularity of a series of quarter-notes similar to, but more extended than, the one that preceded *Love* in line 10. As in that line, this series of quarter-notes gives a quantitative musical emphasis to four of the five unstressed syllables in line 11 (*-ful*, *-els*, *and* and *-ly*); at the same time, its alternate downbeats emphasize the syllables stressed by verbal meter (*youth-*, *Rev-*, *Masks* and *Court-*); in contrast, the opening pair of eighth-notes in phrase IV stretches and, in effect, divides the relatively long duration of the monosyllable *While*: "Whi-l." Similarly, the falling melodic pattern in the settings of *youthful* and *Revels* underscores this falling speech accent (compare the identical pitches of the two syllables in *Courtly*), and the setting of *Masks* to the fifth gives melodic weight to what have been the end of a "normal," six-syllable line (compare the dominant cadence on *houres* and *wine* at the ends of line 2 and 6). The phonetic likeness of *Masks* and the following unstressed syllable, *and*, is underscored musically by the fact that both words are accompanied by a single half-note in the bass—a half-note that effectively links what would have been the end of a "normal" verse-line to the last four syllables in line 11; at the same time, the independent identity of *and* is asserted melodically, by the fact that it is set to the highest note in the phrase. Finally, the fact that line 11 takes more time than any line thus far coincides with the fact that it is set to a single complete phrase—a phrase shorter by two counts than any preceding phrase—whose steady quarter-note rhythm in effect serves to hammer out the length of line 11.

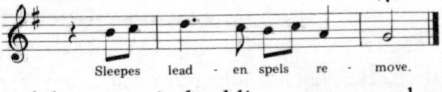

Sleepes   lead - en spels   re - move.

The setting of the stanza's final line returns to the rhythmic and melodic patterning that began musical phrase I and duplicates the five-note melodic figure that concluded the first half of musical phrase II. The shifting intonation of its initial pair of eighth-notes denies the possibility that the natural monosyllabic intensity and length of the word *Sleepes* is great enough to reverse the poem's normal iambic pattern—making the first foot of line 12 trochaic:

/   x
Sleepes lead-. The word *Sleepes* is in any case very strong both phonetically and substantively, and the fact that we hear it sung to two different note pitches gives a particularly insistent instability that at once distinguishes it from the firmly intoned subjects in line 11 and, perhaps, imitates rhythmically the powers of sleep being dispelled by them. Despite the impact of *Sleepes*, the iambic pattern in foot 1 is confirmed musically by the rhythmic and melodic emphasis given to the following syllable, *lead-*, set to a dotted quarter-note—the fifth, and highest note in the phrase—and accompanied by a fifth in the bass. The iambic pattern in the second foot is also asserted musically, not only by the downbeat on the first note of *spels* but by the fact that *-en* is set to a single eighth-note (compare ♫ in line 1 and ♪ in line 9) and *spels* is set

en - large   wax - en

to a pair of eighth-notes which, because they duplicate the setting of *Sleepes,* also emphasize the important phonetic and ideational connections between those two words. The rising accent in *remove* is naturally iambic, but is even more strongly asserted by its setting's close on the tonic cadence. With the metrically unstressed syllable of *remove* sung to a quarter-note and with its stressed syllable held for two beats with a fermata, the line's final foot ends up taking more than twice as long as the preceding foot; in fact, depending on the length of the hold, it may be considerably longer than both preceding feet combined. This sudden musically-dictated slowing is not implicit in its words by themselves; it serves both to accentuate one of the line's internal phonetic unities (the long *e* in *Sleepes* repeated in *re-*) and to underscore the completion of a formal rhyme pair, a third two-line clause and, most importantly, the poem's first stanza.

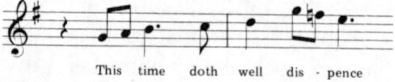

The opening line of stanza 2 is made up of four monosyllables followed by a rising-accent disyllable. The first two metrically stressed words, *time* and *well*, are for several reasons more emphatic than the unstressed words, *This* and *doth;* and the natural iambic pattern in the line's first two feet is effectively reinforced by the relative quantities of the notes to which the four words are set: a pair of eighth-notes for *This,* a dotted quarter for *time*, a single eighth for *doth* and a quarter-note (the fifth) for *well.* That the setting should give musical weight to the line's subject is appropriate, especialy since *This time* echoes *Now*—its adverbial equivalent—the word that began quatrains 1, 2 (where it was set to the same note as *time*) and 3. The special propriety of melodic emphasis on the adverb *well* is at this point less obvious (we have not yet read line 17);[22] but its setting to a dotted quarter-note fifth clearly underscores the phonetic kinship between the word *well* and the first syllable of *leaden* (set to the same note) and *spels* in line 12—a kinship that helps to establish the link between the end of stanza 1 and the beginning of stanza 2. The internal phonetic unity of the verse-line is also pointed out melodically: *This* and the first syllable of *dispence* are set an octave apart.[23] The closure of the verse-line on the second syllable of *dispence* is marked rhythmically by the length of the dotted quarter-note, E, whose lack of special melodic resonance coincides with the unfinished syntax at the end of line 13 (compare similar effects at the end of lines 1 and 5).

The multiplicity of verbal connections in the enjambment between line 13 and line 14 (*dispence/ With*) are echoed musically by the fact that *With* and the first syllable of *dispence* are set to the same high G; this recurrence of the eighth-note root does not particularly suit the declamation of lines 1-2, 5-6, or 17-18. As in every line, the iambic pattern in line 14 is asserted by the pattern of musical meter—an upbeat on the unstressed syllables, a downbeat on the stressed syllables. The iambic pattern in foot 1 is also asserted by the note durations of its setting—an eighth-note on *With* and a quarter-note on *lov-;* at the same time, the congruent rising emphasis of verbal stress and quantity in foot 2 is played down musically, not only because the unstressed syllable of *lovers* and the monosyllable *long* are each set to a pair of eighth-notes but because the entire four-note progression falls from the root to the fifth. The congruence by which *discourse* is set to the dominant cadence at the end of phrase I followed by a rest effectively reinforces the completion of both the verse-line and the clause.

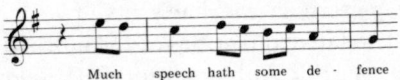

Much   speech hath   some   de · fence

I have already mentioned the contrapuntal interaction between stress and quantity in the first foot of line 15 (like *Sleepes* in line 12, *Much* is a relatively long syllable in an unstressed position). While this effect is somewhat undercut by the shifting intonation of *Much* to a pair of eighth-notes, the first foot still receives more musical weight than the second, *hath some,* which is set to two pairs of eighth-notes, a falling pair and a rising pair; this setting supports the line's verse rhythm, which stresses subject and object rather than verb.[24] At the same time, the melodic play of a pair of falling eighth-notes and a pair of rising ones in the settings of *Much* and *some* points out the simultaneous likenesses—sense and vowel sound—and differences of those two adjectives. The emphasis the second syllable of *defence* gets from its metrical position and from its function in the rhyme scheme is not sustained by note quantity, but it is supported melodically by the fact that *-fence* is set to G. Moreover, since the root here inititiates a five-note melodic ascent that yokes the end of the first half of musical phrase II to the beginning of the second half, it helps to underscore the syntactic and logical interdependence between this and the following line.

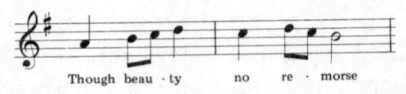

Though beau · ty   no   re · morse

The setting of line 16 complicates the verse rhythm: *Though* (set to the third of three consecutive quarter-notes) is quantitatively more weighted than *beau-* (set to two eighths). And *-ty,* which, like *though,* is unstressed in the verse pattern, is weighted melodically by being set to the fifth, which is also the highest note in the series. Similarly, in the line's second foot, where neither *-ty* nor *no* is very strong in the verse rhythm and where a speaking voice would speed up, the relative stability of a setting in quarter-notes works to slow the line in a way not invited by its words alone. At the same time, because *no* gets what verse stress the foot has and is set to a quarter-note, its rhythmic identity points out its phonetic relation to the line's first word (notice that the same two notes also help point out the phonetic link between *some* and *smooth-* in line 20). The internal phonetic symmetry of line 16 is also underscored by the setting of *-ty* and part of *re-* to the fifth,[25] and achieves additional counterpoint from the fact that a rising speech accent in *remorse* is set to a falling melodic pattern (compare the falling accent in *beauty,* set to an inversion of the same pattern).

All doe not all things well

Line 17 is set to the first half of musical phrase I. The vague and distant sexual suggestiveness in the word *doe* is perhaps made more noticeable by its relatively weighted musical duration; at least the word is rhythmically more emphatic than the two unstressed syllables that flank it. Metrically stressed and set to the quarter-note fifth, the second *all* is also emphatic (compare *nights* and *well* at the same points in lines 1 and 13), as is *things,* whose metrical deemphasis is counterpointed by its syllabic length and by its partial setting to an eighth-note G (compare the less apt imposition of the same melodic energy upon *en-* in line 1, *-neys* in line 5 and *dis-* in line 13). The phonetic asymmetry of *All/all/well,* though it does not recur in other lines set to this music, is nonetheless underscored here by note duration (*well* is half again as long as either *All* or *all*) and by melody (*well* is set to the sixth, *All* and *all* to the root and the fifth).

Some mea - sures come - ly tread

The demanding quantity of the first word in line 18, which plays against its metrical deemphasis, is counteracted rhythmically by its setting to a single eighth-note, but is simultaneously underscored melodically because that eighth-note is the root. The falling speech accent in *measures* is also both asserted and denied musically– asserted because the eighth-notes that get the unstressed syllable are less stable than the single quarter-note of the stressed syllable, denied because *-sures* again rises to the root. The falling accent of the next word is also crossed by its setting, which falls in a pair of eighth-notes from E to D on *come-* but climbs back to E, a firm quarter-note, on *-ly*. *Tread,* the strongest word in the verse line, becomes even stronger given its setting to the dominant conclusion of the phrase.

Some   knot - ted Rid - les   tell

Line 19 is set to the first half of musical phrase II. The slowing effect of the *m/n* juxtaposition in its first two syllables is partially asserted since the intonation of *Some* at two different pitches in effect forces an almost isolated *m* sound against the *n* of *knot-*, and partially denied since *Some* is set unstably to a shifting pair of eighth-notes and since its *m* sound and the *n* of *knot-* are sung at two different pitches. Rhythmic and melodic patterning in the line's music also works to assert and/or deny other of its internal phonetic rhymes: the immediate recurrence of the vowel-plus-*d* sound of *knotted* in the first syllable of *Ridles* is made less audibly apparent because a listener will again hear the short *i* and *d* sounds of *Ridles* sung at two different pitches; in contrast, the dental-plus-*l* consonant sounds in the second syllable of *Ridles* and *tell* are quantitatively emphasized because each is sung to a full quarter-note; the *t*-plus-short *e* pattern in the second syllable of *knotted* and in *tell* is underscored in a different way: one is set to the fifth and one to the root.[26] Finally, the strongly iambic verbal cadence in *Ridles tell*–a disyllable with a falling accent followed by a monosyllabic rhyme word–is played down musically: the line's penultimate stressed syllable is less firmly intoned than the following unstressed syllable, and the duration of its final stressed syllable is relatively undistinguished.

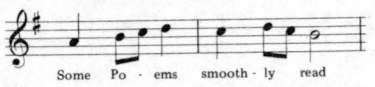

Some Po - ems smooth - ly   read

The close on G of the preceding line initiates an ascent to the fifth in the setting of line 20. Because the syntax of lines 19 and 20 is discontinuous, the unifying effect of the song's opening melodic motif is at this point less appropriate than it was in the settings of lines 3-4, 7-8 or 15-16, each of which was syntactically and logically interdependent. This third consecutive recurrence of *Some* at the beginning of a line is emphasized here by a single quarter-note setting (compare ♩ in line 18 and ♫ in line *Some*   *Some* 19), and that quarter-note followed by two eighths and a quarter-note fifth produces a pattern in note duration and note pitch that, by emphasizing the unstressed syllables in its first two feet, works counter to the line's iambic pattern. The internal phonetic unity of the syllables of line 20 is also stressed musically: we hear the short *e* in *tell* (line 19) and the second syllable of *Poems* sung a fifth apart, the *sm/ms* conjunctions in *Some, Poems* and *smoothly* each sung to a single quarter-note (we heard *Though* and *no* in line 16 sung to the same notes as *Some* and *smooth*-), and the long *e* sounds in the second syllable of *smoothly* and *read* drawn out over three note pitches—the last held for a full two counts.

The iambic verse rhythm at the beginning of line 21 is counteracted musically: the unstressed syllable *The* is set to a quarter-note fifth; the stressed syllable of *Summer* is set to an unstable pair of eighth-notes; and the unstressed syllable of *Summer* is set to the root, a quarter-note that is also the highest note in phrase III. After this point in the line, the rhythmic emphases of words and music become immediately congruent: the stressed syllable of the second foot, *hath,* is underscored by note pitch because it is set to the root one octave lower; and, in the final foot *joyes* is more assertive than *his* for reasons of sound, syntax, substance, note pitch and note duration.

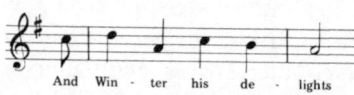

The rhythm of the music to which line 22 is set at once conforms to and subtly counterpoints against the verse rhythm of its words. The setting emphasizes the iambic pattern of the first foot: *And* is set to a single eighth-note, *Win-* to a quarter-note fifth. Furthermore, since the setting of *hath his joyes, And Win-* again repeats the song's opening melodic motif (G-A-B-C-D), it ties the

beginning of line 22 to the end of line 21 and so helps underscore
their ostentatiously parallel syntax, logic and substance. One of the
rhythmic differences between these two lines—the first *his* is
metrically unstressed, the second stressed—is smoothed over
musically by the equal time value of the notes to which they are set.
Similarly, the one-beat durations given to the unstressed syllables
of *Winter* and *delights* (which in effect elongate these relatively
short syllables) smooths out the stress differences in the second and
third feet of line 22 and sets up the even greater lengthening of its
final syllable, *-lights*.

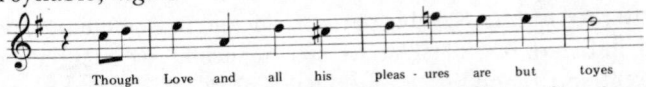

The rhythmic identity of the song's penultimate line is again
marked by the evenness of its quarter-note setting and by its length.
Moreover, as with the penultimate line in stanza 1, the length of
line 23 and the rhythm of its setting are again aesthetically interconnected: we hear each of these lines sung to a complete but (in
context of phrases I-III) truncated musical phrase in which a string
of eight consecutive quarter-notes drives home the fact that the
verse-line has ten syllables instead of the usual six. The iambic
meter of line 23 is initially underscored musically by the congruence of downbeat and verbal stress in the first foot, as well as by
the rising melody and the rhythmic pattern of two eighth-notes
followed by a quarter which opens the phrase. And, while
metrically stressed syllables continue to be stressed by the
downbeat, the length of the unstressed syllable in the fourth foot,
-sures, is underscored melodically: it is set to F, the highest note in
the phrase. The adverbial force of the word *but*—metrically
unemphatic, but crucial to our understanding the line's concession—is similarly brought out by its being sung with the same pitch
and duration as the immediately preceding verb, *are*. Finally,
syntactic coupling by means of the copula *are* is also asserted
musically: the direct object, *toyes*, and the first syllable of part of
the subject, *pleasures*, are both set to the fifth.

Set to the song's shortest phrase, line 24 sounds appropriately
brief. In fact the musical phrase to which it is set is only two beats
shorter than the musical setting for the preceding "long" verse-line,

the effect of whose rhythmic monotony points out the range of syllabic time values in line 24—which runs in length from the eighth-note duration of -*en* to the quarter-note slurring of -*dious* to the dotted quarter duration of *short-* (notice the rhyme-like opposition between the substance of this syllable and the length of its setting) to the half-note with fermata duration of *nights*. The closure manifest at this point in other systems of organization can also be felt in the rhythms of both the verse and the music. For one thing, a musical descent to the tonic cadence is matched verbally by the simultaneously falling speech accents in *shorten* and *tedious*. For another, the unstable setting of the unstressed syllable *They* recurs contrapuntally as the setting of the stressed syllable *te-*; similarly, the second syllable in *tedious* is metrically unstressed but relatively long both verbally (it contains the sounds of two slurred syllables) and musically (its setting to a quarter-note gives it twice the duration of the preceding unstressed syllable, -*en*, set to an eighth-note). The melodic instability of this quarter-note, A, is lessened somewhat by a fifth in the bass, which, because it is also melodically unstable, sets up the *extremely* stable tonic cadence completed in the setting of the next syllable. Finally, the slowing effects of verbal and musical rhythm begun in the unstressed syllable of the line's last foot are augmented in the harmonically resolved, drawn out setting of *nights*—not only the poem's final word but, appropriately, its longest monosyllable.

I opened this chapter with an hypothesis: that our experience of a Campion song's words by themselves is fundamentally different from our experience of those same words sung to their music. The difference is one of kind as well as degree. Among other things, what one hears when one hears a Campion song is a multiplicity of rhythmic congruences produced by a coalescence of two urgently separate but inseparable rhythms, one verbal and one musical. Like the rhythm of any song, the rhythm of a Campion song is physically more complex than the rhythms of either of its parts; it is also in effect more powerful and aesthetically more pleasing. Consider this small but compelling piece of evidence:

nights.

What a listener hears in the full setting of that word is more than just rhythmically conclusive, though it is that too. For, when he comes to the end of line 24, even a reader of the song's words by themselves will be reminded of the *winter nights* in line 1. But he cannot and will not hear in *nights* the reverberations that he can and will hear in

nights

—whose extended length of tonic resolution not only completes line 24 but in effect denies the poem's final assertion that *Love*['s] *pleasures . . . shorten tedious nights* and simultaneously confirms the assertion in line 1: *Now winter nights enlarge*. In a song about the simultaneously increasing and decreasing length of winter evenings, this final coupling of word and note is a paradox: moving us in two ways at once, it calmly but persuasively convinces us both of the immensity of winter nights and of the promise of amorous sport to make them go faster.

Chapter 6

Conclusion

Campion's remarkable aesthetic appeal may be explained in light of a statement that appears early in his *Observations in the Art of English Poesie:* "The world is made by Simmetry and proportion, and is in that respect compared to Musick, and Musick to Poetry: for *Terrence* saith, speaking of Poets, *artem qui tractant musicam,* confounding musick and Poesy together." That Campion, who was skilled in both arts and wrote theoretical treatises on both, would choose to compare music and poetry is not surprising. Nor is it surprising, given the traditional Renaissance idea of art as the imitation of an ordered and harmonious nature, that Campion's aesthetic sense of these two arts would be derived from a larger sense of the natural universe as a resonant whole made of parts held in appropriately balanced relation to one another and to God. Whether or not one cares to see Campion's art as the product of philosophic/religious theory, there is a wealth of evidence to show that Campion's songs were in fact made with a good deal of "Simmetry and proportion." It is the evidence of the songs themselves—the evidence of songs like "Now winter nights enlarge," in which a coupling of words and notes involves the relationship of a multiplicity of identities—identities whose simultaneous likeness and unlikeness pull them simultaneously together and apart.

The principle that governs such relationships—the principle most obviously embodied in rhymes—is perceptible in nature as well as art. Consider the chesnut leaf used by Hopkins to illustrate his theory of aesthetics in *On the Origin of Beauty: A Platonic Dialogue.*[1] The chesnut leaf is pleasing in itself; at the same time, the chesnut leaf with seven leaves—"the middle largest, diminishing towards the stalk, so that those nearest the stalk are smallest"—is more pleasing than the "imperfect" (for nature) six-leaved leaf whose two halves balance each other with perfect symmetry. To be sure, the chesnut leaf with seven points exhibits its own kind of symmetry, but the source of its greater beauty lies in the fact that it is at once symmetrical *and* asymmetrical. Similarly, the oak tree is pleasing not only because it is "a rugged boldly-irregular tree" but because, when seen from a distance, its shape outlines a parabola of "almost mathematical" proportions. The chesnut leaf and the oak are beautiful because in their complex simplicity we apprehend an interrelationship of parts both with themselves and with the whole of which they are parts: parts whose rhyme-like sameness and difference, conformity and non-conformity, cause them to be attracted and opposed at the same time. As Hopkins' imaginary student is led to discover, "All beauty may by metaphor be called rhyme."

What we experience in Campion's "Now winter nights enlarge" is not unlike what we experience in nature. In nature all is flux. Everything in Campion's song, though fixed, is also fleeting. What a listener hears when he hears "Now winter nights enlarge" is a multitude of harmonies among parts moving in and out of different systems of relationship. Every word in the poem functions in a variety of patterns simultaneously—formal, logical, syntactic, semantic, phonetic, rhythmic and so on; at the same time, in conjunction with the note or notes to which it is set, every word also functions in patterns of musical rhythm, melody and harmony. Similarly, in conjunction with the word or syllable it sets, each sound in the music functions in a comparably multiple set of musical and verbal systems. In the mixture of the two complexly ordered systems, one hears words in terms of music and music in terms of words: the mind and the ear listen together to two insistently separate but inseparable versions of the same thing. Because the elements that function in any given pattern may be at once similar and dissimilar, they will be unified and divided in the kind of rhyme-like asymmetrical relation that we find most pleasing: the two time related, phonetically related, syntactically related words *Now* and *houres,* set to G and D, both fit together and do not. The beauty of the pattern lies in the harmony of its parts—parts balanced according to their mixture of regularity and irregularity, consistency and variety, symmetry and change.

No one has ever paid as much attention to a Campion song as I have paid to "Now winter nights enlarge." I doubt, furthermore, that anyone has ever expended this much critical energy upon any single, short "lyric" poem. The reader can decide for himself whether or not my "Much speech hath some defence." In any case, I am certain that the inherent aesthetic value of "Now winter nights enlarge" justifies the time and effort I have given it, that Campion does too, and that my analysis has something important to say about the aesthetics of complex simplicity generally. Songs inevitably seem simple because their words, no matter how complex, come to us overlayed by patterns of notes that persuade us to listen and feel but not think. We hear a song's words penetrated and informed by a medium incapable of referring directly to the world we live in, but one whose rhyme-like effects nonetheless reflect patterns of relationship manifest in countless ways in that world. Music is a simpler and purer medium than literature for this reason: notes are exclusively acoustic phenomena–fixed rates of vibration produced and held for proportionately fixed lengths of time–and words point to things, actions, feelings, ideas. (Auden is wrong: Campion's poems *are* models of *la poésie pure* but they are not "verbal paradises in which the only element taken from the world of everyday reality is the English language"; storms, chimneys, parties on winter evenings, and such are from the world of everyday reality; so, less tangibly, is the range of emotions expressed by the range of Campion's personae in other songs.) It is because of the urgent differences between the two media that their unification in a song like "Now winter nights enlarge" is aesthetically so remarkable. "Now winter nights enlarge" is neither a poem nor a piece of music but something other, a fusion of energies that allows us to experience a greater number of controlled systems of relationship among artistic identities than either verse by itself or music by itself. The special aesthetic value of Campion's songs is in the same way a matter of degree: all songs do this kind of thing. Campion's songs do more of it than most songs.

The evidence I have collected, sorted and classified in this analysis speaks for itself. "Now winter nights enlarge" is as effective in its concentration of verbal patterning as any densely patterned short poem, a Shakespeare sonnet for example; furthermore, because of the added dimension of its music, "Now winter nights enlarge" compels us in ways beyond the command of the most efficient purely literary or purely musical work. Everything in Campion's song harmonizes, but there are so many different harmonies that in shifting from one frame of reference to another a listener finds himself engaged in an experience similar to his experience of the randomness and flux of the real world. It is that randomness and flux that necessitates art, whose imposition of a fixed order upon the unfixed and unstructured raw materials of the real world invites us to experience the world not as it is but as it might be. Because a Campion song multiplies to an astonishingly high degree the number of simultaneous connections among identities in two different artistic media, it comes closer than either verse or music separately to approximating the infinite diversity of relationships among identities in the real world. At the same time, inevitably, there remains an unfathomable abyss between the shaped complexity of a Campion song and the unshaped complexity of the real world. This is as it should be: any work of art that could successfully organize and fix the world once and for all would ultimately obviate the need for art. Meanwhile, to apprehend the multitude of harmonies in a Campion song will continue to be a potentially exciting, bewildering, terrifying and wonderful experience—the experience that Campion had in mind when he wrote:

> Let well-tun'd words amaze
> With harmonie divine.

Appendix of Supplementary Notes

Note 1. Further examples of ideational rhymes in Campion's songs (see Chapter 2, n. 4):

Nearly all of Campion's songs exhibit patterns of ideational rhymes, patterns involving the unification of a pair of terms—nouns, verbs, adjectives—denoting two related but symmetrically opposite ideas. In every instance of rhyme, ideational identities that are both like and unlike pull simultaneously together and apart. Moreover, as "Points define a perifery" (Pound) and the diameter its circle, the unification of polar opposite ideas generally works to define some larger whole parameter—an abstract concept, a field of experience—of which each is an extreme part: summer/winter (time), far/near (space), old/young (age), one/all (quantity), pain/joy (emotion), foul/fair (beauty). In addition to the instances of such patterning in "Now winter nights enlarge"), see the following:

A Booke of Ayres, I: *all/me;* II: *youth/age;* III: *Amarillis/Ladies;* IV: *sunne/shaddowe, night/light, blacke/brightness;* V: *naught/all;* VI: *live/die, pleasure/sorrow;* VII: *receiver/giver, sow/reape;* IX: *all/I alone, soule/body;* XI: *sight/blindness, quench/burned;* XII: *red/white;* XIII: *other pleasures/her;* XIV: *me/they, within/outward, heat/cold;* XV: *rose/lillies;* XVII: *enflame/quench, pain/pleasure, depart/stay;* XVIII: *joys/sorrows, the deepe/the skies;* XIX: *down/up, hill/dale, sleep/awake, black/white;* XXI: *one/all, Father/Sonne, darkness/light;*

The First Booke of Ayres, I: *all/thee;* II: *joyes/sorrows;* III: *All/Thou alone;* V: *night/light;* VII: *vain joyes/heavenly thoughts, earthly pompe/celestial things;* VIII: *joy/sorrow;* IX: *the darksome desart/ Paradice;* XIII: *night/day;* XV: *heaven/earth, good/ill;* XVI: *early/ late;* XVII: *day/night, live/die;* XVIII: *worst/best;* XX: *Summer/ Winter, Jack/Jone;* XXI: *Joys/terrors;*

The Second Booke of Ayres, II: *Once/now*; III: *cloudy/bright*; VII: *the old loves/My sov'raign*; VIII: *joyes/griefe*; IX: *far/near, all my friends/him alone*; X: *all/none*; XIII: *Other beauties/you*; XIV: *seeke/flie, day/night*; XV: *all/none, former/present*; XVI: *my Rivals/I*; XVII: *near/far*; XVIII: *escape/caught, spent/reapt*; XIX: *more/less, one/many*; XX: *old/new, inflame/cold*; XXI: *firmness/wav'ring, joy/grief*;

The Third Booke of Ayres, I: *hee/common lovers*; II: *True love abides/False love is ever flying*; III: *foes/guest*; V: *hence/come*; VI: *one/all, good/not good*; VII: *joy/pain, good/evil*; VIII: *Truth/False, Vertue/Vice, Free/sold, best/worst, poor/rich, hold/give*; IX: *joy/woes*; X: *her/none*; XI: *fair/false*; XIII: *old/new*; XIV: *bad/good*; XV: *all/none*; XVI: *all/thee*; XVIII: *she will/she will not*; XIX: *Others/I only*; XX: *Fire/tears, Rivers/ocean*; XXII: *Nature/Art, wild/tame*; XXIV: *grief/joy*; XXVI: *Spring/Fall, Troylus/Cresseid, well-ordered/neglected, Summer/Winter*; XXVII: *one/more, none/one*; XXVIII: *earth/heaven*;

The Fourth Booke of Ayres, II: *all/one*; III: *thy skin/within, swords/words*; V: *flow/ebbe*; VII: *Rose-buds/snow, Peere/Prince*; VIII: *all/none*; IX: *foul/fair*; X: *Love me/not love me, All/one*; XI: *friend/foe*; XII: *Fals-hood/Truth*; XV: *outward/inward, soul/body*; XVI: *light/night, liv'd/sleep an endless night*; XVII: *Nature/Art*; XIX: *fly/stay*; XX: *True Love/Jealousie, darkness/day, conjecture/truth, age/youth*; XXI: *What I had/what I had not*; XXII: *fire/ice*; XXIII: *May/December*; XXIV: *mind/body, maid/mother*. It should be remarked that most lyric poetry works from such contrasts; think of any five popular songs: four of them will include some kind of A/A' pairing.

Note 2. Further examples of anaphora and anaphora-like patterning in Campion's songs (see Chapter 2, n. 26):

Anaphora (the repetition of a word or words at the start of consecutive lines) and near-anaphora (the repetition of a word or words near the start of consecutive lines or the repetition of a word or words at the start of non-consecutive lines) appears in 54 of Campion's 116 songs. The effect pulls together the beginnings of lines that may or may not be unified by other patterning factors. See *A Booke of Ayres*, I.14-15 (*Let/But let*); 16-18 (*And*); II.1-3 (*Though*); III.6-7 (*Her*); 15-16 (*Give*); IV.4-5 (*Yet follow/Follow*); 8-9 (*Yet follow/Follow*): notice that the pattern of near-anaphora in each of these instances links two separate quatrains; V.7-8 (*I/Had I*), 21-22 (*That*); XVIII.10-11 (*Nor*), 20, 22 (*His*); XX.8-9 (*Of*);

The First Booke of Ayres, II.8, 10-11 (*Nor*); 19-20, 22 (*His*): notice that each of these also provide linkage between stanzas; III.9-10 (*When*); VI.6-7 (*Thou*); 14-15 (*His/Of his*); 26-27 (*None/For none*); 29-30 (*To him*); VII.11-12 (*Such*); VIII.1-2 (*Tune thy/Sing thy*); 11-12 (*Love*); IX. 7-9 (*The*); X.1-2 (*Wise men/Good men*); XI. 1-2 (*Never*); XIII.15-16 (*Ev'n in/In*); 22-23 (*From his/His*); XV.22-23 (*And his/His*); XXI.8-9 (*His*);

The Second Booke of Ayres, I.7-8 (*Now*); II.8-9 (*Who*); IV.1-2 (*O what*); V.2-4 (*The*); 5-6 and 9-10 (*Her*); 14-15 (*And*); VII.7-8 (*Some*); IX.19-20 (*Faire he/That he*); 23-24 (*And too/That too*); XII.1-2 and 4-5 (*The*); 26-27 (*Why*); XV.4-5 (*There is/Why is*); 11-12 (*When/And when*); 22-23 (*Are/Women are*); XVI.18-19 (*And I/I*); XVII.8-9 (*How*); XIX.10-11 (*Is/Or is*); XXI.2-3 (*In you my*);

The Third Booke of Ayres, II.12-13 (*False*); IX.1-2 (*O*); XIII.7-8 (*Thy*); XIV.7-8 (*What*); XV.14-15 (*O let/Let*); XVIII.1-2 (*Thrice*); 2-3 (*Thrice/Then thrice*); XX.15-16 (*Come*); XXIV.2-4 (*Then it/It/That it*); XXVI.6-7 (*All is*); 9-10 (*Thy/And thy*); XXVII.5-6 (*And*); XXVIII.1-2 (*So*); XXIX.6-7 (*Can/Or can*);

The Fourth Booke of Ayres, II.3-4 (*Great/So great*); III.13-14 (*Men/One man*); V.17-18 (*Happy*); VI.1-2 (*So/And so*); VII.13-14 (*Her Eyes like/Her Browes like*): these lines are joined by an ideational repetition as well as by anaphora; IX.2-3 (*I/Guesse I*); 22-23 (*That/Roses that*); 27-28 (*Who shall*); X.1-2 (*Love me or not/Leave me or not*); XII.15-16 (*Fayre you/You*); XIV.3-4 (*Shee*); XIX.30-31 (*Fled/Yet fled*); 33-34 (*Still*); XX.1-2 (*Turne all thy*): notice in this song the continuation of nearly the same pattern in lines 3 and 4 (*Change all thy, And all thy*); XXI.11-13 (*Since what I had/And what I had/A Love I had*); 16-17 (*She*); XXIII.5-6 (*If Love/Loves*).

Note 3. Examples of circular closure elsewhere in Campion's songs (see Chapter 2, n. 42):

In "Now winter nights enlarge" the final line echoes the first line in two different ways: *shorten* opposes *enlarge, nights* duplicates *nights.* A number of other Campion songs also manifest this kind of circular closure, or ring structure, in which elements in the conclusion echo elements in the first line or lines. See, for example, *A Booke of Ayres,* IV (whose first line is echoed throughout): "Follow thy faire sunne, unhappie shaddowe ... The

Sun still prov'd, the shadow still disdained"; VIII: "It fell on a sommers day,/While sweet Bessie sleeping laie . . . She sleepes ev'rie afternoone"; XVI: "Mistris, since you so much desire . . . I climbe to crowne my chaste desire"; *The First Booke of Ayres,* IV: "Out of my soules deapth to thee my cryes have sounded . . . Their sinne-sicke soules by him shall be recured"; *The Second Booke of Ayres,* IX: "Good men, shew, if you can tell,/Where doth humane pittie dwell . . . Where pittie ever yet did bide"; *The Third Booke of Ayres,* IV: "Maydes are simple, some men say . . . Ever let me simple be"; XIII: "Awake, thou spring of speaking grace, mute rest becomes not thee . . . If speech be then the best of graces,/Doe it not in slumber smother"; XX: "Fire, fire, fire, fire!/ Loe here I burne in such desire. . . That else must burne, and with me fall"; XXIII: "Come, O come, my life's delight . . . Come then, and make they flight/ As swift to me as heavn'ly light"; XXV: "Sleepe, angry beauty, sleep, and feare not me . . . That shee in peace may wake and pitty mee"; XXVII: "Never love unlesse you can/Beare with all the faults of man . . . If these, and such like, you can beare,/ Then like, and love, and never feare"; XXIX: "Shall I then hope when faith is fled . . . Faith failing her, Love dyed in mee"; *The Fourth Booke of Ayres,* II: "Respect my faith, regard my service past . . . My faith reward, and from me scandall take"; IV: "Vaile, love, mine eyes, O hide from me . . . To beauties faults must still be blinde."

Again, this kind of structural pattern is a common feature in most lyric poetry. Compare Wyatt's "My lute, awake! Perform the last . . . My lute, be still, for I have done"; Marlowe's "The Passionate Shepherd to his Love": "Come live with me and be my love . . . Then live with me and be my love"; Donne's "A Nocturnal upon St. Lucy's Day": "'Tis the year's midnight, and it is the day's . . . Both the year's, and the day's deep midnight is"; Herbert's "Discipline": "Throw away thy rod,/ Throw away thy wrath . . . Throw away thy wrath"; Blake's "The Tyger" (whose first and last stanzas are identical except for one word); Shelley's "Ode to the Westwind": "O Wild West Wind, thou breath of Autumn's being . . . O Wind/ If Winter comes, can Spring be far behind"; Whitman's "Out of the cradle endlessly rocking . . . (Or like some old crone rocking the cradle, swathed in sweet garments, bending aside,) / The sea whisper'd in me"; and Williams' "Portrait of a Lady": "Your thighs are appletrees/ where blossoms touch the sky . . . I said petals from an appletree."

Note 4. Examples of inexact formal rhymes in Campion's songs (see Chapter 3, n. 1).

Inexact end rhymes—inexact in at least modern pronunciation—occur frequently in Campion's verse, at least once in 69 of his 116 songs. The word he most often rhymes inexactly on is *love*, 18 times with *move* (phonological considerations suggest that the eye rhyme *love/move* had ceased to be a perfect ear rhyme as early as 1500; see Helge Kökeritz, *Shakespeare's Pronunciation* [New Haven, 1953], pp. 31, 243): *A Booke of Ayres*, I, X, XIII, XIX; *The Second Booke of Ayres*, II (*removed*), VI (*moves*), VII, VIII (*removed*), X (*moving*), XIII; *The Third Booke of Ayres*, IX, XI, XV, XXV; *The Fourth Booke of Ayres*, IX, XIX and XXIII; ten times with *prove* (Kökeritz argues that for Shakespeare the *love/prove* rhyme was imperfect [p. 243]; however, Kökeritz also cites Ben Jonson's explicit statement in his *Grammar* [1640] that both *love* and *prove* were pronounced with a short "flat" sound "akin to *u*," that is, with the *u* of "cut"): *A Booke*, I (*reprove*), XII, XV, XVII; *Second Booke*, I; *Third Booke*, III, XI, XVI; *Fourth Booke*, III (*approved*), XXIII; and once each with *grove* (*A Booke*, XVII) and *strove* (*Fourth Booke*, XVII)—both of which could have been pronounced with the short *u* of *love* (see Kökeritz, pp. 233, 244). See also the following (many of these now imperfect rhymes were perhaps or probably exact for Campion—e.g., *boast/frost*, *speak/break*, *fed/lead*, *feasts/ghests*, *there/heare*, *distastes/hasts*, *stone/gone*, etc.; most of them also occur in Shakespeare. The formidable problem of determining precisely how a speaker in early seventeenth-century London would have pronounced these various rhyme words is beyond the scope of this essay; see Kökeritz *passim*.):

A Booke of Ayres, I: *Love/reprove, move/love, come/tomb*; II: *boast/frost*; III: *Ladies/Amarillis*; V: *prove/love, sweare/deare, toong/wrong* and *turne/done/men/shun* (the penultimate line in each stanza rhymes with no other line in the stanza, but the final words in all four of these penultimate lines are related by their different vowel-plus-*n* patterns); VI: *speake/break, sleight/deceit*; X: *move/love*; XI: *scorned/burned*; XII: *prove/love*; XIII: *makes/cracks, move/love*; XV: *love/prove*; XVII: *love/prove, prove/love, come/alone*; XIX: *love/move, fed/lead, mone/one*; XX: *love/move*;

The First Booke of Ayres, IV: *erred/feared*; VI: *feasts/ghests, alone/one*; VII: *record/word*; XII: *threat/great*; XIII: *Fiends/Friends*; XIV: *there/heare*; XIX: *distasts/hasts, windes/finds*; XX: *Feast/best, breake/speake*; XXI: *stone/gone*;

The Second Booke of Ayres, I: *love/prove, love/move*; II: *removed /loved*; III: *returne/mourne*; III: *moves/loves*; VII: *move/love*; VIII: *live/grieve, removed/loved*; X: *loving/moving*; XI: *quarter/laughter*; XII: *winde/kinde, come/blome*; XIII: *move/love*; XIV: *foe/doe*; XV: *wooed/vowed, passion/occasion, moving/roving*; XVI: *were/feare, one/alone*; XVIII: *here/beare, safe/laugh*;

The Third Booke of Ayres, I: *mourne/returne*; II: *alone/gone*; III: *love/prove*; IV: *hearts/deserts, give/beleeve*; VI: *beare/appeare*; VII: *so/two*; IX: *moved/loved*; XI: *love/prove, Love/move*; XIII: *beget/counterfeit, share/are, surpasses/graces*; XV: *none/alone, love/move*; XVI: *love/prove*; XVII: *passe/place*; XX: *Thames/streames*; XXII: *growes/lose*; XXV: *love/move*; XXVI: *holy/folly*; XXVII: *beare/feare*; XXVIII: *have/grave*; XXIX: *gone/none*;

The Fourth Booke of Ayres, I: *distresse/cease*; II: *alone/one*; III: *loved/approved, Amber/chamber, swords/words*; IV: *alone/one*; V: *were/yeare*; VII: *above/move*; IX: *am/name, observ'd/hard, move/love, Gull/pull*; X: *alone/one, were/heare*; XVI: *liv'd/depriv'd*; XVII: *love /strove*; XVIII: *compassion/occasion*; XIX: *cares/teares, rich/beseech, fled/pleade, return'd/mourn'd, mov'd/lov'd, fast/haste, parts/deserts*; XXI: *crave/have, gave/Love*; XXIII: *love/prove*; XXIV: *moved/loved, Order/farther*.

Note 5. Examples in Campion's songs of rhyming and rhyme-like relationships (by assonance, etc.) among end-rhyme words that do not formally rhyme (see Chapter 3, n. 2):

In "Now winter nights enlarge "a number of formal rhyme words are linked across divisions in the formal rhyme pattern by certain shared, non-symmetrically patterned phonetic simiarities—e.g., *houres, towres, blaze, amaze, lights, sights, dispence, discourse, defence, remorse, joyes, delights, toyes* and *nights* all share the sound of terminal voiced or unvoiced *s*; *wine, divine, lights, sights, delights* and *nights* all share the sound of long *i*. The effect in each of these instances is to pull together lines systematically separated by the poem's formal structure. A similar effect is manifest in the following:

A Booke of Ayres, I.1-4, (*live/reprove/dive/revive*): terminal *v*, and 3-6 (*dive/revive/light/night*): long *i*; IV.13-16 (*shineth/night/light/devineth*); V.8-11 (*ensued/prove/eschewed/love*): shared long *u*, complicated by the imperfect rhyming of *love/prove*; VII.14, 17-20, 22 (*sowing/bestowing/observing/changing/abiding/deviding*): final *ing* sound; VIII. 7-10 (*dore/before/neere/heare*): different vowel-plus-*r* sounds; 11-14 (*speake/breake/take/wake*): different long vowel-plus-*k* sounds; X.9-12 (*flie/simpathie/flight/delight*); XI.1-6 (*admiring/ desiring/requiting/blindness/unkindness/delighting*): long *i*; 11-16 (*re- lenting/endles/friendles/lamenting/unredressed/distressed*): short *e* in penultimate syllables; XII.8, 10-12 (*devine/thine/right/despight*);

The First Booke of Ayres, I.9-12 (*grace/place/rage/asswage*): IV.4-6, 10-12 (*erred/feared/reared/secured/assured/recurred*): vowel-plus-*r* in penultimate syllable, short *e*-plus-*d* in final syllable; V.1-4 (*thine/ night/shine/light*); VI. 19-20, 22-23, 25, 27 (*gate/State/make/take/ grace/place*); VII.8, 10-12 (*writer/light/dye/high*); VIII.5-8 (*wayes/ strained/prayse/unfained*); IX.2, 4-6 (*flowers/Bowers/Beare/there*); XIII.21-24 (*stray'd/wide/pray'd/guide*): terminal *d;* XIV.17-24 (*race/ day/deface/lay/sake/remaines/take/braines*): two four-line stanzas linked by a final vowel sound of long *a;* XV.25-28 (*rejoyce/prayse/ voyce/dayes*): voiced and unvoiced *s;* XVI.7-10 (*man/paine/span/ vaine*): long and short *a*-plus-*n;* XVII.2, 4-6 (*light/night/flye/dye*); XIX.9-16: each word in the second stanza ends with a voiced *s* sound; XX.19-20, 23-24 (*make/Cake/breake/speake*);

The Second Booke of Ayres, I.2, 4-6 (*deeme/seeme/me/be*); II. 1-4, 7 (*chained/fained/grace/disdained/place*): long *a;* 1-2, 4-7 (*chained/ fained/disdained/beguiled/smiled/exiled*): terminal *ed;* 9-13, 15 (*increaseth/griefe/ceaseth/reliefe/me/me*); 16-17, 19-21, 24 (*graced/ placed/embraced/proved/removed/loved*): terminal *ed;* V.26, 28, 30, 32 (*fate/late/grace/place*); VI.9-12 (*strive/desire/revive/fire*); VII.1-4 (*right/tyed/delight/bide*); 7-10 (*commends/red/friends/bred*); VIII.2, 4- 7, 10-12 (*removed/loved/pleased/diseased/plighted/delighted/fixed/ mixed*): terminal *ed;* IX.1-2, 4, 6 (*tell/dwell/brest/blest*); 7-8, 10, 12 (*be/me/reliefe/griefe*); 13-15, 17 (*guile/while/disguise/eyes*);19-20, 22, 24 (*me/be/sees/freese*): notice that the corresponding lines in stanzas 1, 2 and 4 are linked by their respective patterns; X.7-10 (*Queene/ heaping/greene/reaping*); 11-12, 14-15, 17-20 (*expresses/kisses/ offenceless/sencelesse/kisse/us/harmlesse/is/us*): terminal voiced or unvoiced *s,* preceded by short *e* in some words; XI.9-12/over- flowne): various *o*-plus-*m/n* combinations; 25-28 (*present/then/ content/men*); XIV.1-2, 7-8 (*die/I/flie/denie*); 12-13, 15-16 (*be/me/ weene/seene*); XV.25, 27, 29, 31 (*strangenesse/plainenesse/jest/blest*);

The Third Booke of Ayres, VII.2, 4, 6-9 (*day/stray/vaine/fain/ delay/pain*); VIII.1-4 (*scorn'd/ador'd/adorn'd/implored*); 6-12 (the whole stanza linked by various long vowel-plus-*m/n* combinations); X.6-10 (the whole stanza linked by long *e* sounds); XIII.9-12 (*offending/enchanting/ending/wanting*); 13-14, 16, 18 (*share/are/other/smother*); XIV.4-12 (the entire poem linked by short *e* sounds in the metrically accented penultimate syllables); XV.3-6 (*findes/shines/sight/delight*); XVI.6-8, 10 (*beare/there/flowres/howres*): vowel-plus-*r*; 9-12 (*flowres/grasse/howres/passe*): terminal voiced or unvoiced *s*; XVIII.1-2, 5-6 (*ayre/chayre/fire/bryer*); 5-6, 11-12 (*fire/bryer/devise/eyes*); XIX.2, 4-6 (*mine/shine/admire/fire*); 7-8, 11-12 (*move thee/love thee/bee/agree*): long *e* in penultimate or final syllables; XX.1-2, 8-9 (*fire/desire/fire/desire*): exact repetition of rhyme words; 10-14 (*fire/desire/flye/denye/dry*); XXIII.1-4, 11-12 (*delight/pine/sight/divine/flight/light*); 7-10 (*enclose/blisse/Rose/is*): voiced or unvoiced *s*; XXIV.7-10 (*redeeme/please/esteeme/ease*); XXV.1, 3, 7, 9, 11-12 (*me/see/sleepes/weepes/three/mee*); XXVII.13-14, 17-18 (*require/retire/beare/feare*); XXIX.13-16 (*gain'd/disgrace/enchain'd/embrace*);

The Fourth Booke of Ayres, II.3-6 (*gaine/paine/alone/one*); IV.1, 3, 7, 9 (*me/be/heale/zeale*); VII.2, 4, 7-10 (*grow/flow/enclose/row/showes/snow*); IX.13-16 (*minde/finde/bide/side*); 25-28 (*Gull/pull/tell/well*); XI.13-16 (*content/profession/repent/discretion*); XII.10, 12-14 (*me/shee/exceedes/needes*); XIII.4-9 (*blinde/finde/minde/spye/dye/flye*); XIV.1, 5-6 (*hell/fuell/cruell*); 7, 11-12); *fled/truthless/ruthlesse*); 5-6, 11-12, 17-18 (*fuell/cruell/truthlesse/ruthlesse/madnesse/sadnesse*): short *e* in metrically unaccented final syllable; XV.5-7, 9 (*shape/Ape/made/shade*); XVI.1, 3, 5-6, 8, 10 (*liv'd/depriv'd/light/night/write/delight*); XVII.7-10 (*fayre/desires/repayre/fires*); XVIII.1-3, 7-9 (*meaning/gleaning/weaning/season/reason/treason*): long *e* in metrically accented penultimate syllables; 7-12 (*season/reason/treason/compassion/fashion/occasion*): terminal vowel-plus-*n*; XIX.19-22 (*return'd/knock'd/mourn'd/lock'd*): terminal consonance in *d*; 32, 34-36 (*minde/behinde/end/contend*); XX.1-4 (*eyes/eares/spies/feares*): final voiced *s*; XXI.13-16, 19-24 (*sweet/see/meete/be/forespeake/feele/weake/steele/grieve/believe*); XXII.1-2, 7-8 (*desire/fire/higher/Fire*); XXIII.13-16, 18, 20-21, 23 (*may/embraces/stay/places/complaine/payne/May/away*); XXIX.5-8 (*moved/loved/resolved/absolved*): *ed* in the metrically unstressed final syllables; 9-14 (*Order/father/mother/another*): *er* in the metrically unstressed final syllables.

Note 6. An account of disyllabic rhymes in Campion's songs (see Chapter 3, n. 3):

Nearly all of Campion's songs contain instances of an informal phonetic relationship among the penultimate syllables in lines whose final syllables rhyme formally—relationships that serve to strengthen the bond between lines paired by their formal rhyme syllables. See, for example:

A Booke of Ayres, II.5-6 (easely broke/sturdie Oke): long e in the penultimate syllables; V.1, 3 (forsake mee/make me); 4, 6 (playing/a-maying); 12, 14 (undooing/wooing); 19, 20 (stranger/danger); 23, 25 (fained toong/deepest wrong): short e in penultimate syllables; 26, 28 (betraying/a-maying); VII.3, 6 (greeting/meeting); 4-5 (neerer/clearer); 7-8 (delighted/united); 14, 17 (sowing/bestowing); 15-16 (receiver/giver); 20, 22 (abiding/deviding); VIII.11-12 (to speake/to breake): the identity of to and to helps establish the sufficiency of what is now, and may have been, the imperfect phonetic likeness of speake and breake; 17-18 (he smild/beguild); X.7-8 (did tend/did end); 9-10 (doeth flie/simpathie): vowel-plus-th; XI.1-2 (admiring/desiring); 4-5 (blindness/unkindness); 11, 14 (relenting/lamenting); 12-13 (endles/friendles); XII.2, 4 (in thee/pitie mee); XIII.2, 5, 7 (despite/guiltie spright/delight): long e in penultimate syllables; 4, 6 (terror makes/thunder cracks): vowel-plus-r helps to establish the sufficiency of what again may have been an imperfect rhyme; 8, 10 (of joyes/but toies): schwa in the penultimate syllables; 13, 16 (on mee/tyrannie): vowel-plus-n; 19, 21 (pleasure move/her love): vowel-plus-r; 20, 22 (banish/vanish); XV.6-7 (smiling/beguiling); 13-14 (dying/crying); XVI.7-8 (little higher/Cupids fire): short i; XVII.1, 3 (desire/retire); 6, 8 (denie not/flie not); 22, 24 (pleasure/treasure); XVIII.2, 4 (is free/vanitie): short i; XIX.8, 10 (lovers mone/ev'rie one): the v-r combination in lovers reappears in ev'rie; 12, 14 (faire armes/Paramours harmes): vowel-plus-r; 25, 27 (Lillies white/cheekes alight): long e-plus voiced s in the penultimate syllable of one line repeated as long e-plus-unvoiced s in the syllable preceding the penultimate one in the other line;

The First Booke of Ayres, I.1-2 (-ing spright/-ing night); II.2, 4 (is tree/-itie); III.1-3 (-chayning/fayning/-mayning); 4-6 (turned/burned/mourned): vowel-plus-r in the metrically accented penultimate syllables; 7-9 (-claymed/blamed/famed); 10-12 (-rused/-cused/-bused): notice that all three lines in each stanza of this song are linked by their disyllabic rhymes; IV.1-3 (sounded/grounded/-founded); 4-6 (erred/feared/reared); 7-9 (-lying/flying/-scrying); 10-12 (-cured/-sured/-cured): again, each line in every stanza is linked disyllabically; V.1, 3 (of thine/but thine); VI.1-2 (bright day/thy way); 3, 6, 8 (-member/-vember/ember); 4-5 (with feasts/British ghests): short i in the penultimate syllables, again

helping to establish the sufficiency of what may have been an imperfect
rhyme; 7, 9 (*excede/-sed deed*): short *e*; 12, 15, 17 (*-gations/Nations/
-blations*); 19-20, (*the gate/the State*); VII.1, 3 (*-tyred minde/I finde*): long
i in the syllable preceding the penultimate one in one line recurs in the
penultimate syllable of the other line; 7, 9 (*expresse/them lesse*); VIII.9, 11
(*effect/respect*); 10, 12 (*-peasing/pleasing*); IX.8, 10 (*endues/infuse*);
X.17-18 (*Statues then/to men*); XI.5-6 (*paradice/our eyes*): vowel-plus-*r*
in the syllable preceding the penultimate one in the first line repeated in a
different vowel-plus-*r* combination in the penultimate syllable of the
second line; XII.8, 10 (*revive/deprive*); XIII.1, 3 (*mine eye/I spye*); 5, 7
(*hath drawne/doth dawne*); 17, 19 (*I rais'd/I prais'd*); 18, 20 (*-stored
sight/-during night*): vowel-plus-*r* combinations in the syllables preceding
the penultimate ones in both lines; XIV.2, 4 (*we sat/begat*); XVII.11-12
(*denye/wee dye*); XVIII.1, 4 (*-sever/ever*); 2-3 (*Eagles flye/is high*); 5, 8
(*crowned/drowned*): *ou*-plus-*n* in the metrically accented penultimate
syllables; 9, 12 (*-fusion/-lusion*); 13, 16 (*-dored/-stored*); XXI.1-2 (*as
stone/and gone*): short *a*; 18-19 (*wreaths gay/decay*); 25-26 (*hop't
fame/but name*);

The Second Booke of Ayres, I.13, 15 (*content/consent*); 14, 16 (*-er
finde/-er kinde*); II.5-6, 8 (*-guiled/smiled/-iled*); 9, 11 (*-creaseth/
ceaseth*); 13, 14 (*leaves me/-ceives me*); 17-18, 20 (*graced/placed/
-braced*): long *a-s* in the metrically accented penultimate syllables; 21-22,
24 (*proved/-moved/loved*); 29, 31 (*languish/anguish*); IV.2, 4
(*-ceeding/-ceeding*); 5-6 (*to be/to mee*); 7, 9 (*-y griefe/reliefe*); V.2, 4 (*-ly
flow/-ly blow*); 6, 8 (*-er fade/her shade*); 22, 24 (*effect/neglect*); VI.2, 4
(*denye/shee flye*); 25, 27 (*the hard/demand*):schwa, or perhaps long *e*, in
the penultimate syllables; 26, 28 (*distaste/imbrac't*); 30, 32 (*be sought/be
caught*): note the various sorts of parallelisms between the words that
precede this pair—*They should be sought/They will be caught;* VIII.2, 4
(*-moved/loved*); 5-6 (*pleased/-eased*); 8, 10 (*plighted/-lighted*); 11-12
(*fixed/mixed*): short *i-x* in the metrically accented penultimate syllables;
17-18 (*-turneth/burneth*); IX.21, 23 (*is caught/is taught*); 22, 24 (*bait he
sees/makes men freese*): long *a* in the syllables preceding the penultimate
ones in both lines; X.3, 6 (*sowing/stowing*); 4-5 (*-ceiver/giver*); 8, 10
(*heaping/reaping*); 13, 16 (*loving/moving*); 14-15 (*-fencelesse/sence-
lesse*); XI.7, 9 (*pleasure/measure*); 8, 10 (*quarter/laughter*); 13, 15
(*-vised/-prised*); XII.2, 4 (*hath tam'd/hath inflam'd*); 5, 7 (*-ly
breathe/beneath*): a probable long *e* in both penultimate syllables, which
helps establish the sufficiency of long *e*-plus-different *th* sounds in the
final syllables; 6, 8 (*bowers/flowers*); 21, 23 (*doth view/anew*); schwa;

30, 32 (*this case/little grace*): short *i* in one penultimate syllable repeated in the syllable preceding the penultimate one in the second line; XIV.11, 14 (*will close/it goes*); 20-21 (*-lesse spright/as night*): unvoiced and voiced *s*; 23-24 (*it foe/will doe*); XV.2, 4 (*move me/love me*); 10, 12 (*flye me/-nye me*); 17, 19 (*licenc'd/silence*); 18, 20 (*passion/-casion*); 21, 23 (*men say/then they*); 22, 24 (*moving/roving*); 25, 27 (*strangenesse/plainenesse*); 26, 28 (*doting/-voting*); 30, 32 (*passion /fashion*); XVI.8, 10 (*desire/retire*); 22, 24 (*I were/I feare*); XVIII.8, 10 (*flying/crying*); 12, 14 (*pouring/-vouring*); 22, 24 (*sleeping/keeping*); 28, 30 (*blamed/-named*); XIX.2, 4 (*playing/-laying*); 9, 11 (*others /smothers*); 13-14 (*duely/truly*); 15, 17 (*to field/to weilde*); 16, 18 (*shipping/slipping*); 20-21 (*duely/truly*); XX.12, 14 (*is shee/will shee be*): short *i* in the penultimate syllable of one line repeated in the syllable preceding the penultimate one in the other line, whose penultimate syllable (*shee*) duplicates the final syllable of the first line; 16, 18 (*regard/reward*); XXI.1, 3 (*-fuse mee/-cuse me*); 7, 9 (*wav'ring/-fav'ring*);

The Third Booke of Ayres, I.1-2 (*spare not/care not*); 11-12 (*dying /flying*); 13-14 (*ever/never*); 17-18 (Adonis/*none is*); III.1-3 (*move mee/love thee/-bove mee*); 4-6 (*-jecting/-fecting/-tecting*); 7-9 (*reason/season/treason*); VI.4-6 (*-some growes/a Rose/of those*); 7-9 (*reject/effect/respect*); VII.1, 3 (*answers/dancers*); 10, 12 (*freedome/ needs them*); VIII.11-12 (*containe/and plaine*); IX.1, 3 (*moved/loved*); 5-6 (*much blisse/of this*); X.3, 5 (*despaire/as fayre*); 8-9 (*of steele/the heele*); XI.14, 16 (*to Love/to move*); XIII.4, 6 (*creating/rating*); 9, 11 (*-fending/ending*); 10, 12 (*-chanting/wanting*); 15, 17 (*-passes/graces*); 16, 18 (*other/smother*); XIV.1-3 (*-versing/-hearsing/-versing*); 4-6 (*-tends us/-friends us/sends us*); 7-9 (*-senting/-venting/-tenting*); 10-12 (*-pressed/-sessed/-blessed*): another song in which all three lines in each stanza are linked by disyllabic end rhymes; XVI.7-8 (*-ance beare/-tons there*); 10, 12 (*the grasse/shall passe*); XVII.11-12 (*-redrest/be possest*): long *e* in the penultimate syllable of one line repeated in the propenultimate syllable of the next line; 14, 16 (*disdaine/in vaine*); XIX.1, 3 (*named/ -flamed*); 7, 9 (*move thee/love thee*); XX.8-9 (*my fire/my desire*): penultimate syllable of one line duplicated in the propenultimate of the next line; 10-11 (*fire, fire/my desire*); XXI.3-4 (*are plac't/are grac't*); 11-12 (*am I/envy*); XXIII.2, 4 (*-gour pine/more divine*); 5-6 (*unkinde/enclin'd*); 13, 15 (*-tion can/of Man*); XXVI.1-2 (*clearly/ dearly*); 3-4 (*-reaved/-ceived*); 5-6 (*-stayned/fayned*); 7-8 (*blessed/ Cresseid*); 11-12 (*holy/folly*); 13-14 (*wonder/thunder*); 15-16 (*dying/ -vying*); XXVII.13-14 (*require/retire*): XXVIII.5-6 (*to converse/too perverse*); XXIX.1, 3 (*is fled/is dead*);

The Fourth Booke of Ayres, I.2-3 *(dying/crying)*; 6, 10 *(this light /despight)*; III.1-2 *(loved/-proved)*; 7-8 *(Amber/chamber)*; 13-14 *(glory/story)*; 17-18 *(live true/of new)*; VI.8, 10 *(unknowne/love growne)*; VIII.1-2 *(the Spheares/the yeares)*; 3-4 *(above/Midas move)*; 6-7 *(t'advance/that dance)*; IX.17-18 *(doth move/not love)*; 27-28 *(can tell/as well)*; XI.6, 8 *(pleased/-eased)*; 10, 12 *(weeding/bleeding)*; 14, 16 *(-fession/-cretion)*; XII.3, 5 *(obtaine/doth gaine)*; 9, 11 *(debase/-ies grace)*; 16, 18 *('tis true/as you)*; XIII. 13, 15 *(from paine/complaine)*; XIV.3-4 *(-mire it/-sire it)*; 5-6 *(fuell/cruell)*; 11-12 *(truthlesse/ruthlesse)*; 15-16 *(-cover/lover)*; 17-18 *(madnesse/sadnesse)*; XV.8, 10 *(they view/ -ways true)*; 11-12 *(is eterne/discerne)*: short *i*-plus-*s* in the propenultimate syllable of one line echoed in the penultimate syllable of the next line; XVIII.1-3 *(meaning/gleaning/weening)*; 4-6 *(-tayneth/fayneth/ -plaineth)*; 7-9 *(season/reason/treason)*; 10-12 *(-passion/fashion/ -casion)*: another song with each line in each stanza linked disyllabically; XIX.2, 4 *(my cares/my teares)*; 26, 28 *(-ly parts/deserts)*; XX.2, 4 *(to eares/to feares)*; XXI.11-12 *(I crave/I have)*; XXII.11-12 *(your heele/you feele)*; XXIII.1, 3 *(desire/retire)*; 2, 4 *(with love/-ish prove)*; 6, 8 *(-ny not/flye not)*; 9, 11 *(-ed sing/-fit bring)*; 10, 12 *(-sure sleepes/-er keepes)*; 14, 16 *(-braces/places)*; 17, 19 *(in this/amisse)*; 18, 20 *(complaine/man payne)*; XXIV.1-2 *(please mee/ease mee)*; 3-4 *(sicknesse/quicknesse)*; 7-8 *(resolved/absolved)*.

Note 7.   Trisyllabic rhymes in Campion's songs (see Chapter 3, n. 3):

A number of Campion songs contain instances of phonetic relationships among the two syllables that precede the formal rhyme syllables— relationships that again serve to strengthen the connection between lines paired formally by their end-rhyme syllables:

A Booke of Ayres, I.12-14 *(fortune ends/mourning friends)*; III.21, 23 *(have pillowes/of willowes)*; IV.1, 4 *(-py shaddowe/-pie shaddowe)*: these lines are identical throughout except for the initial *Yet* in line 4—*Follow thy faire sunne, unhappy shaddowe/Yet follow thy faire sunne, unhappie shaddowe;* 5, 8 *(depriveth/reviveth)*: these lines are also nearly identical throughout; 15, 16 *(-ie shineth/devineth)*; V.15, 17 *(thy pleasure/the treasure)*; 22, 24 *(misfortune/importune)*; VII.9, 11 *(armes enchayning /entertaining)*: four rhyming syllables—vowel-plus-*r* in *armes* and *-ter,* *en-* duplicated in both lines; XI.3, 6 *(requiting/delighting)*; 9, 10 *(lovers fortune/powers importune)*; XII.5-6 *(thou shalt prove/without love)*: a trisyllabic pairing in which the phonetically linked syllables *thou* and *-out* do not correspond metrically; notice also the different *th* sounds in *thou* and *with-* and the terminal *t* sounds in *shalt* and *-out;* XIII.9, 11 (*-ly delight/-ie require*); 14, 16 (*-es gracing/embracing*); XVIII.33, 35 (*amorous/Avernus*);

The First Booke of Ayres, IV.4-5 (*have erred/and feared*); 7, 9 (*relying/descrying*); 10, 12 (*secured/recured*); VI.30, 33 (*none other/can smother*); XII.5-6 (*heav'ns just rod/hand of God*); XIII.14, 16 (*Angels, flye/dangers lye*); XX.13-14 (*the fathers joy/the mothers boy*): ideational as well as phonetic rhyme;

The Second Booke of Ayres, II.5-6 (*beguiled/-ly smiled*); III.11-12 (*never be/-member me*); IV.8, 10 (*appeared/hath cleared*); 11-12 (*and divine/and she is mine*); VIII.14, 16 (*repenting/relenting*); IX.7-8 (*Saint there be/-maines for me*); XI.1, 3 (*divided/decided*); 2, 4 (*must bed thee/must wed thee*); 14, 16 (*restrayning/-ly fayning*); XV.1, 3 (*neglected/rejected*); 6, 8 (*it burneth/it mourneth*); 14, 16 (*prevented/re-pented*); XVIII: 2, 4 (*-ty smiling/beguiling*); 18, 20 (*of pleasure/loves treasure*); XIX.6-7 (*hath it duely/with him truly*): a loosely trisyllabic pair—terminal *th* in *hath* echoed in *with*, short *i* in *it* echoed in *him;*

The Third Booke of Ayres, I. 1-2 (*heares me not/mee forgot*): the order of the vowel-plus-*r* and long *e* patterns inverted in propenultimate and penultimate syllables; II.5-6 (*embracing/disgracing*); 7-8 (*in blind-nesse/unkindnesse*); III.8-9 (*in reason/is treason*); IX.2, 4 (*-relenting /repenting*); 9, 11 (*despayred/-repayred*); XI.7, 9 (*that deceive/craft receive*); XIII.3, 5 (*discourses/discourses*); XIV.1, 3 (*conversing/convers-ing*); 7-8 (*presenting/preventing*); XXVI.9-10 (*neglected/dejected*); XXVII.9-10 (*scorn'd in none/serv'd in one*): a complexly ideational as well as phonetic rhyme pair; XXVIII.1, 3 (*thy fond sute/thy tongue mute*): propenultimate syllables identical in both lines, penultimate syllables related by different *o*-plus-*n* sounds; XXIX.17-18 (*I am free/dyed in mee*);

The Fourth Booke of Ayres, I.7-8 (*all sorrow/Ile borrow*); IV.5-6 (*light alone/shine on one*): ideational as well as phonetic pairing; 7-9 (*try to heale/by too much zeale*); V.9-10 (*all there were/all the yeare*); IX.25-26 (*silken Gull/blossome pull*); XI.2, 4 (*submission/condition*); XIV.9-10 (*could borrow/-bled sorrow*): vowel-plus-*d* in the propenultimate syllables; XVII.11-12 (*thus resolve at last/then becomes the chast*): informal phonetic relations between three pairs of syllables; XIX.11-12 (*them brake forth/from the North*): vowel-plus-*m* in propenultimate syllables, *th* in propenultimate syllable of line 11 echoed in *th* in penultimate syllable of line 12; XX.1, 3 (*all thy thoughts to eyes/all thy friends to spies*): identity of *all, thy* and *to*, terminal *t/d*-plus-*s/z* in *thoughts* and *friends;* 13, 15 (*word and looke/golden hooke*): terminal *d* in propenultimate syllable, vowel-plus-*n* in penultimate syllables; XXIII.22, 24 (December/*remember*); XXIV.5-6 (*be moved/-ly loved*); 9-10 (*holy Order/no farther*): loosely trisyllabic pairing of long *o* in *holy* and *no* and vowel-plus-*r* in the first syllables of *Order* and *farther;* 11-12 (*a mother/another*).

Note 8. Rhyming or rhyme-like relationships (e.g., by anaphora) at the beginning of formally end-rhymed lines (see Chapter 3, n. 4):

In many of Campion's songs pairs of lines that are pulled together by the formal rhyme pattern are also pulled together by a phonetic relationship between their opening word or words. See, for instance:

A Booke of Ayres, I.9-10 (*No drum/Unless*): short *u*-plus-*m* in second syllable of one line repeated as short *u*-plus-*n* in first of second line; 13-14 (*When/Let*); 17-18 (*And/And*); II.1-2 (*Though/Though*); 5-6 (*The/But*): incidental repetition of short *u* in modern dialects; III.7, 9 and 27, 29 (*Her when we/But when we*); 17, 19 (*Who when we/But when we*); 8, 10 (*She/She*); 11, 13 (*If/But if*); 12, 14 (*She gives me/We must give*): phonetic likenesses coupling ideational opposition; IV.1, 4 and 5, 8 (*Followe/Yet follow*): lines 1 and 4 are in fact nearly identical: *Follow thy faire sunne, unhappy shaddowe/Yet follow thy faire sunne, unhappie shaddow;* repeating this pattern with variation, lines 5 and 8 are nearly identical only until their last four syllables: *Follow her whose light thy light depriveth/Yet follow her whose light the world reviveth;* VIII.1-2 (*It fell/While sweete*): chiasmic pairing of syllables with vowel-plus-*t* and vowel-plus-*l;* 7-8 (*Jamy/She lay*): another more strongly assertive example of chiasmic order, this time in syllables with long *e* and long *a* (note also the ideational and syntactic links between *Jamy* and *She*); 11-12 (*Bessie vow'd/He resolv'd*): repetition of long *e* and terminal *d* in second and third syllables; 19-20 (*Jamy then/Bessie*): long *e* in second syllables, the short *e* in third syllable of one line repeated in the first syllable of the next; IX.1, 3 (*The/The*); X.7-8 (*All/Still*): the pattern of vowel-plus-*l* in these lines is complicated by the repetition of *still* as the fifth syllable in each line (*All that I soong still/Still she was first, still*); XI.1-2 (*Faire, if you/Sweete, if you*): first syllables unrelated phonetically but parallel by syntax and logic, anaphora-like repetition of the second and third syllables; 3, 6 (*Grace deere love/Flie both love*): no phonetic relation between first syllables— which are nonetheless related as imperative verbs expressing opposite commands, anaphora-like repetition of third syllables; 4-5 (*Fond, but if/False, if*): alliteration in *f* in first, syntactically parallel but ideationally opposed syllables, third syllable of line 4 repeated as the second in line 2; 9-10 (*Fates if/Stars if*): anaphora-like repetition of the second syllables, no phonetic relation between the first though they are again parallel by syntax and logic; 11, 14 (*Yield reliefe by/Helpe to ease my*): vowel-plus-*l* in first syllables, long *e* in third syllables, long *i* in fourth syllables; XII.1, 3 (*Thou are not/Thou are not*); 2, 4 (*For/Nor*); 8, 10 (*My thoughts/I'le not*); XIII.2, 5 (*View/As, to*); 9, 10 (*All her/Other*): anaphora-like repetition of vowel-plus-*r* in second syllables; 15, 17 (*And her/Her*); XV.6-7 (*For by thy/I see thy*); 13-14 (*So that/The old*): chiasmic ordering of long *o* in first and fourth syllables surrounding the alliteration of *th* in the second and third syllables; XVI.3-4 (*In your faire/Yet never*): alliteration of *y* in *your* repeated in *Yet*, vowel-plus-*r* repeated in both third syllables and in the second syllable of the first line; 13-14 (*Nor woe/So*); XVII.9, 11 (*Have I/Time shall*): chiasmic pattern in which short *a* in the first and fourth syllables surrounds long *i* in the second and third syllables; 10, 22 (*In this/With the*): parallel sequence of short *i* in first syllables followed by alliteration in *th* in the second; 14, 16 (*My lips/Die, die in*); 18, 20 (*And not/That*): repetition of short *a* and vowel-plus-*t*; 22, 24 (*Securenes/O farewell*): vowel-plus-*r* in second syllables, short *e* in third; XVIII.6, 8 (*In harmeles/Nor sorrow*): vowel-plus-*r* combinations; XIX.11, 13 (*That/That*); 12, 14 (*Your/Your*): a second pairing of identical words, creating an alternating abab phonetic sequence at the beginning of these four lines that corresponds to the abab sequence of their end-rhyme words, *blew/armes/rue/harmes*; 18, 20 (*holds/no*); 22, 24 (*All you/Will make you*); 29, 31 (*All you/Bids you*); XX.8, 10 (*Of masks/And*): short *a;* 11-12 (*When/Then*): phonetic anaphora in the repetition of *en* in two temporal adverbs whose pairing by sound is also echoed in their pairing by syntax and logic. This two-part *When/Then* construction condenses and mirrors the poem's overall two-part logical structure, an extended "when" clause in stanza 1— *When thou must home to shades of underground,* etc.— being answered by an extended "then" clause in the first four lines of stanza 2— *Then wilt thou speake of banqueting delights.* The explicit pattern in *When/Then* in this poem thus runs, *When* (lines 1-6), *Then* (lines 7-10), *When* (line 11) *Then* (line 12).

The First Booke of Ayres, I.3-4 (*Lord, light/For, blinde*); 5-6 (*Sunne/But*); 7-8 (*Fountaine/Sweet showres*): *ou* dipthong connecting two ideationally connected words; II.6, 8 (*In harmlesse/Nor sorrows*): vowel-plus-*r* combinations; III.1-2 (*Where are all thy/Whither are thy*); 7-9 (*Yet in/That none/When*): vowel-plus-*t*, vowel-plus-*n*, short *e*; 10-12 (*When/Let/None*): two unifying patterns, one in short *e* and one in vowel-plus-*n*; IV.1-3 (*Out/Let/Lord*): vowel-plus-*t*, alliteration in *l*; V.2, 4 (*Shall I/I should*): chiasmic ordering of alliteration in *sh* surrounding a repetition of long *i*; 5, 7 (*But my/That I*); 14, 16 (When/Endlesse); 17, 19 (*In thy/Though I*); 18, 20 (*To thy/Yet thy*): though metrically unstressed, all of the second syllables in quatrain 5 are linked phonetically by long *i*; they are also linked by syntax and logic, the three second person pronouns at once attracted and opposed to the single first person pronoun; VI.4-5 (*Thou receiv'd/Come, chiefest*): long *e* in second syllables followed by *f/v*-plus-dental in third; 12, 17 (*In your/With your*): the disyllabic rhyme here matches the disyllabic rhyme at the end of these two lines (*-gation/ -blation*); 16-18 (*But this light/Prayse the Lord*): an all but unnoticeable chiasmus of schwa sounds in the incidental conjunction and article (*But/the*) surrounding a pair of similar but different vowel-plus-*s* sounds in the adjective and imperative verb (*this/Prayse*), alliteration in *th* in the second two syllables, alliteration in *l* in the two third syllables (which are also linked ideationally); 31-32 (*This/That*): common alliteration in *th* of two correlative adjectives whose potential syntactic agreement is broken when the second (*That*) proves to be a conjunction ([so] *that thine own renowne might see*); 34, 36 (*May/May*); VII.7, 9 (*All/Celestiall*); 8, 10 (*Is but/Yet*); 11-12 (*Such beames they/Such heate they*): unity of sense as well as sound; VIII.2, 4 (*Sing thy/Sometime*); 9, 11 (*Love/Love*); IX.7, 9 (*The Wolfe his young ones/The Lyons Welpe*): anaphora-like repetition of the definite article followed by two ideationally aligned nouns (one a subject and one modifying a subject) minimally connected by sound (shared *l*) and themselves followed by two ideationally related nouns also minimally connected by sound (alliteration in *w* in *ones, Welpe*); X.11-12 (*Such undooe/Of mankinde*): short *u* assonance in first pair of syllables, vowel-plus-*n* in second pair; 13, 15 (*Kindnesse/Blessed*): minimally assertive chiasmus of dental in first and fourth syllables surrounding short *e*-plus-*s* in second and third syllables; 14, 16 (*Conscience/Long ere*): sequential pairing of schwa-plus-*n* in first pair of syllables followed by short *e* in second pair (note recurrence of short *e* sound in five of the six second syllables in this quatrain: *Kindnesse, Conscience, Blessed, ere* and *Honest*); XI.1-2 (*Never weather-beaten/Never tyred*): anaphora in first word followed by repeated short *e* in two ideationally related adjectives; XII.1, 3 (*Lift up/The Lord*): minimally assertive chiasmus of alliteration in *l*-plus-terminal dental in the first and last words surrounding short *u* assonance in the second and third; 7, 9 (*With chearefull/Remorce for all*): vowel-plus-*r* and *f*-vowel-*r* combinations; 11-12 (*Strive then/The Sonne*): chiasmic pairing of alliteration in *s* around alliteration in *th*, complicated by an additional more strongly assertive pairing of the two second syllables by shared vowel-plus-*n*; XIII.2, 4 (*Pilgrim-like, I/Which, blinded, I*): patterns in short and long *i*; 10, 12 (*Drest with/That winning*): sequential pairing of first syllables by terminal *t* and second syllables by alliteration in *w*-plus-short *i*; 18, 20 (*My restored/The Lord*): no phonetic relation in first pair of syllables but the *or*-plus-dental spread out across the third and fourth syllables of line 18 (*re-stor-ed*) is telescoped to *ord* in the second syllable of line 20; 21, 23 (*And, since I/His grace I*); 22, 24 (*From his/Henceforth*): another multiply chiasmic pattern in which the *fr* sound in the first syllable is spread apart in *forth* and the second and third syllables alliterate in *h* and terminate in voiced and unvoiced *s* sounds; XIV.9, 11 (*Is then/O Salem*): an interesting repetition of vowel-plus-*s* condensed in the first syllable of line 9 and spread across the first two syllables of line 11, followed by short *e* assonance-plus-*m/n* in the respective second and third syllables of each line; 21, 23 (*Curst Babels seede/Blest shall they be*): a kind of trisyllabic beginning rhyme involving terminal *st* consonance in the first pair of ideationally opposed words, short *a*-plus-*l* spread out across the second and third syllables of line 21 condensed in the second syllable of line 23, and long *e* repeated in the fourth syllables of both lines (note also the phonetic relations between Babels and *Blest*: alliteration in *b*, the reordering of *bels* in the second syllable of Babels to *bles* in *Blest;* and the corresponding near-trisyllabic end rhyme in these lines: *Salems sake/babes that take*); 22, 24 (*Just ruine/And 'gainst*): moderately assertive chiasmus involving soft and hard *g* sounds followed by terminal *st* consonnance (cf. *Blest/Curst*) in the first and last words surrounding vowel-plus-*n* patterns in the third syllable of one line ("rue-in") and the first syllable of the next; XV.2, 4 (*Prayse our God/Is hee not Lord*): sequential patterning of vowel-plus-voiced *s* in the first pair of syllables, schwa-plus-dental in the third pair, and terminal *d* sound in the third syllable of line 2 and the fourth of line 4, also equal by logic (notice also the pattern of vowel-plus-*r* in *our* and *Lord*); 5, 7 (*Sing wee/With voyce*): another chiasmic pairing of *s* consonnance in the first and fourth syllables surrounding an alliteration in *w* in the second and third; 9, 11 (*First who/Whom*); 10, 12 (*From the East/When in the Seas*): a quasi-trisyllabic rhyme composed of vowel-plus-*m/n* in the first pair of syllables, a repetition of the definite article, and patterns of long *e*-plus-unvoiced *s* and unvoiced *s*-plus-long *e* in *East/Seas;* 13, 15 (*Hee/Who*): alliteration in *h* of the third person and interrogative pronoun (*Who* stands here for the object "what people" in a question whose answer in line 16 is again *hee*); 18, 20 (*Wayting/To ayde*); 26, 28 (*Sounding/And*); XVI.2, 4 (*That sleep'st*/*'Tis not*): minimally assertive but unusual chiasmus pairing similar vowel-plus-*t* sounds around a secondary chiasmus of *st*/*t*-vowel-*s*; 7, 9 (*Get up, get up*/*Yeelds but the*): barely noticeable dentals at or near the end of both first syllables (same metrical position, different speech stress), chiasmic pattern of short *u*-plus-plosive/plosive-plus short *u* in second pair of syllables, repeated short *u* sound in *up, up* repeated in *but the;* 11-12 (*One*/*Then*); XVII.2, 4 (*For, while*/*And I still*): conjunction of long *i*-plus-*l* in the second syllable of one line pulled apart in the second and third syllables of the next: *I* (sti)*ll*; XVIII.6-7 (*New joyes*/*Such*): no phonetic relation between the first pair of syllables, but a faint chiasmus in *joyes*/*Such* of initial soft *g* and final *ch* surrounding voiced and unvoiced *s*; XIX.1, 3 (*Lighten, heavy*/*Yeeld thy brest*): vowel-plus-*d*/*t* in first pair of syllables (*l*-plus-vowel in one reversed to vowel-plus-*l* in the other); 2, 4 (*The*/*The*); 14, 16 (*Th'unmoved*/*To view*): notice the ideational similarity coupled with phonetic dissimilarity in what follows: *Th'moved water*/*To view a streame*); XX.3-4 (*Doe their weeke*/*Devotely*); 5-6 (*Skip and*/*And helpe*); 9-10 (*Well can*/*And tell*); 13-14 (*Tib is all*/*And little*): a mildly assertive trisyllabic rhyme composed of *d*/*t* in first pair of syllables, short *i* in second pair, and terminal *l* consonnance in third pair (note the corresponding disyllabic end rhyming in these lines, *fathers joy*/*mothers boy,* also an ideational double rhyme pair made up of two simultaneously attracted and opposed possessive nouns followed by their two ideationally equivalent objects); 15-16 (*All their*/*And care*); 17-18 (*Jone can*/*And*); 19-20 (*Shee can*/*And*): pattern of short *a*-plus-*n* in previous two lines duplicated here (*Jone* and *Shee* are not related phonetically but are equal by logic); 21-22 (*Jacke knowes*/*And his*): note the recurrence of *And* at the start of every other line in this stanza; 31-32 (*Yet for*/*Securer*); XXI.1-2 (*All*/*For* Hally); 3, 5 (*Hally*/*All*): same vowel-plus-*l* sounds as in previous two lines chiasmically reversed and repeated in first pair of syllables here; 8-9 (*His Iv'ry*/*His Rosie*): ideational as well as phonetic rhyming of second two words (white/red); 10-11 (*Eyes that*/*His bright*); 20-21 (*Then*/*None*): 24-25 (*Quencht is*/*His hop't*): chiasmic ordering of terminal *t* sounds in first and fourth syllables enclosing *is* sound in second and third; 27-28 (*For him*/*Since more*): another phonetic chiasmus, pairing *or* sounds around a pair of short *i* sounds.

See also, *The Second Booke of Ayres,* I.1, 3 (*Vaine*/*Prayse*); 2, 4 (*Whose*/*Count those*); 7, 9 (*How faire an*/*What hart cannot*); 13, 15 (*So bitter*/*Ah, but*); 14, 16 (*Unhappy men*/*Else uncouth*); 17-18 (*Let us then*/*Men must*); II. 5-6 (*But*/*By*); 9, 11 (*My love*/*While*); 17-18 (*A Goddesse so*/*In her most*); III.1-2 (*Harden*/*Ne'er let*); 3-4 (*Once true happy/Both as one*); 5-6 (*But/What*); IV.1, 3 (*O what/What*): note true anaphora in lines 1-2 (*O what/O what*); 2, 4 (*O what/From*); 7, 9 (*Shee that alone/Shee now alone*): compare the ideational unity and division in what follows—*in cloudy griefe/with bright reliefe;*V.2, 4 (*The Rivers/The Winds*); 6, 8 (*Her/To Harbour*); 10, 12 (*Her/Her*); 17, 19 (*Her roses/Their boughs*); 22, 24 (*High wonders/My words*); 29, 31 (*And/Content*); VI.6, 8 (*Then/And*); 17, 19 (*Wise shee is, and/Fayre she is, and*); 22, 24 (*'Tis/If*); 30, 32 (*As they are faire/As they are wise*): trisyllabic anaphora followed by phonetically non-related adjectives that are nonetheless closely aligned by logic; note the phonetic, logical and syntactic parallelism in what follows: *they should be sought/they will be caught;* VII.11-12 (*Medowes/Though Roses*); 13, 15 (*Free/Shee*); VIII.1, 3 (*O deare/Where*); IX.7-8 (*Oh/Some hope*); 16, 18 (*My simple/By which my*); 19-20 (*Faire he/That he*); 27, 29 (*And not/That*); 29, 30 (*But rather/Where pittie*); X.3, 6 (*Growne ripe in/Rich in*); 7, 9 (*Kisse/Kisses*); XI.8, 10 (*Pay/Put*); 13, 15 (*Why were/Women are*); XII.2, 4 (*The Winter/The kinde*); 18, 20 (*Loves/Doth*); 26, 28 (*Why die/Am I*); 30, 32 (*Too justly/'Twill yeeld*); XIII.5, 7 (*Other/Such*); 6, 8 (*In you/To*); 14, 16 (*That/And*); 17-19 (*Which when/Woman*); XIV.1-2 (*Pin'd/And*); 3, 6 (*Doe/To*); 9-10 (*In my bed/It breeds*); XV.9, 11 (*Should I then/When I*); 14, 16 (*Which/Where*); 18, 20 (*To discourse/Loosing wisht*); 21, 23 (*Yet our/Women are*); 25, 27 (*When I/I pittie men*); 29, 31 (*While wee/Maydes, I see*); 30, 32 (*At their/That*); XVI.5-6 (*If another/'Tis but*); 15-17 (*When/When*); 19, 20 (*I am neerer/Hid in your*); XVII.1, 3 (*Come away/When loves*); 2, 4 (*Thy/They*); XVIII.5-6 (*No; you mock't/When you got*); 8, 10 (*Ile clip your/And keep you*); 18, 20 (*So/So*); 22, 24 (*When/Which*); XIX.1, 3 5 (*A secret/Yet/At*); 2, 4 (*I kindly welcome for/His desires, whole or*); 5-6 (*His owne he/Yet twits me*); 13-14 (*His owne enough/Yet still he twits me*); 15, 17 (*Wise Archers beare/Should Warriors learne*); 16, 18 (*The Venturer/Or thrive faire*); XX.1-2 (*Her rosie/Are Spheares*); 8, 9 (*More worthy/That her*); 10-11, 13 (*Oh, could she/Or that shee/Doe or speake*); 16, 18 (*Though she/Are only*); XXI.8, 10 (*My/Yet my*); 11-12 (*Oh wretched griefe/My onely griefe*);

The Third Booke of Ayres, I.5-6 (*Had/His*); II.7-8 (*When/Or vexe*); 9-10 (*If my/Why is*); 11-12 (*True love/False love*); 13-14 (*False then/Once false*); 15-16 (*Hee that/Shall*); III.1-2 (*Were my/But thy*); 5-6 (*Then/Friendship*); 7-8 (*While I/Thy*); IV.2, 4 (*They, forsooth/Maides were*); 14-16 (*But let/Ever let*); V.5-6 (*How/Hence*); 7-8 (*Come, come delight/Feele once heate*); 9-10 (*The lovers/Proud of*); 13-14 (*And/That*); VI.4-5 (*Tis thy beauty, foolish/Which who views*); 8-9 (*Then art/For the*);

10, 12 (*But/But*); VII.1, 3 (*Kind are/Breaks time*); 2, 4 (*But her/From their*); 8-9 (*Can true/Converting*); 11, 13 (*When/When*); VIII.1-2 (*O grief, O spight/Truth far exil'd*): r-vowel-*f*/*f*-vowel-r in second syllables, long *i*-plus-dental in fourth syllables; 3-4 (*Free Justice/Right cast*): ideational relation of *Justice* and *Right*; IX.10, 12 (*Distaste/Admit*); X.6-7 (*Her must/The more*); 9, 10 (*But cannot/The last*); XI.2, 4 (*Their /Their*); 5-6 (*Then/The*); 11-12 (*Yet some, I/But such by*); 13, 15 (*O why had/O would*); 17-18 (*Yet doe/To*); XIII.7-8 (*Thy voice is as an/Thy speech is as an*); XIV.1-3 (*What/Wealth/Woman*); 4-5 (*If weary/When with*); 7-8 (*What pretty/What we get*); 11-12 (*Good Wife/Bad with*); XV.1-2 (*Fire that/Flowers that*); 3-4 (*How can/Or can*); note short *a* in second syllable of lines 1-4 here; 11-12 (*Then will/As well*); XVI.7-8 (*With thee/Wee the*); 9, 11 (*Other/And thus*); 15, 17 (*Twenty/When*); 19-20 (*Thus/But*); XVII.1, 3 (*Shall I/Shall I*); 2, 4 (*When/Will*); 5-6 (*Let me not/Tell the long*); 11-12 (*So may/Ere my*); XVIII.1-2 (*Thrice tosse /Thrice sit*); 7-8 (*This/That*); XIX.8, 10 (*Challenge then/Let me call*); 11-12 (*State/Yet*); 17-18 (*To be thine/Ile love thee*); XX.1-2 (*Fire, fire/Loe here I*); 3-5 (*That/Out/Cannot*); 10-11 (*Fire/There*); 15-16 (*Come/Come*); XXII.2, 4 (*Since/Those little*); 7, 9 (*Palme tree/Free*); 11-12 (*What/Wilde*); XXIII.1, 3 (*Come, O come/Love loves no*); XXIV.2, 4 (*Then it harbours/That it scarce*); 5-6 (*Truest hearts/To despayre are*); 11-12 (*Wisedome/As if*); 17-18 (*Better/Then*); XXV.11-12 (*Pleade, sleepe/That shee*); XXVI.3-4 (*Shortly wilt/Little*); 5-6 (*This is/All is*); 9-10 (*Thy/And thy*); XXVII.1-2 (*Never/Beare*); 5-6 (*And/And*); 13-14 (*Men/Make*); 17-18 (*If these, and such like/Then like, and love*); XXVIII.5-6 (*An houre with thee I/For I would not be*); 7, 9 (*But roofes/The grove*); 13, 15 (*Since then/Till then*); 17-18 (*A heavenly/But never*); XXIX.1, 3 (*Shall I then/Or can I*); 2, 4 (*Can I seeke love/Poorely he lives*);

The Fourth Booke of Ayres, I. 2-3 (*All delayes/Many lost sighes*); 9-10 (*To tell my once/I dye alone*); II.3-4 (*Great/So great*); III.3-4 (*For this dost/And play'st*); 5-6 (*Thy glasse/That*); 13-14 (*Men that/One man*); IV.7, 9 (*Griefes past recur/The pure*); V.11-12 (*But th'attyres/That the wives*); 17-18 (*Happy man, Content that gives/Happy Dame, content that lives*); VI.2, 4 (*And so/O*); 8, 10 (*They now to/Alas, how soone*); VII.2, 4 (*When/Wherein*); 5-6 (*There Cherries/Till Cherries*); VIII.12, 15 (*And bent his/And Phoebus*); 13-14 (*Then/That*); IX.1-2 (*Young and/I have*); 3-4 (*Guesse/Men*); 9-10 (*Yet/Men*); 21-22 (*As/That*); 23-24 (*Roses/ Growe*); 27-28 (*Who shall not I/Who shall, would I*); X.1-2 (*Love me or not/Leave me or not*); 9-10 (*Could I enchant/Her would I charme*);

XI.13, 15 (*Command thy/Of Kindness*); 14, 16 (*And shame/That made*); XII.3, 5 (*Easely could/Fals-hood*); 7-8 (*Love forbid/Or in*); 10, 12 (*A simple truth/Truth*); 13, 14 (*Prayse is/Wealth, pris'd*); 16, 18 (*You know it/But to*); XIII.4-6 (*No eyes are/So fayre/Then strike, O*); 7-8 (*Is my fond sight/Close ayming at/Shoot home, sweet*); 10-12 (*O then we/And heale/O hope*); 13, 15 (*At large/Yet, Love*); X.3-4 (*Shee/Shee*): note phonetic rhyming throughout these two lines—*Shee wounds them that desire it/Shee kils them that admire it*; 5-6 (*Give her/No fire*); 15-16 (*My raving/I liv'd*); 17-18 (*The first step/Is the excesse*); XV.7-9 (*Eyes that/All's but*); 8, 10 (*What can/And*); 11-12 (*Reasons/Ev'n*); 17-18 (*What, or/But for*); 23-24 (*Let our/For pure*); XVI.7, 9 (*Be't eyther/'Tis their best*); XVII. 7, 9 (*Should/Shee*); 9, 10 (*That/That*); XVIII.4, 6 (*Learne to speake/Lookes a-squint*); XIX.13, 15 (*Then to/To them*); 14, 16 (*That/And*); 11-12 (*But a/As a*): compare *But, alast/With a* (17-18) and *Not a/For a* (23-24); 20, 22 (*And at her/Her*); 31, 33 (*Yet fled/Still did*); 35-36 (*Till/With*); XX.1, 3 (*Turne all thy/Change all thy*); 2, 4 (*Turne all thy/And all thy*); XXI.5-6 (*Yet/What*); 11-12 (*Since what I had/And what I had*); 13, 15 (*A Love I/Once by*); 20, 22 (*That never/Yet am*); XXIII.2, 4 (*Calme/Can*); XXIV.1-2 (*Faine would I/When my*); 9-10 (*Sure, I/When I*); 11-12 (*Yet I/As I*).

Note 9. Rhyming or rhyme-like relationships (e.g., by anaphora) at the beginning of lines that do not formally rhyme (see Chapter 3, n. 5):

In many of Campion's songs pairs of lines that are not pulled together by a formal rhyme connection are nonetheless paired by an informal phonetic connection between their opening word or words. Here are some examples:

A Booke of Ayres, I.6, 8 (*Then must/Then bloudie*); 10-11 (*Unless/But*); 14-15 (*Let/But let*); 16-17 (*And/And*); II.1, 3 (*Though you/Though youth*); 2, 3 (*Though/Though*); 4-5 (*Yet embers/The tender*); 8, 10 (*Yet stubs/Know buds*); III.5-6 (*Nature/Her*); 6-7 (*Her/Her*); 14-16 (*We must give/Give them/Give me*); 20-21 (*She/These*); 22, 25 (*And beds/And fresh*); IV.1-2 (*Followe/Though*); 4-5 and 8-9 (*Yet follow/Follow*); 5-6 (*Follow/Though*); 15-16 (*That/And*); 18, 20 (*The sunne/The sun*); V.8, 10 (*Had/Unhap-*); 10-11 (*Un-/This un-*); 16-17 (*What didst thou not/So didst thou rob*); 17-18 (*So/Which so*); 21-22 (*That/That*); 22-23 (*That/When flat*); 23-24 (*When/They en-*); 26-27 (*If this/But this*); VIII.2, 4 (*While/Light*); 5, 7-8, 10-12, 14, 16, 18-19, 22, 24

(*Jamy/Jamy/Jamy/She lay/She/Bessie/He/She/She/To see/Jamy/Deceiv'd/She sleepes*): the presence of long *e* at or near the beginning of these twelve lines pulls them together in relations that underscore the ideational and syntactic relations among most of these same words—e.g., *She/Bessie* and *He/Jamy*; IX.1, 4, 6 (*The Sy-/But I/Over mine*); 3-4 (*The/But*); 7-8 (*Yet/And then*); 9, 11 (*Which/Since*); 15-16 (*Beare/Where*); X.7-8 (*All/Still*); 9, 11 (*Yet/Then let*); XI.6, 8 (*Flie/Ile*); 13-14 (*Hope/Helpe*); XII.2, 4 (*For/Nor*); 8-10 (*My/Thy/I'le*); XIII.2, 4 (*View her/Her*); 6-7 (*The/But*); 8-9 (*All/Millions*); 10-13, 15, 17 (*Other/To her/My for-/For/And her/Her*): vowel-plus-*r* combinations in six lines; XIV.3-4 (*To/Who*); 10, 12 (*For/Poore*); XV.1-2 (*When/As yet*); 6-7 (*For by thy/I see thy*); 11, 13 (*That/So that*); 12, 14 (*But/The*); XVI.4-5 (*Yet/It*); 6, 8, 10, 12-13 (*Nor where/There, there/There/For/Nor*); 13-14 (*Nor woe/So*); XVII.5-6 (*If love/Loves*); 6-7 (*Heere/O tarrie*); 19, 21-22, 24 (*Your/Feare/Securenes/O farewell*); XVIII.8, 10-11 (*Nor sorrow/Nor armour/Nor*); 15-17 (*The horrours/And terrours/Thus scorning*); 18-19 (*That fate/He makes*); XIX.3-4 (*Bids you/You*); 27, 29 (*Shall/All*); 33, 34 (*On de-/She*); XX.8-9 (*Of/Of*); 10, 12 (*And all/Then tell*); XXI.5-6 (*Heav'n is/His*); 8-9 (*Both/O*); 15-16 (*Guide my/Of thy*); 21-22 (*But when/O then*);

The First Booke of Ayres, II.10-11 (*Nor/Nor*); 15-17 (*The horrors/And terrors/Thus, scorning*); III.9-10 (*When/When*); IV.6-7 (*Ev'n/Thee*); V.2-4 (*Shall I/Might thy/I*); 11-12 (*They/Blaze*); 17-20 (*In thy/To thy/Though I/Yet thy*); 4, 6-7 (*Thou/Thou/Thou*); 14-16 (*His/Of his/But this*); 26-27 (*None/For none*); 29-30 (*To him/To him*); VII.6-7 (*Will/All*); 9-10 (*Celestiall/Yet fullest*); 11-12 (*Such/Such*); VIII.1-2 (*Tune thy/Sing thy*); 4-5 (*Sometime/Strive*); IX.2-3 (*Like/Thy*); 4-5 (*Nor/There*); 7-8 (*The Wolfe her young ones/The foxe his Cubbs*): ideational as well as phonetic correlations; X.1-2 (*Good men/Wise men*); 3, 5 (*Feeble/Hee*); 6-7 (*Beares/Some there*); 12-13 (*Of mankinde/Kindness*); 18, 20 (*Honest/Foster*): terminal *st* in metrically noncorresponding syllables; 22-23 (*Wholesome/All so*); XI.1-2 (*Never/Never*); 2-3 (*Never tyred/Then my*); XIII.3, 5 (*What/But*); 15-16 (*Ev'n in/In*); 22-23 (*From his/His*); XIV.19, 21 (*Hurle/Curst*); 21-23 (*Curst/Just/Blest*); XV.3-4 (*His/Is*); 10-11 (*From/Whom*); 17-18 (*Angels/Wayting*); 22-23 (*And his/His*); XVI.11-12 (*Yet/Then*); XVII.4-5 (*And I/times*); 6-7 (*So/But, O*): note the ideational rhyme in the fourth syllables of these lines—*So ev'ry day/But, O yee nights*; XVIII.4-5 (*Then/When*); 8-9 (*That worldly/Farewell, World*); XX.6-7 (*And/Lash*); 10, 12 (*And tell/And turn*); 17, 19 (*Jone can/Shee can*); 25, 27 (*Now, you scorn/Though you court-*); 27, 29 (*Though/Though*); notice that the word *And* begins lines 6, 10, 12, 14, 16, 18, 20, 22, 24, 28 and 30; XXI.2-3 (*For* Hally/Hally); 6, 8 (*Ev'ry/Iv'ry*); 9, 11 and 23, 25 (*His/His*); 9, 10 and 11, 13 (*His/Eyes*); 16-17 (*Adorn'd/glory*); 27-28 (*For/Since more*);

The Second Booke of Ayres, I.10-11 (*Who, seeing/Shee*); 15-18 (*Ah, but/Else un-/Let us/Men must*); II.6-7 (*By love/In some*); 15, 17 (*A Goddesse/A Goddesse*); 28-29 (*For none/No wonder*); III.8-9 (*Who/Who*); IV.1-3 (*O what/O what/What*); V.2-3 (*The/The*); 5-6 and 9-10 (*Her/Her*); 14-15 (*And/And*); 16, 18 (*Let heav'n/And when*); 23-24 (*O why/My*); 26-27 (*Woe worth/For, though*); 28-30 (*That/And/That*); VI.5-6 (*Worse then/Then*); 17, 19-20 (*Wise she/Fayre she/That she*); 21-22 (*If/'Tis*); 22-23 (*'Tis but/What*); VII.7-8 (*Some/Some*); VIII.10-11 (*Alike/Why*); 15-16 (*As snow/So*); IX.2-3 (*Where/Farre*); 6-7 (*And onely/Oh*); 9-10 (*Prayer or/From her*); 12, 14 (*Or/The more*); 23-24 (*And too/That too*); X.6-7 (*Rich/Kisse*); XI.4-5 (*Sure wee/Pre-*); 14-15 (*Are/Women are*); XII.1-2 and 4-5 (*The/The*); 16-17 (*That/What*): terminal *t;* 17-18 (*What/Loves*): schwa assonance; 26-28 (*Why/Why/Am I*); 29-32 (*O beautie/Too justly/Unkindly/'Twill yeeld thee*); XIII.12-13 (*For/Sweet, afford*); 12, 14 (*For that/That*); 16, 18 (*And fill/All shall*); 19-20 (*Woman/Or man*); XIV.21, 23 (*For that/That*); 16, 18 (*And fill/All shall*); 19-20 (*Woman/Or man*); XIV.21, 23 (*For it/Be it*); XV.4-5 (*There is/Why is*); 6-7 (*It freezeth/Looseth*); 25-26 (*When I/With my*); 28, 30 (*Their/At their*); XVI.6-7 (*'Tis/Is*); 7-9 (*Is this/Your wisht/Suspicions*); 13-14 (*Still/Is*); 18-19 (*And I/I*); 20-21 (*Hid in/Is this*); 23-24 (*Some/So much*); XVII.3-4 (*When loves/They must*); 8-9 (*How/How*); 9-10, 12 (*How many/When/Attending*); XVIII.1, 3, 5 (*Come you/Thinke you/No; you*): note also *When you* in line 6, which is end-rhymed with line 5—*day/away;* 11-12 (*Sooner/And number*); 16-18 (*Which/Such/So rich*); 17, 19 (*Such/But*); 21, 23 (*Would/Would*); XIX.2-3 (*I/Yet my*); 4, 6 (*His/His*); 10-11, 13 (*Is/Or is/His*); 15-16 (*Wise Archers/The Venturer*): ideational as well as phonetic pairing; XX.2-3 (*Are/Her*); 7-8 (*More/Fore*); 13-14 (*Doe or/For*); 17-18 (*For/Are*); XXI.2-3 (*In you my/In you my*); 7-8 (*Why/My*); 10, 12 (*Yet I/My*);

The Third Booke of Ayres, II.4-5 (*That/But*); 12-13 (*False/False*); IV.1-2 (*Maydes/They*): ideational as well as phonetic pairing; 5-6 (*Truth/Few*); 7-8 (*Then/When*); 9-10 (*Love/But*); 11-12 (*Rather/Ever*); V.14-15 (*That/Action*); VIII.10-11 (*Though/Old*); IX.1-2 (*O/O*); 10-11 (*Distaste/Great*); X.7, 9 (*The/The*); XI.3-4 (*Now kinde/Their kindnes*);

XIII.3-4 (O/Old); 7-8 (Thy/Thy); 10-11 (Hast/And); 12-13 (Other/Some); 17-18 (If/Doe it); XIV.9-10 (Sorting all/All); XV.2-3 (Flowers/How); 4-5 (Or/Fayre); 10-11 (Yet/Then); 14-15 (O let/Let); XVI.2-3 (Doe but fixe/Little sute); XVII.3-4, 6 (Shall/Will/Tell); 5-6 (Let/Tell); 9-10, 12 (For/Or/Ere); 14-15 (Which/'Tis); 16-17 (To/Doe); XVIII.2-3 (Thrice/Then thrice); 4-5 (And murmur/Goe burne); 6-7 (These/This); XIX.2-3 (Since thy/For by); 10, 12 (Let/Yet); 15-16, 18 (I/In thine/Ile); XX. 16-17 (Come/Some); XXI.2-3 (With her/To heare her); 6, 8 (Such love as this/Such love as this); 7, 9 (When all/And all); XXII.2-3, 5, 7-9 (Since she/Though she/That she/Palme tree/Leave/Free); 10, 12 (And for/Wilde borne); XXIII.4, 6 (The/The); 10-11 (In them/Come); XIV.2-3 (Then it/It); 3-4 (It/That it); 9-10 (That/Halfe); 10, 12 (Halfe/As if); 13-14 (Yet no/Growne); XXV.10-11 (Dreames/Pleade); 11-12 (Pleade, sleepe/That shee); XXVI.1, 3 (Silly/Shortly wilt); 4-5 (Little/This); 6-7 (All is/All is); 10, 12 (And/And); XXVII.1, 3 (Never/Men); 6-7 (And/Men that); 14-15 (Must/Sometimes); XXVIII.1-2 (So/So); 4-5 (And/An); 13-14 (Since then I can/In heaven I am); 14-15 (In heaven/Till then); XXIX.1-2 (Shall I/Can I); 2-3 (Can/Or can); 4, 6 (Poorely hee/Shee); 7-8 (When I/When I); 16-17 (As shee/But shee);

The Fourth Booke of Ayres, I.7, 9 (To/To); 8-9 (Yet/To tell); II.7, 9 (Some/Such); III.4, 6 (And play'st/That first); 12-13 (Then/Men); 13-14 (Men/One man); IV.1-2 (Vaile/The plagues); 3, 5 (If beauty/Who); 7-8 (Griefes past/That greater); V.6-7 (That before/Dames of yore); 16-17 (For let man/Happy man); VI.1-2 (So/And so); 3-4 (As I/O why); VII.1-2 (There is/Where Roses); 4-5 (Wherein/There): note the chiasmus at the start of lines 1-2 and 4-5 (There/Where/Where-/There); 6-7 (Till Cherry/Those Cherries); 13-14 (Her Eyes like/Her Browes like); VIII.12-13 (And bent/Then); IX.2-3 (I/Guesse I); 10-11 (Men that/As glad); 16-17 (Ever/Where); 22-23 (That/Roses that); 26-27 (Shall/Who shall); X.6, 8 (Her to/Who); 10, 12 (Her would I/So would I); XI.7-8 (Love/He must); 9-10 (These thorny/Or); 13-14 (Command/And); XII.2-3 (Heaping/Easely); 11-13 (Great is/Truth is/Prayse is); 15-16 (Fayre you/You); XIII.9-10 (Shoot home/O); XIV.1-2 (Beauty/Aye me); 2-3 (Aye me/Shee); 7-8 (Pittie/Aye mee); 14-15 (Aye/My); XV.4-5 (Whose forme/Fairenesse); 6-7 (Is/Eyes); 6-8 (Is but/Eyes that/What); 19-20 (Love in the/Not in the); XVI.1-2 (Since she/Sweete shee); 3, 5 (Why/Why); 6-7 (Better to/Be't eyther true); XVIII.3-4 (Nurces/Learne); XIX.4-5 (With grace/They); 19-20 (So backe/And at); 22-23 (Her/Not a word); 27-28 (That make/As they); 30-31 (Fled/Yet fled); 33-35

(Still/Still/Till); XX.1-2 *(Turne all thy/Change all thy)*; 13-14 *(Wrest every/Racke ev'ry)*; XXI.7-8 *(Thanks be/No maladies)*; 10-11 *(Yet live/Since)*; 12-13 *(And what I had/A Love I had)*; 16-17 *(Shee/She)*; XXII.1, 3 *(Beauty/About you)*; XXIII.5-6 *(If Love/Loves)*; 18-19 *(Or/There)*; XXIV.4-5 *(And that, oft I/Oft have I)*; 10-11 *(When I/Yet I)*.

Note 10. Phonetic anadiplosis in Campion's songs (see Chapter 3, n. 6):

Phonetic anadiplosis—the linking of the end of one line to the beginning of the next by assonance, consonance, alliteration, etc.—occurs frequently in Campion's verse; its effect is to provide immediate continuity from one verse-line to the next, and so to counteract the formal separation between lines. Here are some examples:

A Booke of Ayres, I.10-11 *(love/But)*; 13-14 *(ends/Let)*; II.1-2 *(old/Though)*; 2-3 *(cold/Though)*; 9-10 *(boast/Know)*; III.4-5 *(maide /Nature)*; 11-12 *(Amarillis/She gives)*; 13-14 *(Ladies/We)*; 25-26 *(Amarillis/With)*; IV.1-2 *(shaddowe/Though)*; 4-5 *(shaddowe/Follow)*; 5-6 *(-eth/Though)*: terminal *th* becomes initial *th*; 13-14 *(-eth/There)*; V.13-14 *(done/When)*; 20-21 *(men/When)*; VI.5-6 and 11-12 *(speake/Ev'n)*; VII.10-11 *(lips/With)*; 12-13 *(is/As)*; 21-22 *(lips/Let)*; VIII.11-12 *(speake/He)*; IX.12-13 *(left/Griefe)*: terminal fricative; 15-16 *(sure/Where)*; X.4-5 *(love/But)*; 5-6 *(paine/Then)*; 8-9 *(end/Yet)*; XI.13-14 *(friendles/Helpe)*; XII.2-3 *(thee/Thou)*; 8-9 *(-vine/Thy)*; XIII.18-19 *(bee/She)*; XV.4-5 *(prove/To)*; 6-7 *(smiling/I)*; XVI.3-4 *(rest/Yet)*; 7-8 *(higher/There)*; 10-11 *(lyes/Those)*; 15-16 *(higher/I)*; XVII.4-5 *(prove/If)*: terminal voiced and unvoiced fricative; 22-23 *(pleasure/ Then)*; XVIII.2-3 *(Free/From)*; 9-10 *(towres/Nor)*; 11-12 *(flie/From)*; 23-24 *(Inne/And)*: vowel-plus-*n*; XIX.21-22 *(vigill/All)*: the pattern in vowel-plus-*l* provides linkage between not only lines but stanzas; 27-28 *(-light/Love)*; XX.1-2 *(ground/And)*; 5-6 *(love/From)*; 11-12 *(thee/ Then)*; XXI.2-3 *(creator/Author)*: ideational as well as phonetic linkage; 6-7 *(thunders/One)*; 16-17 *(devinenes/Cleanse)*: linkage between stanzas; 21-22 *(-nes/O then)*;

The First Booke of Ayres, I.9-10 *(grace/The faint)*; II.2-3 *(free/From)*; 9-10 *(towres/Nor)*; 23-24 *(Inne/And)*; IV.4-5 *(erred/Therefore)*; 7-8 *(-lying/In thy)*; v.2-3 *(night/Might)*; 3-4 *(shine/I)*; 8-9 *(-in/Cleanse)*; 18-19 *(five/Though I)*; VI.8-9 *(-ber/for)*; 11-12 *(Lord/In your)*; 15-16 *(-tions/But)*; 23-24 *(take/Lay)*; VII.1-2 *(minde/And)*: terminal *nd*; 3-4 *(finde/From)*; 7-8 *(-presse/Is)*; 9-10 *(lesse/Yet)*; VIII.2-3 *(sorrow/ Though)*; 9-10 *(-fect/Sweetest)*; IX.4-5 *(Bowers/There)*; 5-6 *(Beare/But)*:

alliteration in *b*; X.7-8 (*seeke/Making*); 12-13 (*societie/Kind-*): *societie* rhymes formally with *tye*; 13-14 (*cold/Con-*); 17-18 (*then/Hon-*); 19-20 (*flow/Foster*): alliteration in *f*; 21-22 (*grow/Whol-*); XI.4-5 (*rest/Ever*); XII.8-9 (*revive/Re-*); 10-11 (*-prive/Strive*); XIII.8-9 (*sight/Straight*): terminal *t*; 9-10 (*hell/Drest*); XIV.2-3 (*sat/Sweet*): alliteration in *s* and *t*; 5-6 (*there/Our*); 11-12 (*Forget/Forget*); 12-13 (*hand/Fast*); XV.20-21 (*ill/All*); XVI.6-7 (*gate/Get*); 10-11 (*vaine/One*); XVII.4-5 (*night/Times*); XVIII.2-3 (*flye/For*); 4-5 (*ever/When*); 14-15 (*blisse/Whose*): terminal *s*; XIX.2-3 (*Fled/Yeeld*): alliteration in *l* and *d*; 10-11 (*-sues/Whose*); 11-12 (*hasts/Her*); XX.8-9 (*hayre/His*); 14-15 (*hee/His*); 16-17 (*powre/Glor-*);

The Second Booke of Ayres, I.9-10 (*move/Who*); 15-16 (*-sent/Else*); II.3-4 (*grace/Straight*); 5-6 (*-guiled/By*); 8-9 (*exiled/My*); 23-24 (*rest/Where*); IV.6-7 (*mee/Shee*); 11-12 (*divine/Since I*); V.2-3 (*flow/The groves*); 5-6 (*fayre/Her*); 16-17 (*more/Her*); 25-26 (*worth/Woe-worth*); 26-27 (*fate/For*); 31-32 (*not/Nor*): *n* allitertion in logically related monosyllables; VI.10-11 (*-sire/More*); 11-12 (*-vive/I*); 20-21 (*loves/If*): vowel-plus-fricative, the third word in line 12 is also *love*; 27-28 (*-mand/Want*): different *a* sounds preceding *n*-dental; VII.10-11 (*bred/Medowes*); 15-16 (*ground/And*); VIII.10-11 (*-lighted/Why*); 13-14 (*teares/Our*); 16-17 (*-lenting/Vexed*); IX.3-4 (*seeke/So*); 15-16 (*-guise/My*); 17-18 (*eyes/By*); 18-19 (*-fused/Faire*); 20-21 (*be/But*); 24-25 (*freese/From*); X.1-2 (*is/As*); 5-6 (*giver/Rich*); 14-15 (*-fencelesse/As those*); XI.4-5 (*thee/Pre-*); 5-6, 11-12, 17-18 (*more/Here's*); XII.1-2 (*winde/The Winter*); 3-4 (*kinde/The kinde*); 13-14 (*come/From*); 23-24 (*anew/To*); 29-30 (*accus'd/Too*); XIII.12-13 (*be/Sweet*): linkage between stanzas; XIV.14-15 (*goes/Tis*): terminal *s*; 18-19 (*it/That* terminal *t*; XV.6-7 (*burneth/Looseth*); 19-20 (*-lence/Loosing*): initial *l* and terminal *s/z* in the rhyming syllables; XVI.10-11 (*-tire/While*); 12-13 (*say/Still made*); 17-18 (*stand/And*); XVII.1-2 (*-lights/Thy*); XVIII.8-9 (*flying/Smothring*); 9-10 (*heape/And keepe*); 26-27 (*laugh/But if*): terminal *f* sound in the rhyming syllables; XIX.5-6 (*-dresse/His*): terminal unvoiced and voiced *s* sounds; 8-9 (*flowes/No*); 12-13 (*Rose/His owne*); 16-17 (*shipping/Should*); XX.3-4 (*-locke/Make*); 7-8 (*rare/For*); XXI.3-4 (*me/My*);

The Third Booke of Ayres, I.3-4 (*delay/Dayes*); 5-6 (*use/His*); 7-8 (*mourne/For*); II.12-13 (*flying/False*); III.4-5 (*objecting/Then*); 5-6 (*affecting/Friendship*); IV.1-2 (*say/They*); 3-4 (*obey/Maides*); V.5-6 (*this/Hence*); VI.7-8 (*poore/For*); VII.2-3 (*day/Breakes*); 7-8 (*faine/Can*): terminal *n*; 12-13 (*them/When*); VIII.9-10 (*owne/Though*);

IX.3-4 (*loved/Fond love*); X.1-2 (*-lent/Let*); 5-6 (*fayre/Her*); 8-9 (*steele/The Grecian*); XI.12-13 (*so/O*); XIII.1-2 (*thee/The*); 8-9 (*-feit/For*); 10-11 (*-chanting/And*); XIV.6-7 (*us/What*); 8-9 (*-venting /Sorting*); XV.1-2 (*fed/Flowers*); 5-6 (*sight/Sweet*); 9-10 (*you/Yet*); XVI.2-3 (*prove/Little sute*); 3-4 (*win/Way*); 8-9 (*there/Other*); 10-11 (*grasse/And thus*); short *a*-plus-*s* combination at the end of one line pulled apart in two words in the next line; 14-15 (*be/Twenty*); 17-18 (*kinde/And*); 18-19 (*thee/Thus*); XVII.4-5 (*lett/Let*): phonetic identity in words that are syntactically and logically different; 11-12 (*-drest/Ere*): *r*-plus-short *e* in one syllable reversed in the next; XIX.5-6 (*-mire/I*); 8-9 (*place/Say*); 9-10 (*thee/Let me*); 10-11 (*grace/State*); XX.1-2 (*fire/Loe here I*); 4-5 (*braine/Can-*); 6-7 (*Thames/Dread*); 9-10 (*-sire/Fire*); 10-11 (*fire/There*); 15-16 (*downe/Come*); 16-17 (*drowne/Some*): in both of these instances patterns of different *o* sounds and nasals repeat; XXI.1-2 (*blisse/With*); 8-9 (*sow/Such*); XXII.1-2 (*so/Since*); 2-3 (*me/Though she*); 4-5 (*she/That she*); 8-9 (*-ceede/Free*); XXIII.1-2 (*-light/Let*); 6-7 (*thee/Thou*); XXIV.10-11 (*ease/Wise-*); 13-14 (*can/Growne*); 15-16 (*Man/That*); 17-18 (*blest/Then*); XXV.6-7 (*kinde/My*): linkage between stanzas; 9-10 (*weepes/Dreames*); 11-12 (*thee/That shee*); XXVI.2-3 (*man/Men*); 6-7 (*-pent/Men*); 14-15 (*-tire/Sometimes*); XXVIII.1-2 (*sute/So rude*); 15-16 (*minde/And*); XXIX.5-6 (*free/Shee*); 7-8 (*-vents/When*); 17-18 (*free/Faith*);

The *Fourth Booke of Ayres*, I.9-10 (*delight/I dye*); II.3-4 (*gaine/So great*); 6-7 (*one/Some*); 11-12 (*sake/My faith*); III.4-5 (*eyes/Thy*); 6-7 (*within/'Tis*); 7-8 (*Amber/And*); V.1-2 (*be/But*); 6-7 (*dyes/Dames*); 11-12 (*land/That*); 13-14 (*descend/And*); 15-16 (*frame/For*); VI.2-3 (*sight/As I*); 9-10 (*all/Alas*); VII.15-16 (*kill/All*); VIII.3-4 (*-bove/But*); 8-9 (*kinde/That quite*); 9-10 (*minde/And*); IX.1-2 (*I am/I have*); 14-15 (*finde/Like*); 18-19 (*love/If*); 21-22 (*past/That*); 23-24 (*last/Roses that*); 25-26 (*Gull/Shall*); 29-30 (*be/Love hee*); X.6-7 (*mee/Envy*); 9-10 (*were/Her*); XI.2-3 (*-mission/Is*); 8-9 (*diseased/These*); XII.4-5 (*force/Fals-*); XIII.3-4 (*so/No*); XVI.2-3 (*me/Shee*): phonetic likeness, ideational opposition; 4-5 (*it/Give*); 14-15 (*me/My*); 17-18 (*-nesse/Is*); XV.17-18 (*bin/But*); 19-20 (*-got/Not*); 21-22 (*hot/Her*); XVII.7-8 (*fayre/That were*): vowel-plus-*r* combinations; 8-9 (*-sires/Shee is admir'd*); 11-12 (*last/Shee hath*); XIX.3-4 (*wise/With*); 8-9 (*-light/I*); 19-20 (*-turn'd/And*); 22-23 (*lock'd/Not*); 23-24 (*finde/For*); 31-32 (*fast/As*); 33-34 (*haste/Still*): alliteration in *st*; 23-24 (*-hinde/till I*); XX.10-11 (*youth/True*); 13-14 (*looke/Racke*); XXI.1-2 (*kill/Come*); 3-4 (*still/This*); 12-13 (*have/A love*); 15-16 (*meete/Shee*); 16-17 (*be/She*);

XXII.3-4 (*rest/Yet*); 7-8 and 15-16 (*higher/There*); 10-11 (*borne/For*);
11-12 (*heele/His*); XXIII.4-5 (*prove/If Love*); 12-13 (*keepes/O come*);
13-14 (*may/Let's chayne*); 22-23 (*December/When*); XXIV.1-2
(*mee/Maides*); 6-7 (*loved/But*).

Note 11. Phonetic epanilepsis in Campion's songs (see Chapter 3, n. 7):

Phonetic epanilepsis—the repetition of sounds at the beginning and end
of a verse-line, as in "Now winter nights enlarge," line 11 (*While...Sights*)
and line 17 (*All...well*)—also occurs frequently in Campion's songs; its
effect provides unity to the individual verse-line, and so reinforces the
formal separation between verse-lines. Consider the following examples:

A Booke of Ayres, I.10 (*Unles...love*): schwa; 13 (*When...ends*): short
e-plus-*n*; 14 (*Let...friends*); 15 (*But...come*); II.1 (*Though... old*); 10
(*Know...frost*): *frost* rhymes with *boast;* III.3 (*Give... Amarillis*): short *i;*
15 (*Give...love*); 21 (*These...pillowes*): terminal voiced *s;* IV.1 (*Followe...shaddowe*); V.4 (*When...maidenhead*); 8 (*Had...ensued*): terminal
d; 13 (*But...done*); 27 (*But...shun*); VI.6 and 12 (*Ev'n...breake*): rhymes
with *speake;* VII.13 (*As...kisses*); 14 (*Growne...sowing*); VIII.12
(*He...breake*): rhymes with *speake;* 19 (*Jamy...play*); 22
(*Deceiv'd...deceit*); IX.2 (*And...cast*); 8 (*And...stands*); 14 (*When...gone*);
15 (*Beare...sure*); X.6 (*Then...againe*); XII.8 (*My...divine*); 10 (*I'le...thine*);
XIII.1 (*See...me*); 15 (*And...find*); 20 (*And displeasing...banish*); XIV.9
(*And...fain'd*); XV.6 (*I see...beguiling*); XVI.4 (*Yet...brest*); 8
(*There...fire*); 16 (*I...desire*); XVII.1 (*Your...desire*); 4 (*Doe...prove*); 11
(*Time...requite*); 13 (*Then...come*); 19 (*Your...heart*): *r* sounds; 22
(*Securenes...pleasure*): short *e* and *ur* sounds; XVIII.7 (*Whome...delude*);
13 (*Hee only...behold*): long *e*, long *o* and *l* sounds; XIX.2, 9, 23, 26, 30
(*the Fairie...Proserpina*): vowel-plus-*s,* long *e;* 12 (*Your...armes*); 14
(*Your...harmes*); XX.1 (*When thou...ground*); 6 (*From...move*): *f/v, m;* 9
(*Of Turnies...of knights*); XXI.13 (*Rescue...darknes*): short *e, k* and *s;*

The First Booke of Ayres, II.7 (*Whom...delude*); 13 (*Hee only...behold*);
III.7 (*Yet...-claymed*): "clai-med"—short *e*-plus-dental; 9 (*When...
famed*): "fai-med"—short *e* and nasal; 10 (*When...perused*); 11
(*Let...excused*); IV.1 (*Out...sounded*); 2 (*Let...grounded*); 5 (*Therefore
...feared*); V.3 (*Might...shine*); 4 (*I...light*); 6 (*On...sinne*); 10 (*At
thine...white*); VI.1 (*Bravely...day*); 15 (*Of...-tions*); 31 (*This hee...thee*);
VII.9 (*Celestiall...lesse*); VIII.10 (*Sweetest...appeasing*); IX. 5 (*There...
Beare*); X.10 (*Vexe...bent*); 18 (*Honest...men*); 20 (*Foster...showres*);
XI.1 (*Never...shore*); 2 (*Never...more*); 3 (*Then...brest*); XII.2

(*What...threat*); 8 (*Thy...-vive*); XIII.17 (*Straight...rais'd*); 18 (*My...sight*); XIV.4 (*And...begat*); 8 (*Some...sung*); 9 (*Is...fit*); XV.14 (*That...stand*); 19 (*Arm'd...send*); 24 (*Their...swerve*); XVI.3 (*Rise... sight*); 4 (*'Tis...begin*); XVII.5 (*Times...flye*); (*When...-sest*); XVIII.4 (*Then...ever*); 5 (*When...-ed*); 15 (*Whose...is*); XIX.1 (*Lighten...spright*); 6 (*And...minde*); 13 (*Skies...windes*): rhymes with *findes* XX.9 (*Well...Ale*); 10 (*And tell...tale*); 23 (*Make...breake*); XXI.6 (*Ev'ry...mee*); 10 (*Eyes...grace*); 11 (*His...face*);

The Second Booke of Ayres, 1.3 (*Prayse...prove*); 11 (*Shee...mee*); II.4 (*Straight...-dained*); 6 (*By...smiled*); 17 (*A Goddesse...graced*); 21 (*But love...proved*); 31 (*It is...anguish*); IV.7 (*Shee...griefe*); 9 (*Shee...reliefe*); 12 (*Since I...is mine*); V.5 (*Her...fayre*); 23 (*That...late*); 31 (*Content ...not*); VI.4 (*From...five*); 6 (*Then...burne*); 12 (*I...fire*); 31 (*When...well*); VII. 7 (*Some...commends*); VIII.4 (*Yet...loved*): "lov-ed"; 8 (*When...-ed*); 10 (*Alike...-lighted*); 12 (*Must...mixed*); 17 (*Vexed...-eth*); IX.5 (*She...meeke*); 21 (*But...caught*); X.2 (*As...kisses*); 3 (*Growne...sowing*); 5 (*Of...giver*); 7 (*Kisse then...Queene*); 13 (*Of...loving*); 15 (*As those...sencelesse*); XI.6 and 18 (*Here's...dore*); 7 (*Tenants...pleasure*); 11 (*Consider...more*); 12 (*Here's...store*); 13 (*Why...-vised*); 15 (*Women... -ed*); 16 (*Sleeping...-ing*); XII.3 (*And...kinde*); 4 (*The kinde...-flam'd*); 6 (*Out...bowers*); 13 (*The...come*): schwa; 14 (*From...unknowne*); 18 (*Am...men*); XIII.2 (*that...sight*): terminal *t;* 3 (*Whom...view*); 7 (*Such...love*); 13 (*Sweet...sight*); 20 (*Or...faire*); XIV.1 (*pin'd...die*); 3 (*Doe...-fuse*); 6 (*To...muse*); 17 (*Would...wit*); XV.9 (*Should...wooed*); "woo-ed"; 10 (*Seek-...mee*); 11 (*When...-ed*); 19 (*While...silence*); 25 (*When...-nesse*); 30 (*At...passion*); 32 (*That...fashion*); XVI.8 (*Your... -sire*); 15 (*When...hand*); 17 (*When...stand*): short vowel-plus-*n* in both these examples; 22 (*Would...were*); 25 (*And...-tend*); XVII.2 (*Thy... there*); 7 (*Is shee...is shee*); 11 (*These...close*); XVIII.1 (*Come...-ton*); 7 (*When...fled away*); 8 (*Ile...flying*); 11 (*Sooner...starres*); 13 (*Tell... Temmes*); 17 (*Such...was*); 19 (*But...reapt*); 20 (*So trustlesse...treasure*); 23 (*Would...were*); 26 (*And...laugh*); 30 (*And...unnamed*): nasals and dentals; XIX.3 (*Yet...-lesse*); 11 (*Or...-ers*); 17 (*Should...weilde*); XX.7 (*More...rare*); 18 (*Are...-ward*); XXI.4 (*My...-prise*);

The Third Booke of Ayres, I.1 (*Oft...not*); 4 (*Dayes...day*); II.1 (*Now...not*); 7 (*When...-nesse*); 12 (*False...flying*); III.5 (*Then...-fecting*); 6 (*Friendship...-tecting*); IV.1 (*Maydes...say*); 10 (*To...Jew*); V.7 (*Come...braine*); 11 (*Poore...-dure*); 13 (*And...minde*); VI.8 (*Then...-fect*); VIII.9 (*O...growne*); X.2 (*Let...spent*); XI.1 (*If

Love...love); XIII.11 (*And...ending*); 15 (*As...-passes*); XIV.5 (*When...
friend us*); 9 (*Sorting...-ing*); 11 (*Good...-ed*); 12 (*Bad...blessed*); XV.1
(*Fire...fed*); 7 (*But...none*); XVI.1 (*If...love*); 2 (*Doe...prove*); 3
(*Little...win*); 9 (*Other...flowres*); 23 (*And...fast*); XVII.2 (*When...set*); 4
(*Will...lett*); 12 (*Ere...-sest*); XVIII.8 (*That...have*); XIX.6 (*I...fire*); 16
(*In...pen*); XX.1 and 10 (*Fire...fire*); 6 (*Come...Thames*); 11 (*There...
-sire*); 15 (*Come...downe*); 16 (*Come...drowne*); XXI.2 (*With...is*); XXII.3
(*Though...shew*); 8 (*Leave...-ceede*); XXIII.6 (*The...thee*); 10 (*In...is*);
XXIV.17 (*Better...blest*); 18 (*Then...best*); XXV.1 (*Sleepe...me*); 4
(*Those...spoke*); 11 (*Pleade...thee*); XXVI.1 (*Silly...clearly*); XXVII.6
(*And speake...repent*): *n*-plus-dental, *p*, long *e*; 8 (*Make...more*);
XXVIII.1 (*So...sute*); 5 (*An houre...converse*): vowel-plus-*n*, vowel-plus-*r*;
6 (*For...perverse*): *f/v*, vowel-plus-*r*; 10 (*Gray...place*); 17 (*A heavenly
...have*); XXIX.2 (*Can...gone*); 6 (*Shee...mee*); 7 (*When...-vents*);

The Fourthe Booke of Ayres, I.10 (*I...-spight*); II.3 (*Great...gaine*); 4 (*So
great...paine*); 9 (*Such...thus*); III.2 (*To...-proved*); 6 (*That...within*); 11
(*Is't...swords*): *s* and dentals; 17 (*'Tis...true*); IV.4 (*Suffice...kinde*); 7
(*Griefes...heale*); 9 (*Affection...strict*); V.1 (*Ev'ry...be*); 3 (*Borrow'd...
best*): alliteration in *b* and dental; 12 (*That...stand*); 13 (*Once...descend*);
14 (*And...amend*); 15 (*Aid...frame*); VI.9 (*Not...all*); VII.7 (*Those...
-close*); VIII.6 (*Then Pan...t'advance*); 10 (*And...trance*); IX.12
(*When...wooe*); 15 (*Like...bide*); 18 (*Venus...love*): ideational as well as
phonetic rhyming; 21 (*As...past*); 22 (*That...last*); 23 (*Roses...
over-blowne*); 24 (*Growne...alone*); 26 (*Shall...pull*); X.8 (*Who loves...to
one*); 10 (*Her...heare*); XI.8 (*He...diseased*); 12 (*But...bleeding*); 13
(*Command...content*): alliteration in hard *c*, *m/n* and dental; XII.7
(*Love...thrive*); 11 (*Great...grace*); 15 (*Fayre...fayre*); 16 (*You...true*);
XIII.1 (*O...bow*); XIV.7 (*Pittie...is fled*): short *i* and dental; 13 (*Sor-
row...Fury sing*): *s*, vowel-plus-*r*; 16 (*I liv'd...lover*); 18 (*Is...-nesse*);
XV.11 (*Reasons...eterne*); 12 (*Ev'n...discerne*); 13 (*Soule...so*); 23
(*Let...meete*); XVI.1 (*Since...liv'd*); 3 (*Why...-priv'd*); 4 (*For-...borne*); 5
(*Why...light*); 6 (*Better...endlesse night*): short *e*, dental; 7 (*Be't...fain'd*):
terminal dental; 8 (*That...write*): terminal dental again; 11 (*O...so*);
XVII.5 (*To...hue*); 11 (*Rest...last*); XVIII.4 (*Learne...pertayneth*); 5
(*Hee...he fayneth*): phonetic likeness in metrically corresponding syllables
in these two lines; XIX.3 (*I...wise*); 5 (*They...awake*); 13 (*Then...fled*); 20
(*And...knock'd*): alliteration in *n* and terminal *d*; 21 (*Where...mourn'd*);
30 (*Fled...lov'd*); XX.2 (*Turne...eares*): Vowel-plus-*r*; 17 (*For...free*);
XXI.1 (*If...kill*); 2 (*Come...paine*); 5 (*Yet...guesse*); 8 (*No...-noy*); 12
(*And...have*); 16 (*Shee...be*); 17 (*She gave...shee gave*); XXII.4 (*Yet...

brest); 8 and 16 (*There...fire*); XXIII.1 (*Your...-sire*); 14 (*Let's chayne...embraces*): short *e*, *m/n* and *s/z*; 23 (*When...-way*); XXIV.5 (*Oft...moved*): "mov-ed"—*f/v* and terminal dental; 9 (*Sure...Order*).

Note 12. Further examples of expanding and contracting sound patterns (see Chapter 3, n. 8):

Patterns of expanding and contracting alliteration—in which pairs of consonants appear in different combinations with one another, in one order or the reverse order and either joined together or split apart by intervening consonant and/or vowel sounds—are very highly concentrated in Campion's verse. The following is an account of some of these patterns in *The First Booke of Ayres*, XX:

> When thou must home to shades of under ground,
> And there ariv'd, a newe admired guest,
> The beauteous spirits do ingirt thee round,
> White Iope, blith Hellen, and the rest,
> To heare the stories of thy finisht love,
> From that smoothe toong whose musicke hell can move:
>
> Then wilt thou speake of banqueting delights,
> Of masks and revels which sweet youth did make,
> Of Turnies and great challenges of knights,
> And all these triumphes for thy beauties sake:
> When thou hast told these honours done to thee,
> Then tell, O tell, how thou didst murther me.

One pattern involves the dentals *d* and *t* in expanding and contracting combinations with the nasals *m* and *n*. In line 1, *m* and *t* are separated by the sound of *us* in *must* and by a word break in *home to*; *n* and *d* appear next to each other in *under* and *ground*. The same conjunction recurs in the first word of line 2, *And;* the same two sounds are divided in the reverse order in *ariv'd, a newe*, and are reversed again (again with an intervening short *a*) in *newe admired*, in which *m* also appears juxtaposed with and separated from two different *d* sounds. In line 3, nasals and dentals are spread apart in *do ingirt;* they are joined in the reverse order in *round,* and reappear in that same combination in *and* in line 4. In line 6, *t* is divided from *m* by a word break and the sound of *s: that smoothe*. In the second stanza, nasal precedes dental by a word division and the length of one syllable in *Then wilt* (7), and by roughly the same amount of time in *banquet-* (7); they are contracted in *and* (8) and all but contracted in the reverse order in *did make* (8). They pull apart in the same order in *Turnies*

(9) and, in the reverse order, in *knights* (9). They come back together in the next word, *And* (10), and are inverted and separated in *triumphs* (10). In line 11, they are more widely separated in *When thou hast*, and come back together in the reverse order in *done*. In line 12, they appear separated by only a word division in *Then tell*, and reappear in the same order but pulled apart in *didst murther*.

The dentals *d* and *t* also occur in combination with various *r* sounds. In line 1, *r* follows *d* in *under*; it precedes *d*, with the time between the two sounds increased, in *ground*. In line 2, *d* and *r* are separated by the length of one syllable and a word division in *And there*; the distance between the two sounds in reverse order is roughly the same in *ariv'd*; *r* occurs in two combinations with *d* in *admired*. Nasals and dentals are pulled together in line 3 in *ingirt*, and are reversed and separated in *round*. In line 4, they are separated in *rest*; they reappear in the next two lines, divided in *To hear*, brought closer in *stories*, and reversed and expanded in *From that*. In line 9, an *r* sound follows a dental in *Turnies* and *and great*, and precedes one in *great* by itself. The two sounds are contracted in *triumphes* (10), are inverted and separated by voiced *s* and a word division in *honours done* (11), and are separated by one syllable and a word break in *didst murther* (12).

The dentals *d* and *t* also occur in combination with various *r* sounds. In line 1, *r* follows *d* in *under*; it precedes *d*, with the time between the two sounds increased, in *ground*. In line 2, *d* and *r* are separated by the length of one syllable and a word division in *And there*; the distance between the two sounds in reverse order is roughly the same in *ariv'd*; *r* occurs in two combinations with *d* in *admired*. Nasals and dentals are pulled together in line 3 in *ingirt*, and are reversed and separated in *round*. In line 4, they are separated in *rest*; they reappear in the next two lines, divided in *To hear*, brought closer in *stories*, and reversed and expanded in *From that*. In line 9, an *r* sound follows a dental in *Turnies* and *and great*, and precedes one in *great* by itself. The two sounds are contracted in *triumphes* (10), are inverted and separated by voiced *s* and a word division in *honours done* (11), and are separated by one syllable and a word break in *didst murther* (12).

The sound of *d* or *t* also expands and contracts with the sound of voiced or unvoiced *s*. In line 1, a dental and sibilant are contracted in *must*, and are contracted in the reverse order in *shades*. The two sounds reappear together in *guest* in line 2 and, inverted, in *spirits* in line 3, which pulls together the *t* and *s* sounds of *beauteous*. They are contracted again in *rest* (4) and are contracted and then expanded in *stories* (5), a word that also figures in a pattern in which *t* and *s* are widely separated: *To hear thy stories*. They are divided in *smoothe toong* (6), inverted and contracted in *delights* (7), reversed and pulled apart in *sweete* (8), reversed again and divided in *Turnies* (9), and then contracted in *knights* (9). They are expanded in *triumphes* (10), brought closer in *beauties* (10), joined in reverse order in *hast* (11), all but joined in *honours done* (11) and in fact joined in *didst* (12).

The nasals also appear in combination with the fricatives *f* and *v*. In line 1, the sound of voiced *f* (*v*) is separated from *n* by a word break and schwa in *of under*. Their distance is increased in *ariv'd, a newe* (2); unvoiced *f* comes close to a nasal in *finisht* (5), and is somewhat more divided in *From* (6); voiced *f* follows a nasal in *move* (6). The two sounds reappear inverted and separated by only a word break in *Of masks* (8), and are pulled apart in the reverse order in the next two words: *and revels*. They are inverted and expanded in *Of Turnies* (9), and then are contracted in *of knights* (9) and *triumphes* (10).

Nasals also come together and pull apart in combination with various *r* sounds. In line 1, *n* and *r* are divided in *under* and, in the reverse order, in *ground*. Nasal and *r* sounds are separated in line 2 in *And there*, are more widely separated in *ariv'd, a newe*, and are pulled closer together in *admired*. They occur chiasmically in line 3: first with *n* before *r* in *ingirt*, then reversed in *round*. They are separated in *And the rest* (4), brought close together in *From* (6), pulled apart in *masks and revels* (8), contracted in *Turnies* (9), expanded in *triumphes* (10), brought closer in the reverse order in *honours* (11) and *murther* (12), and are inverted and separated by only a word division in *murther me*.

These same patterns occur in many other songs. Here are some examples: Dentals and nasals expand and contract in *A Booke of Ayres*, I.1-6 (*My sweetest, and, And, not, heav'ns great lampes doe* [alternating *n, t, m, d*], *Into, and, But soone, must, night*); III.1-5 (*not, must, and, kind, wanton, countrey, maide, Nature, disdaineth*); IX.1-2 (*curten, night, And, silent*); *The First Booke of Ayres*, I.6-7 (*mists, and, darknes, compar'd, Fountaine, wounds*); VII.1-3 (*To Musicke, bent, my retyred, mind, And, faine would, But in, comfort, find*); The Third Booke of Ayres, VIII.1-3 and 6-9 (*kinde, no day, time, dancers, And, vaine./ O did, but onely, Can true, converting*); and XXI.7-8 (*golden, times, did know, When all did, yet none*).

The dentals come together and pull apart with various *r* sounds in *A Booke of Ayres*, I.1-6 (*sort, our deedes, great, strait, strait again revive, ever-during*); III.1-5 (*care not, praide, kind Amarillis, countrey, Nature, art*); *The First Booke*, VII.1-6 (*retyred, comfort, finde:/ From, true, record, ev'ry note, word*); *The Second Booke*, XI.14-18 (*dores, Are not, restrayning, are most, surprised, grace me yet, little more, barre not, dore*); XVI.1-4 (*strangenesse, frets, hat, perswade, Art, secret*); *The Third Booke*, III.1-2 (*Harden, tyred, hart, flinty rage, Ne'er let, teares, constant griefe*); and *The Fourth Booke*, VI.1-6 (*discourse, right, Nature, for beauties, grac't, words, better, better take*).

There are good examples of dentals expanding and contracting with voiced and unvoiced *s* sounds in *A Booke of Ayres*, I.1-6 (*sweetest, let us, sort, deedes, Let us, heav'ns great, lampes doe, west, straight, But, soon, set, is our little, must*); X.1-2 (*Saint, accents, sweet, Haste, sad, noates*); XIV.11-12 (*brests, his court, Cupid sits, sits, nails for cold*); *The First Booke* I.4-6 (*desires, wander as, stray, starres, underlights, mists, darknes*); *The Second Booke*, XVIII.1-4 (*false-ey'd, crafty smiling, to escape, words*); *The Third Booke*, XXVIII.1-2 (*So hot so, mad is, fond sute, So rude, so tedius*); *The Fourth Booke*, III.1-5 (*joy'st, most, dames, this dost, disguise, play'st, Sycophant, t'observe, councel'st, t'adorne thy skin*); and VI.1-6 (*sweet, sweet is, discourse to, so delightful, sight, taste, Was it, beauties, grac't, words*).

The nasals *m/n* appear in combination with the fricatives *f/v* in *A Booke of Ayres*, V.8-13 (*foreseene, prove/ Unhappie, event, Maides foreknow, feare naught*); XIII.1-4 and 12-15 (*flies enrag'd, from, me/View, swift then, mov'd, My fortune, frownes, blowne affections, find*); *The First Booke*, VII.2-4 (*faine, vaine, comfort, finde, From, heav'nly*); X.3-5 (*vant, revenge, alone forgive that can*); *The Second Booke*, VI.1-6 (*Faine, my love, love and, From, motion if, paine is feare, fancy*); VII.14-18 (*unmoved, ev'ry ground, And favours, ev'ry time, loves with mine, sov'raigne, and fayre*); VIII.14-18 (*fond, heav'nly, melts love, Vexed kindnesse, soone fals, off, and , flame*); X.11-18 (*Dove alone, fervencie, most loving, offencelesse, And void, moving, love and, envie*); and *The Fourth Booke*, IV.1-5 (*love, mine, from, private will not, proves kind, heav'ns.*

Finally, nasals also expand and contract with various *r* sounds in *A Booke of Ayres*, XII.1-4 (*not faire, red and, ornaments, art not, mee, Nor, faire nor, nor*); XXI.3-6 (*number, Harmonie, framed, throne, perpetually shining, devine power, thunders*); *The Second Booke*, III.9-12 (*admire, triumph, art onely, time there, never, remember me* [*r, m, m, r, m*]); *The Third Booke* VII.7-10 (*Nature, growne, Poore in, desert, in, name rich, proud of shame, are not, your owne, honour*); X.6-7 (*Her must, or none, none breathes, more, my despayre*); and *The Fourth Booke* XVIII.2-4 (*learne, Nurces, children, Learne, first, then, pertayneth*).

Note 13. Phonetic unity in individual verse-lines (see Chapter 3, n. 9):

Any Campion line is very likely to repeat certain key sounds. Here are some good examples:

A Booke of Ayres, I.1 ("My sweetest Lesbia, let us live and love"): short *e* and vowel-plus-*s* three times each, *l* four times); II.4 ("Yet embers live when flames doe die"): short *e* and *m/n* three times each, *f/v*, voiced *s* and *d* each twice; III.15 ("Give them gold that sell love"): *g*, short *e*, *th* and *v* twice each, *l* three times; IV.1 ("Followe thy faire sunne, unhappy shaddowe"): *f*, short *u*-plus-*n* and long *o* twice each; VII. 22 ("Let us reape, loves gaines deviding"): *l*, long *e* and schwa twice each, *s/z* and *d/t* three times each; VIII.2 ("While sweete Bessie sleeping laie"): *l*, long *e* and *s* three times each, *b/p* and *w* twice each; IX.1 ("The Sypres curten of the night is spread"): long *i*, *th*, *pr* and *n* twice, *d/t* three times, unvoiced *s* four times; X.2 ("Haste you, sad noates, fall at her flying feete"): *s*-plus-dental in *Haste* reversed in *sad* and in *noates*, *d/t* four times, *f* three times, *l* twice; XII.3 ("Thou art not sweet, though made of meer delight"): *d/t* six times, nasal three times, *th*, vowel-plus-*r* and long *e* twice each; XVI.16 ("I climbe to crowne my chast desire"): long *i* four times, *m/n* three times, hard *c* twice, s-plus-dental in *chast* inverted in *desire;* XIX.14 ("Your Paramours harmes"): vowel-plus-*r* four times, voiced *s* and *m* twice each; XXI.17 ("Cleanse my soule, O God, thy bespotted Image"): *m/n* and *s/z* three times, long *i*, long *o*, *l* and *b/p* twice each;

The First Booke of Ayres, I.5 ("Sunne and Moone, Starres and underlights I see"): *m/n* six times, *s/z* five times, vowel-plus-*nd* three times, long *i* twice; IV.12 ("Their sinne-sicke soules by him shall be recured"): short *i* and initial *s* three times, vowel-plus-*l* twice; VIII.1 ("Tune thy Musicke to thy hart"): long *u* three times, *th* and long *i* twice; IX.8 ("The Foxe his Cubbs with false deceit endues"): *s/z* five times, *d/t* three times, *f* twice; X.10 ("Vexe them to peace are bent"): short *e* three times, *th* and *b/p* twice; XI.1 ("Never weather-beaten Saile more willing bent to shore"): vowel-plus-*r*, short *e* and *m/n* four times each, *b-t* combinations twice; XII.11 ("Strive then, and hee will help; call him, hee'll heare"): initial *h* five times [some of these instances were eye rhymes only perhaps—the *h* not pronounced], *l* four times; XIV. 19 ("Hurle downe her wals, her towres deface"): vowel-plus-*r* four times, *s/z* three times, *ou* diphthong twice; XVI.3 ("Rise now, and walke the wayes of light"): chiasmic pattern of a pair of long *i* sounds enclosing a pair of initial *w* sounds; XX.28 (And revell in your rich array"): *r*-plus-vowel three times, vowel-plus-*r* twice;

The Second Booke of Ayres, I.18 ("Men must be men, and women women still"): ostentatious patterning in *m* and *n;* III.7 ("Silly Tray-tresse, who shall now thy carelesse tresses place"): vowel-plus-*s*/*z* five times; V.3 ("The groves and medowes swell with flowres"): *s*/*z* four times, long *o*, *w* and *l* twice each; VIII.5 ("While fond feare may colour finde, Love's seldom pleased"): *l* five times, *f*/*v* four times, long *i* twice; X.7 ("Kisse then, my harvest Queene"): hard *c*, short *e*, vowel-plus-*n* and unvoiced *s* twice each; XIV.1 ("Pin'd I am, and like to die"): long *i* four times, short *a* and *m*/*n* twice; XVI.7, 14, 21 and 28 ("Is this faire excusing? O no, all is abusing"): vowel-plus-*s* five times, long *u*-plus-*ing* and long *o* twice each; XX.8 ("For these are old, and shee so new"): vowel-plus-*r*, long *e* and long *o* twice each;

The Third Booke of Ayres, II.14 ("Once false proves faithfull never"): *f*/*v* five times, terminal unvoiced *s* twice; IV.1 ("Maydes are simple, some men say"): alternating sequence of *m*/*n* and *s* sounds; VIII.11 ("Old Stories onely goodnesse now containe"): *n* five times, long *o* and terminal unvoiced *s* twice; X.3 ("Should she now fixe one smile on thee, where were despaire"): initial *sh* in first two words, vowel-plus-*r* in last three words, *m*/*n* four times; XIII.1 ("Awake, thou spring of speaking grace, must rest becomes not thee"): chiasmus of a pair of long *a* sounds and a pair of hard *c* sounds enclosing a pair of *sp* sounds; XIV.12 ("Bad with bad in ill sute well, but good with good live blessed"): phonetic patterning in words also coupled ideationally; XVII.4 ("Will you finde no fained lett"): chiasmus of vowel-*l* and *l*-vowel pair surrounding pairs of *f* and *n*-*d* sounds; XVIII.3 ("Then thrice three times tye up this true loves knot"): *th* and *t* four times each, long *i* and *m*/*n* three times each; XX.4 ("Out of mine idle empty braine"): *m*/*n* four times, long *i* twice; XXII.12 ("Wilde borne be wilde still, though by force made tame"): *d*/*t* five times, *b*, *l* and *m*/*n* three times each, long *i* and long *a* twice each; XXVII.11 ("For what is courtship, but disguise"): short *i* three times, short *u*-plus-*t*, *or* and gutteral *c*/*g* twice each; XXVIII.10 ("Gray Snakes the meadowes shrowde in every place"): long *a* three times, vowel-plus-*d* twice;

The Fourth Booke of Ayres, I.3 ("Many lost sighes long I spent, to her for mercy crying"); long *i* and vowel-plus-*r* each three times, *l* and short *o* twice each; III.1 ("Thou joy'st, fond boy, to be by many loved"): *oi* dipthong and *f*/*v* twice each, vowel-plus-*r* three times; V.4 ("Native grace becomes a face, though ne'er so rudely drest"): *s*/*z* five times, vowel-*r*/*r*-vowel sounds four times, long *a* three times; VII.7 ("Those Cherries fayrely doe enclose"): terminal voiced *s* four times, long *o* and *er* twice each;

IX.25-26 ("Yet nor Churle, nor silken Gull/Shall my Mayden blossome pull"): *m/n* seven times, *l* six times, vowel-plus-*r* three times; XIV.16 ("I liv'd too true a lover"): chiasmus of a pair of long *u* sounds enclosed within pairs of *l*-vowel-*v* sounds; XV.24 ("For pure meetings are most sweet"): vowel-plus-*r* three times, *m* and long *e* twice each; XVI.12 ("Happy are they that neyther know"): *th* three times, short *a*, vowel-plus-*r* and *n* twice each; XXI.16 ("Shee would, but ah, it would not be"): a pair of long *e* sounds enclosing three vowel-plus-*t* combinations, a pair of schwa sounds, and *would/would*.

Note 14. Musical amplification of a song's text (see Chapter 4, n. 11):

Campion frequently underscores words related by a phonetic, syntactic and/or semantic likeness by setting them to notes related by a rhythmic and/or melodic likeness. Here are some examples of this kind of coincidence of musical and verbal energy:

A Booke of Ayres, I: the rhyme syllables of the first couplet in each stanza (*love/-prove, mee/be, ends/friends*) are set to the same quarter-note (A); a five-note descent from the fifth to the root imitates the sense of the words it sets in line 3 (*heav'ns great lampes doe dive*); II: music underscores the ideational rhyming of *young* and *old* in line 1 (both set to A), *hot* and *colde* in line 1 (one set to C and one to C sharp) and *youth* and *age* in line 3 (both set to D); IV: the second syllables of *unhappy* in line 1 and *unhappie* in line 4 are both set to D, an effect intensified by the fact that the second D is held three times as long as the first; VI: the setting of *highest* in line 3 imitates its sense (*high-* is set an octave above the three preceding words); the phonetic relations among the rhyme syllables in the second couplet in each stanza (*-peare/cleare, sing/spring*) are underscored by their settings to G and D, the root and fifth; the refrain-like effect of a repetition of the words *the stringes doe breake* at the end of each stanza is intensified by the fact that in each line the words repeat to new music (a similar repetition amplifies the substance of the words *her sighes*); IX: their respective identical settings underscore the phonetic likeness of the "a" and "b" rhyme syllables in each quatrain (*spread/-red* and *cast/-gast*, etc.); seven of the ten syllables in the first and third lines of each stanza are set to the same note, D, a fact that helps to underscore phonetic relationships among some of these syllables in line 1 (*The Sypres . . . the night . . . spread*), line 3 (*. . . weaker cares . . . are con-. . .*), line 9 (*. . . Ghosts . . . am one . . . those*), line 13 (*Griefe, ceaze . . . will still . . .*) and line 15 (*Beare . . . there . . . sure*); X: the phonetic likeness of *Saint* in line 1 and *noates* in the same metrical position of line 2 (shared *s, n* and *t* sounds) is underscored because both words are set to A; the next syllable in each line, *fol-* and *fall,* are both set to C; the rhyme syllables in the first couplet of both stanzas (*sweet/feete* and *tend/end*) are set to A; their settings to the root and fifth underscore the likeness and difference of the "b" rhymes (*move/love* and *doeth flie/-pathie*) and the "c" rhymes (*flight/-light*); XVI: the formal and thematic importance of the refrain words *But a little higher* (repeated twice in each of lines 9 and 15) is underscored musically by the fact that when sung they are repeated four times in each line; a melodic pattern that is raised a whole step in each repeat imitates the sense of these words; the different phonetic likenesses in the enjambments *higher/There* (7-8) and *higher/I* (15-16) are underscored by the identical settings of all four words; XX: in each stanza the "a" rhymes (*ground/round,* etc.) are set to A and the "b" rhymes (*guest/rest,* etc.) are set to G;

The First Booke of Ayres, V: the second and fourth lines in each stanza (the "b" rhyme lines) are connected by the identical rhythmic patterns of their settings; IX: there is a chiasmic pattern in the B section that underscores the phonetic likeness between the first word in line 5 (*There,* set to B flat) and the last word in line 6 (*there,* set to B) and between the last word in line 5 (*Beare,* set to a whole-note G) and the first word in line 6 (*But,* set to a half-note G); XI: the obvious syntactic, ideational and phonetic parallelisms between the last lines in each stanza are underscored by their identical settings; XII: the nearly identical rhythmic and melodic proportions of their settings underscore the various verbal likenesses between the second line in each stanza (*Pilgrim-like I cast,* etc.) and the last five syllables of the fourth line in each stanza (*I securely passed,* etc.); XVI: the rhyme syllables in the final couplet of each stanza (*late/gate* and *blisse/is*) are joined by their fifth-first settings; XVII: the identical settings of *my last night* in line 4 and *day wee dye* in line 6 amplify their ideational connection; the recurrence of a refrain line at the end of each stanza (*So ev'ry day wee live, a day wee dye*) is made more insistent by the fact that when sung some of its words are repeated—*So ev'ry day, so ev'ry day, wee live, wee live, a day wee dye*); XVIII: an ascending chromatic progression (A-B flat-B-C-C sharp-D) imitates the sense of the words it sets in line 3—*For his steep hill is high* (the setting is not similarly appropriate to the corresponding words in lines 7, 11 or 15); *tri-* in line 4 is set to a D held twice as long as the D that sets *high* in line 3; the same two notes underscore phonetic relationships between the corresponding words in stanza 2 (*see/beames*) and stanza 3 (*trimm'd/charm'd*); XXI: the variously vital second words in the fourth line of each stanza (*sweet, bright, wreaths* and *hop't*) are underscored rhythmically by their setting to four sixteenth notes; the recurrence of a brief refrain in each stanza (*weepe with mee*) is intensified by the fact that in each stanza it repeats three times;

The Seconde Booke of Ayres, I: phonetic epanilepsis in line 3 (which begins and ends with *pr: Prayse . . . prove*) is marked by the identical setting of both words; identical settings also underscore phonetic and/or ideational parallelisms between certain metrically corresponding words in the first and second stanzas: *Love* (1) and *love* (7), *beauty* (2) and *golden* (8), *prove* (3) and *move* (9), *false* (5) and *faith* (11), *me* (5) and *me* (11), *women* (6) and *woman* (12); II: phonetic parallelisms between certain metrically corresponding words are again underscored by their identical settings: *chained* (1) and *graced* (17), *fained* (2) and *placed* (18), *hopes* (3) and *heav'n* (19), *-dained* (4) and *-braced* (20), *But* (5) and *But* (21), *And with . . . grief* (10) and *And will . . . -liefe* (26), *-liefe* (12) and *griefe* (28); III: in line 7, *tresse* is set to G and *-lesse, tress-* and *place* are each set a fifth above, to D; the informal phonetic similarities of the corresponding rhyme syllables in both stanzas are emphasized by their identical settings: *rage* (1) and *place* (7), *-swage* (2) and *grace* (8), *kinde* (3) and *thine* (9), *minde* (4) and *mine* (10); V: the "b" rhymes in each stanza (*fade/shade, -dore/more,* etc.) are each set to G; VII: the words in the last line of each stanza (*And* Ros'mond *was as sweet as shee,* etc.) are emphasized by repetition: *And* Ros'mond, *and* Ros'mond *was as sweet, was as sweet, was as sweet as shee;* the occurrence of *o* sounds in the second syllables of these same lines (Ros-, Ros-, *sov-*) is underscored by their identical settings, as is the syntactic sameness and difference of the fourth styllables (*was, are, is*) by their identical settings; XI: the "a" rhymes in each stanza (*divided/decided,* etc.) are set to the same notes; so are the "b" rhymes (*must wed thee/must bed thee,* etc.); the insistent effect of the refrain words in lines 5 and 6 of each stanza (*yet* [or *then*] *a little more:/Here's the way*) is intensified by their musically dictated repetition: *yet a little more, yet a little more, yet a little more:/Here's the way, the way, the way;* XIII: a rhyme-like musical effect of identical rhythmic and melodic patterns connects the otherwise unconnected first three syllables of the "a" rhyme lines in each stanza (*There is none/Whome mine eyes,* etc.); phonetic and logical similarities at the end of the third lines in stanzas 1 and 2 are amplified by the identical settings of the words *affect to view* and *effect of love;* XVII: a relation between the openings of the first lines in each stanza (*Come away/Is shee come*) is underscored by the musically dictated repetition of these words: *Come away, come away/Is shee come, is shee come;* XXI: the repetition of words to new music at the beginning of the fifth line in each stanza underscores connections in sound and sense between *O bitter griefe* and *O wretched me;* other musically dictated repeats underscore variously connected phrases in the first lines of each stanza (*Where shall I refuge seeke*/*Why should my firmnesse finde*);

The Third Booke of Ayres, I: the words *Oft have I sighed* and *Had he but lov'd* at the start of the first lines in each stanza are repeated three times to new music, an effect that amplifies the phonetic connection between *Oft* and *lov'd* and the phonetic and grammatic connection between *have* and *Had;* the recurrence of the words *O yet I languish still* in the third line of both stanzas is similarly remarked by the fact that in each stanza these words are repeated to new music; IV: phonetic likeness between the penultimate syllables of the third line in stanzas 2, 3 and 4 (*-ly, be* and *be-*) is underscored by the setting of these syllables to an ascending series of five sixteenth notes; V: identity of the fourth syllables in the first lines in stanza 1 and 4 (*all* and *all*) and phonetic likeness between the same syllables in stanzas 2 and 3 (*powers* and *teares*) is underscored by the identical setting of these syllables; similarly, near identity of the fifth syllables in the third lines of stanza 2 and 4 (*make* and *makes*) and phonetic likeness of the same syllables in stanzas 1 and 3 (*ease* and *dream-*) is underscored by the identical setting of these syllables; VII: phonetic and syntactic relations between lines 1 and 3 of the first stanza (*Kinde are her answeres*/*Breaks time,as dancers*) and phonetic relations between the same lines in stanza 2 (*Lost is our freedome*/*Why doe wee neede them*) are underscored by the identical setting of these lines; the exclamatory *O* at the start of the sixth line in both stanzas is set to the same dotted quarter-note, the fifth; VIII: relationships among the following metrically corresponding syllables in the two stanzas are amplified by their identical settings: O/O (line 1 of each stanza), O/O (1), *to*/*to* (1), *poor*/*-ture* (1), *Jus-*/*but* (3), *vaine*/*hon-* (4), O/O (5), *such*/*just* (6), and *as*/*and* (6); IX: the metrically unaccented *ing* rhymes in the second and fourth lines of both stanzas are all set to the same whole note G; verbal relationships at the start of the seventh line in both stanzas (*O heare mee speake*/*O deare delight*) are amplified by the musically dictated repetition of words in each of these phrases: *O heare, O heare, O heare mee speake, O heare mee speake,* etc.; a similar musically dictated repetition of words in the eighth lines of both stanzas underscores the ideational opposition between *my woes* and *reliefe;* XVII: the epigrammatic conclusion of each stanza (*Tell the long houres at your dore*/*Ere my long love be possest*/*While these cold nights freeze me dead*), and in particular the semantic content of the third words in each of these lines (*long, long* and *cold*), are intensified by the repetitions dictated by their settings: *Tell the long, long houres, tell the long houres at your dore,* etc.; XXIX: the identity of words at the end of the fifth lines in stanzas 1 and 3 (*and I am free*) is underscored by the identity of their settings; similarly, verbal identity at the end of the sixth lines in stanzas 1 and 2 (*in loosing mee*) is underscored by the identical settings of these words; identical settings also emphasize various connections between metrically corresponding syllables in different stanzas: *I/I /My* (line 1 of each stanza); *when/mine/-dome* (nasals in line 1), *I/I* (line 2 in stanzas 1 and 2); *I/I* (line 3 in stanzas 1 and 3); *faith/fail-* (line 6 in stanzas 2 and 3);

The *Fourth Booke of Ayres,* I: a repetition of words to new music in the last line of each stanza amplifies the near identity of *Ile dye* and *I dye;* IV: identical settings underscore phonetic similarities between these metrically corresponding syllables: *hide/try* (line 1 in each stanza), *me/heale* (1), *plagues/great-* (2), *be/zeale* (3), *Suf-/Af-* (4), *she/be* (4), *proves/too* (4), *heav'ns/em-* (5), *one/blinde* (6); VII: the refrain line at the end of each stanza (*Till Cherry ripe themselves doe cry*) is amplified by the repetitions dictated by its setting: *Till Cherry ripe, till Cherry ripe, till Cherry ripe, Cherry ripe, ripe, ripe, Cherry ripe, Cherry ripe themselves doe cry;* Davis' note on the setting of this line (p. 174) calls attention to an effect of musical and ideational discord: "the music beneath the word 'Cherry ripe' is taken from a London street seller's cry (and thus undercuts, with its earthy commercialism, the high Petrarchan style of the rest of the song)"; X: an identical setting underscores the rhyme-like relationship of words at the beginning of the first couplet in stanza 1 (*Love me or not/ Leave me or not*) and the first couplet in stanza 3 (*Could I enchant/Her would I charme*); XII: phonetic likeness between certain syllables in line 1 of each stanza is amplified by their identical settings: *guile* and *guild* in line 1 of the first stanza are both set to D, as are the metrically corresponding syllables in line 1 of the third stanza, *winde* (probably pronounced "wynde") and *pride; Love* and *thrive* in line 1 of the second stanza are both set to B, as are the metrically corresponding syllables in line 1 of stanza 3, *Praise* and *-ceedes;* XVII: the"a" rhymes in each stanza (*love/strove,* etc.) are each set to A, the "b" rhymes (*parts/Arts,* etc.) to B flat; identical settings also underscore various incidental relationships between metrically corresponding syllables: *in/mine* (line 2 in each stanza), *-ly/de-* (2), *is/is* (3), *-ture/-ers* (3), *while/still* (3), *she/re-* (3), *grace/dai-* (4), *Shee/Shee* (6: musical identity contradicts the logical non-identity of these two identical pronouns— the first refers to Nature and the second to a lady), *had/hath* (6), *make/-comes* (6), *true/chast* (6); XXIV: the effect of music repeated for each stanza of a song is suggested in a song that has only one stanza by the fact that the setting of the first line in each couplet is repeated as the setting of the second line in each couplet.

Note 15. The rhythmic counterpointing of quantitative length against metrical unstress (see Chapter 5, n. 14):

The slowing effect produced when a quantitatively demanding syllable falls in an unstressed metrical position of the verse-line occurs frequently in Campion's songs. The syllable that receives contrapuntal emphasis is often especially important to the semantic content and/or phonetic patterning of the line. There are good examples in:

A Booke of Ayres, I.3 ("Let us not way them: heav'ns great lampes doe dive"); III.25 ("And fresh Amarillis"; here and elsewhere, notice that the line's rhythm may be further complicated by the presence of relatively short syllables in metrically stressed positions–*Āmarillis*); IV.1 ("Followe thy faire sunne, unhappy shaddowe"); 9 ("Follow those pure beames whose beautie burneth"); VIII.2 ("While sweete Bessie sleeping laie"); 16 ("She dreamp't not what he would doo"); 22 ("Deceiv'd in her owne deceit"); IX.13 ("Griefe, ceaze my soule, for that will still endure"); 14 ("When my cras'd bodie is consum'd and gone"); 15 ("Beare it to thy black denne, there keepe it sure"); XI.3 ("Grace deare love with kind requiting"); XIII.6 ("The voice of heav'ns huge thunder cracks"); 15 ("And her proude thoughts too well to find"); XVI.8 ("There, there, O there lies Cupids fire"); XVII.16 ("Die, die in sweete embracing"); 21 ("Feare yeelds no delay"); XIX.17 ("This night by moone-shine leading merrie rounds"); XX.6 ("From that smoothe toong whose musicke hell can move"); 9 ("Of Turnies and great challenges of knights"); 12 ("Then tell, O tell, how thou didst murther me");

The First Booke of Ayres, I.3 ("Lord, light me to thy blessed way"); 7 ("Fountaine of health, my soules deepe wounds recur"); 8 ("Sweet showres of pitty raine, wash my uncleannesse pure"); IV.2 ("Let thine eares my plaints receive, on just feare grounded"); 12 ("Their sinne-sicke soules by him shall be recured"); VI.1 ("Bravely deckt, come forth, bright day"); 5 ("Come, chiefest of the *British* ghests"); 34 ("May blest *Charles* thy comfort be"); VII.3 ("But in vaine joyes no comfort now I finde"); XIII.16 ("In faire disguise black dangers lye"); 19 ("And with loud voyce I prais'd"); 18 ("Cryed in *Jerusalems* sad day"); 19 ("Hurle down her words, her towres deface"); XV.19 ("Arm'd millions he doth send"); XVI.5 ("Seek heav'n early, seeke it late"); 10 ("Yet burnes out thy lifes lampe in vaine"); 12 ("Then watch, and labour while time is"); XVII.1 ("Come, chearfull day, part of my life, to me"); 5 ("Times fatall wings doe ever forward flye"); XVIII.10 ("False light with many shadowes dimm'd"); 11 ("Old Witch with new foyles trimm'd"); XIX.11 ("Whom soone after Violence hastes"); XX.3 ("Doe their weeke dayes worke, and pray"); 18 ("And decke her windowes with greene boughs"); XXI.1 ("All lookes be pale, harts cold as stone"); 7 ("Joyes drown'd in teares must be"); 22 ("No more may his wisht sight returne");

The Second Booke of Ayres, I.10 ("Who, seeing cleare day once, will dreame of night"); II.2 ("Fond hart, by favours fained"); 11 ("While her sweet bounty ceaseth"); III.7 ("Silly Tray-tress, who shall now thy careless tresses place"); 9 ("Who shall thy bright eyes admire"); VI.16 ("A wound long hid growes past recure"); 31 ("When true theeves use falsehood well"); VII.9 ("Pale lookes have many friends"); 17 ("Let the old loves with mine compare"); VIII.16 ("So melts loves hate relenting"); XII.10 ("On her bright eastern hill"); XIV.7 ("The same thing I seeke, and flie"); XV.2 ("Whose good parts might move me"); XVI.8 ("Your wisht sight if I desire"); XVIII.15 ("Then the thick-show'd kisses here"); XX.5 ("All out of one smooth Curral Rocke");

The Third Booke of Ayres, I.4 ("Dayes seeme as yeares, when wisht friends breake their day"); 7 ("O yet I languish still, still constant mourne"); 8 ("For him that can breake vowes, but not returne"); II.2 ("Since she proves strange I care not"); 3 ("Fain'd love charm'd so my delight"); 12 ("False love is ever flying"); 14 ("Once false proves faithfull never"); IV.5 ("Truth a rare flower now is growne"); 11 ("Then a young mans vowes beleeve"); 13 ("Love they make a poore blinde childe"); V.7 ("Come, come delight, make my dull braine"); VI.7 ("If to one thou shalt prove true, and all beside reject"); VIII.2 ("Truth far exil'd, False art lov'd, Vice ador'd"); 8 ("Poore in desert, in name rich, proud of shame"); 12 ("And the true wisedome that is just, and plaine"); IX.13 ("Dye, wretch since hope from thee is fled"); XI.1 ("If Love loves truth, then women doe not love"); 5 ("Then as a Seaman the poore lover fares"); 18 ("To have fayre women false, then none at all"); XIII.5 ("The words which thy rich tongue discourses"); XIV.3 ("Women onely are mens good, with them in love conversing"); 11 ("Good wife is the good I praise, if by good men possessed"); XVI.17 ("When to all Ile prove more kinde"); 21 ("Those sweet houres which wee had past"); 23 ("And, could'st thou fly ne'er so fast"); XVII.6 (Tell the long houres at your dore"); 12 ("Ere my long love be possest"); 16 ("To attend loves joyes in vaine"); 18 ("While these cold nights freeze me dead"); XVIII.1 ("Thrice tosse these Oaken ashes in the ayre"); 3 ("Then thrice three times tye up this true loves knot"); 6 ("These

Screech-owles fethers, and this prickling bryer"); XX.6 ("Come *Trent,* and *Humber,* and fayre Thames"); 7 ("Dread Ocean, haste with all thy streames"); 12 ("Wilde borne be wilde still, though by force made tame"); XXIII.3 ("Love loves no delay: thy sight"); XXV.9 ("And in her slumber, see! shee close-ey'd weepes"); 11 ("Pleade, sleepe, my cause, and make her soft like thee"); XVIII.9 ("The grove is charg'd with thornes and the bold bryer"); 10 ("Gray Snakes the meadowes shrowde in every place"); 15 ("Till then, for Hopes sweete sake, rest your tir'd minde");

The Fourth Booke of Ayres, I.3 ("Many lost sighes long I spent, to her for mercy crying"); 4 ("But now, vaine mourning, cease"); 5 ("Ile dye, and mine owne griefes release"); III.9 ("Youths should the Field affect, heate their rough Steedes"); 11 ("Is't not more joy strong Holds to force with swords"); 14 ("One man for one brave Act hath prov'd a story"); IV. 1 ("Vaile, love, mine eyes, O hide from me"); 5 ("Who can usurp heav'ns light alone"); VI.6 ("That her grac't words might better take"); 10 ("Alas how soone is this love growne"); VII.2 ("Where Roses and white Lillies grow"); VIII.1 ("To his sweet Lute *Apollo* sung the motions of the Spheares"); IX.15 ("Like thirst longing, that doth bide"); 24 ("Growe lesse sweet, then fall alone"); X.3 ("O, that her grace would my wisht comforts give"); 11 ("But love enforc'd rarely yeelds firme content"); XI.5 ("Though Bryers breede Roses, none the Bryer affect"); XIII.9 ("Shoot home, sweet *Love,* and wound him, that hee may not flye"); XV.1 ("Are you what your faire lookes express"); 24 ("For pure meetings are most sweet"); XVII.11 ("Rest, jealous thoughts, and thus resolve at last"); XVIII.4 ("Learne to speake first, then to wooe, to wooing much per-tayneth"); XXIII.1 ("Your faire lookes urge my desire"); 6 ("Loves pleasure, deare, deny not"); 20 ("That breedes no man payne").

Note 16. The rhythmic counterpointing of quantitative shortness against metrical stress (see Chapter 5, n. 17):

Campion frequently creates an illusion of speed by placing a quantitatively undemanding syllable in a stressed metrical position of the verse-line. Some examples occur in lines that simultaneously counterpoint quantitative length against metrical stress—e.g., *A Booke of Ayres,* III.25 ("And fresh Ămarillis"); *The First Booke,* VII.3 ("But ĭn vaine joyes no comfort now I find"); *The Third Booke,* XVIII.5 ("The Screech-owles fethers, aňd this prickling bryre"); Other examples may be found in:

A Booke of Ayres, V.5 ("Ĭf such danger be in playing"; here and elsewhere, notice that the metrical emphasis given to a relatively short syllable may help to indicate the line's syntactic structure and/or its substance); 7 and 28 ("Ĭ will gŏ no more a-maying"); VIII.1 ("Ĭt fell ŏn a sommers day"); 3 ("Ĭn her bowre, ŏn her bed"); IX.16 ("I'le flie to hĕr againe, and sue for pitie tŏ renue my hopes distressed"); XIII.16 ("With what unequal tyrannĭe"); XIV.4 ("Who art so cruell aňd unsteadfast growne"); 5 ("For nature, cald for bў distressed harts"); XV.5 ("Tŏ deceive the powers above"); XVIII.12 ("From thunders vĭolence"); 24 ("And quiet Pilgrimăge"); XIX.2, 9, 16, 23 and 30 ("The fayry queen Proserpină"); XX.4 ("White Iopĕ, blith Hellen, aňd the rest");

The First Booke of Ayres, IV.8 ("Ĭn thy sacred word I'le trust, to thee fast flying"); VI.18 ("Prayse the Lord, for onely on great and mercifŭll is hee"); VII.5 ("Thy power, O God, thy mercies tŏ record"); VIII.10 (Sweetest Sacrifĭce, all wrath appeasing"); IX.5 ("There lives no Vulture, nŏ devouring Beare"); 12 ("Not one of them in Paradĭce remaynes"); X.12 ("Of mankind, societĭe"); XIII.4 ("Which blinded, Ĭ securely past"); XVI.16 ("*Jerusa*lĕm be not the ground"); XIX.8 ("It ĭs the ruine of mankind"); XX.4 ("Devoutely ŏn the holy day"); XXI.3 ("*Hally,* ĭn whose sight");

The Second Booke of Ayres, I.12 ("But prov'd a woman, ăs all others be"); II.32 ("From Paradĭce to part"); V.10 ("Tŏ represse my school'd desire"); IX.14 ("Tħe more ĭs my woe the while"); X.12 ("Her fervencĭe in kisses"); XII.24 ("To gratifie the Spring"); XVI.5 ("Ĭf another you affect"); XVIII.13 ("Tell the Osiers ŏf the *Temmes*"); XXI.11 ("O wretched me, that mў chiefe joy should breede");

The Third Booke of Ayres, IV.8 ("Bў their follies, then deserts"); VIII.12 ("And thĕ true wisedome that is just, and plaine"); XI.3 ("Now kind and free of favour ĭf they prove"); 5 ("Then as a Sea-man thĕ poore lover fares"); 10 ("It is a womans nature tŏ beguile"); XIII.7 ("Thy voyce is ăs an Eccho cleare which Musicke doth beget"); 8 ("Thy speech is ăs an Oracle which none can counterfeit"); XIV.6 ("Salamănder-like, with fire"); XIX.16 ("Ĭn thine honour Hymnes Ile pen"); XXI.11 ("So lov'd, so blest, in mў belov'd am I"); XXII.6 ("If pray'rs prevaile not, Ĭ can doe no more"); XXIV.6 ("Tŏ despayre are most enclin'd"); XXV.7 ("My words have charm'd her, fŏr secure shee sleepes"); XXIX.13 ("So mў deare freedome have I gain'd");

The Fourth Booke of Ayres, I.8 ("Yĕt a small time ŏf complaint, a little breath Ile borrow"); III.4 ("And play'st the Sycophănt t'observe their eyes"); 16 ("Who would record it, ĭf not to his shame"); VIII.3 ("And all the Mysteriĕs above"); 10 ("And held him rapt as ĭn a trance"); IX.8 ("Tŏ be proud, nor tŏ despayre"); XII.16 ("You know it, aňd 'tis true"); XIV.6 ("No fire ĭs more cruell"); XVII.5 ("To form her too too beautifŭll of hue"); XIX.36 ("Wĭth a spirit tŏ contend"); XXIII.5 ("Ĭf Love may perswade").

Notes: Chapter 1

1. Thomas Campion, Preface to "Two Bookes of Ayres," *The Works of Thomas Campion*, ed. Walter R. Davis (New York: W. W. Norton & Co., 1970), p. 55. I quote Campion throughout from this edition.

2. A. H. Bullen, *Elizabethans* (London: Chapman and Hall Ltd., 1925), p. 127.

3. Ezra Pound, *A B C of Reading* (New York: New Directions, 1960), p. 84.

4. A. H. Bullen, ed., *Lyrics from the Song-Books of the Elizabethan Age* (London: John C. Nimmo, 1887), p. vi.

5. Percival Vivian, ed., *Campion's Works* (1909; rpt. Oxford: Oxford Univ. Press, 1966), p. 1v.

6. Miles Kastendieck, *England's Musical Poet* (New York: Oxford Univ. Press, 1938), p. 199.

7. Roy Fuller, "Fascinating Rhythm," *The Southern Review,* IX (1973), 857-872.

8. John T. Irwin, "Thomas Campion and the Musical Emblem," *SEL* (Winter 1970), 121-124. Irwin's article, which begins to suggest some of the complexity I find in "Now Winter Nights Enlarge," in effect justifies my own further attention to that song.

9. Hallet Smith, *Elizabethan Poetry* (Cambridge: Harvard Univ. Press, 1966), pp. 287, 281.

10. W. H. Auden, ed., *Selected Songs of Thomas Campion* (Boston: David R. Godine, 1972), p. 9.

11. Pound, p. 14.

12. Auden, p. 11.

13. William Hazlitt, *Lectures on the Literature of the Age of Elizabeth* (London: George Bell, 1899), p. 174.

14. A. H. Bullen, ed., *The Works of Dr. Thomas Campion* (London: The Chiswick Press, 1889), p. xvi.

15. A. H. Bullen, ed., *Thomas Campion, Songs and Masques with Observations in the Art of English Poetry* (London, 1903).

16. Ernest Rhys, ed. *The Lyrical Poems of Thomas Campion* (London: J. M. Dent & Co., 1895), p. xxv. It is interesting to note the praise which Bullen himself received for his discovery. Swineburne, for instance, to whom Bullen sent every edition he put out, had this to say about the importance of the Chiswick Press Campion: "In issuing the first edition of Campion's *Works* you have added a name to the roll of English poets, and one that can never be hence forward overlooked or erased. Certainly his long neglected ghost ought now to be rejoicing in Elysium. (*Letters from Algernon Charles Swineburne to A.H. Bullen*, London, 1910, p. 21.) See also these stanzas by Edmund Gosse:

> Bullen, well done!
>   Where Campion lies in London-land,
>   Lulled by the thunders of the Strand,
> Screened from the sun,
>
> Surely there must
>   Now pass some pleasant gleam
>   Across his music-haunted dream,
> Whose brain and lute are dust.

(Quoted by Amy Cruse, *The Elizabethan Lyrists and their Poetry* [London, 1913].)

17. Kastendieck, p. 70.

18. C. S. Lewis, *English Literature in the Sixteenth Century* (Oxford: Oxford Univ. Press, 1954), pp. 552-553.

19. Douglas Bush, *English Literature in the Earlier Seventeenth Century* (New York: Oxford Univ. Press, 1962), p. 102.

20. Auden, p. 11

21. Quoted by Kastendieck, p. 44.

22. Rhys, p. viii.

23. Vivian, p. 355.

24. See Bruce Pattison, *Music and Poetry of the English Renaissance* (London: Methuen & Co., 1970). For an account of a modern editor's difficulty in separating and arranging in metrical form the madrigal lyric from its music, see also Edmund Fellowes, ed., *English Madrigal Verse, 1588-1632* (Oxford: Oxford Univ. Press, 1967), pp. xxi-xxiv.

25. Kastendieck, pp. 46-47.

26. Ralph W. Short, "The Metrical Theory and Practice of Thomas Campion," *PMLA*, LIX (1944), 1004.

27. Walter R. Davis, ed., *The Works of Thomas Campion*, p. xiii. Davis argues that Campion's reputation was forced into decline because of Eliot's "elevation of John Donne and the other 'metaphysical' poets to major status as the really important poets of the English Renaissance, and of metaphysical wit and the complex image as the major evidences of

literary worth." This does not seem to be entirely true. Witness Short's article. Eliot's own remarks on Campion deserve notice: "I should say that within his limits there was no more accomplished craftsman in the whole of English poetry than Campion. I admit that to understand his poems fully there are some things one should know: Campion was a musician, and he wrote his songs to be sung. We appreciate his poems better if we have some acquaintance with Tudor music; and we want not merely to read them, but to hear some of them sung, and sung to Campion's own settings" ("What is Minor Poetry?" *On Poets and Poetry* [rpt. New York: Farrar, Straus, 1957]).

28. Edward Lowbury, Timothy Salter, and Alison Young, *Thomas Campion, Poet, Composer, Physician* (London: Chatto & Windus, 1970), p. 32.

29. Catherine Ing, *Elizabethan Lyrics* (London: Chatto & Windus, 1951), p. 150.

30. Borrowing a question from Bertrand Bronson, "When is a ballad not a ballad?" (answer: when it does not have its music), one sees the logic of calling Campion's songs without their music "poems."

31. W. Chappell, *Popular Music of the Olden Time* (London, 1855), quoted by Kastendieck, p. 31.

32. Kastendieck, p. 42.

33. Quoted by Kastendieck, , pp. 32-33.

34. Thomas Morley, *A Plaine and Easy Introduction to Practical Music* (1957: rpt. New York: W. W. Norton & Company, 1973), p. 9.

35. Quoted by Lowbury, Salter, and Young, p. 32.

Notes: Chapter 2

1. For purposes of this chapter I shall restrict "meaning" to its most basic sense, as concerned with the reference of verbal symbols and their syntactic relations to the outside world of things and their real relations. A poem in this sense has substantive "meaning," a paraphrasable content; we can talk about what it is talking about.

2. Yvor Winters, "The 16th Century Lyric in England: Part III," *Poetry: A Magazine of Verse,* LIV (1939), p. 37.

3. Anticipating objections here and from time to time in what is to come, let me caution the reader against taking any reference to potential meaning as an assertion of its unique presence in the context in question. I do not

think that "airy" nothing is a nesty nothing and I do not take "know" as a negative.

4. Other obvious examples of ideational rhyme pairs in "Now winter nights enlarge" are *enlarge/discharge, blaze/o'erflow, Summer/Winter* and *enlarge/shorten*. For an account of the presence and function of ideational rhymes elsewhere in Campion, see Note 1 of the Appendix.

5. *OED*, s.v. *shall*, B.II.3, 6, 8g and i.

6. Although line 5 as printed by Davis is not end-stopped by any mark of punctuation, and so runs on into line 6, because two different independent syntactic units are completed in *Let now the chimneys blaze/And cups o'erflow with wine*, the lines are not strictly speaking a "run-on" pair. (There is a comma after *blaze* in the 1613 printed edition.)

7. Though line 11 is punctuated by a comma after *sights*, the sense of lines 11-12 is also clearly "run-on."

8. This will be a good place for a note on the presence and function of adjectives in this stanza. Though the "a" rhymes in quatrain 3—*lights* and *sights*—are subjects governing the verbs of their respective clauses, the full subject of the verb *remove* is not merely *Courtly sights* but the entire noun phrase *youthfull Revels, Masks, and Courtly sights*. In a sense, then, the syntactic rationale for making line 11 the longest line in the stanza (ten syllables instead of six) has been to accomodate the stanza's longest subject. That subject is large because it is made up of three different nouns modified by two different adjectives (three if we understand [youthfull] *Masks*). Modifying adjectives have already figured in the postponement of the quatrain's first verb until the second line of its clause—*Shall waite* being figuratively pushed out of line 9 by the length of its modified subject, *yellow waxen lights*. This pattern of a compound adjective followed by its noun recurs with variation elsewhere in the stanza, once in the subject *well-tun'd words* in line 7 (both modifiers monosyllabic rather than disyllabic, the first an adverb) and once again in *Sleepes leaden spels* in line 12 (a direct object rather than subject, its first word a possessive noun). Moreover, adjectives are present in each of the stanza's two-line syntactic units. This in itself is not surprising—adjectives always amplify—but notice in passing that neither of the stanza's "short" syntactic units (lines 5 and 6) contain adjectives, and that their doubling helps to account for the subtle pattern of syntactically increasing subjects in the last three of the stanza's independent clauses: *well-tun'd words; yellow waxen lights; youthfull Revels, Masks, and Courtly sights*.

9. For example, "Now winter knights enlarge/The number of their whores." The hours/whores pun is common (see *As You Like It* II.vii.26-28: "from hour to hour, we ripe and ripe,/And then from hour to hour, we rot and rot;/And thereby hangs a tale"); so is night/knight. Here and elsewhere I will cite passages from Renaissance works as evidence that the kinds of potential meaning I find in "Now winter nights enlarge" were in

fact potentially inferable by Campion's audience—an audience of early seventeenth century readers. Most of the passages I refer to come from Shakespeare because his works are widely known; because they were widely known then, and presumably reflect potential meaning patterns in current usage; and because Shakespeare and Campion were nearly exact contemporaries (1564-1616, 1567-1620).

10. *OED* s.v. *love*, 5.: "The personification of sexual affection, usu. masculine, and more or less identified with the Eros, Amor, or Cupid of classical mythology; formerly sometimes feminine, and capable of being identified with Venus." *OED* gives this example from *Love's Labor Lost* IV.iii.380: "Forerun faire Love, strowing her way with flowers."

11. There is more than a simple grammatical connection between the two adjectives in lines 9-10, since the word *hunny* refers to a substance whose color and whose hollow, chamber-like honeycomb are, respectively, *yellow* and *waxen*. Notice, incidently, that the word *hunny* preceding *Love* gives additional support to the personification inpled in *Love* by itself, since the sweet viscous fluid produced by bees is also by extension a term of endearment ("sweetheart," "darling"), again used to address a beloved person, one's "love." See *OED,* s.v. *honey, 5.,* which gives this example from *Timon of Athens* II.i.24: "My sparrow, my hony, my duck, my cony." Notice also the momentary potential of seasonal comment in the juxtaposition of *yellow waxen:* "which have grown old," "waxed yellow"; and the parallel between fire and liquid in lines 5-6 and the same pair in lines 9-10, a parallel casually augmented by the similarity in shape between chimneys and candles.

12. *OED,* s.v. *wait,* 14.f, j and 6.b; compare the similar play in Shakespeare's Sonnets 57, 58 and 97.

13. Compare Campion's even more overt sexual reference in the refrain to *A Booke of Ayres,* III ("I care not for these Ladies"), discussed more fully below, and in *The Fourth Booke of Ayres,* XXII ("Beauty, since you so much desire").

14. See the Introduction to *Ben Jonson: Selected Masques,* edited by Stephen J. Orgel, (New Haven: Yale University Press, 1970). Campion himself wrote three such entertainments, *The Lord Hay's Masque* (1607), *The Lord's Masque* (1613), and *The Somerset Masque* (1614), each of them celebrating a different wedding.

15. Compare Prospero's "Be cheerful, sir, our revels now are ended" after his masque in *The Tempest* (IV.i.147-48); the *OED* does not record this sense specifically.

16. *OED,* s.v. *sight,* I.1: "a spectacle."

17. *OED,* s.v. *spell,* 3.

18. The fact that the Roman festival of the god of lead, Saturnalia (held in mid-December), was a time of unrestrained revelling adds support to the

underlying ideational connection between subject and object in lines 11 and 12.

19. In all of Campion's two-stanza poems the second stanza reflects on the first to some degree. For clearly explicit comment in a second stanza on a first, see especially *A Booke of Ayres*, VI, VII, X, XII and XIV; *The First Booke of Ayres*, VII; *The Second Booke of Ayres*, II and X; *The Third Booke of Ayres*, VII, VIII, IX, X, XX, XXI, XXII and XXV; *The Fourth Booke of Ayres*, II, IV and XVI.

20. Notice also the ideational kinship between *long discourse* (line 14) and the increasing length of *winter nights*.

21. *OED*, s.v. *dispense*, I.1

22. The *OED* gives this example from Sidney's *Arcadia* (1590): "I would and could dispense with these difficulties."

23. *OED*, s.v. *dispense with*, 13, 14. *OED*'s example is from *Timon of Athens* III.ii.93: "Men must now learne with pitty to dispence."

24. Notice that line 14 by itself is still a prepositional phrase; *With*, therefore, is pivotal: it turns in two directions, stands and operates in two different syntactic microcosms simultaneously.

25. Line 17 repeats with variation several patterns of syntax and logic from the preceding quatrain: the pairing of the quasi-superlative adjectives *All* and *all* (one pronominal) echoes the pairing of two positive adjectives, *Much* and *some* (line 13); the negative adverb *not* echoes the negative adjective *no* (16); the present indicative verb *doe* echoes the auxillary *doth* (13); and the spread-apart verb-adverb combination *doe . . . well* echoes the reverse combination in *well dispence (13)*.

26. Although the triplication of the pronomial adjective *Some* at the beginnings of lines 18, 19 and 20 is the only true instance of anaphora in "Now winter nights enlarge," the duplication of *Let* and *Let* at the beginnings of alternate lines (5 and 7) is anaphora-like. For other examples of anaphora and anaphora-like patterns in Campion, see Note 2 of the Appendix.

27. *OED*, s.v. *do*, B.16.b. See also *A Booke of Ayres*, V: "Maides forknow thir own undooing,/ But fear naught till all is done"; VIII: "Then his hands learn'd to woo,/ She dreampt not what he would doo"; *The Second Booke of Ayres*, XIV: "Be it friend, or be it foe/Ere long Ile trie what it will doe'; *The Fourth Booke of Ayres*, V: "Ev'ry Dame affects good fame, what ere her doings be"; and IX:

> Yet my lips have oft observ'd
> Men that kisse them presse them hard,
>   As glad lovers use to doe
>   When their new met loves they wooe.
>
>   ...
>
> Were not women made for men?
> As good 'twere a thing were past
> That must needes be done at last.

28. *OED*, s.v. *conversation*, 3., which gives this example from *Richard III* III.v.31: "His conversation with Shore's Wife." Compare Hamlet's "If you be honest, and faire, your Honesty should admit no discourse to your Beautie" (III.i.108), where "Honesty' is a synonym for Ophelia's chastity, and "Beautie" for her physical body (compare *beauty* in line 16 of this poem).

29. For thing as "penis," see the Fool's remark in *King Lear* I.v.55-56: "She that's a maid now, and laughs at my departure/Shall not be a maid long, unless things be cut shorter." For *thing* as "vulva," see *The Two Gentlemen of Verona* III.ii.355-60:

> *Speed.* "Item: She is too liberal."
> *Launce.* Of her tongue she cannot, for that's writ down she
> is slow of, of her purse she shall not, for that I'll keep shut.
> Now, of another thing she may, and that I cannot help.

30. For potential suggestions in Shakespeare of *all* meaning "penis" ("awl"), see *Julius Caesar* I.i.22-24: "Truly, sir, all that I live by is with the awl. I meddle with no tradesman's matters nor women's matters, but with awl"; *A Midsummer Night's Dream* I.ii.85: "Some of your French crowns have no hair at all"; *Henry IV, Part 2* V.iii.32-36 (Silence's song): "Be merry, be merry, my wife has all"; and *Cymbeline* I.vi.120-23: "to be partner'd/ With tomboys hir'd . . . with diseas'd ventures/ That play with all infirmities for gold." See also Sonnet 31.14: "all the all of me"; 40.4: "All mine was thine" and 13: "Lascivious grace, in whom all ill well shows"; 61.14: "From me far off, with others all too near"; 75.9: "Sometime all full with feasting on your sight" and 14: "Or gluttoning on all, or all away"; and 124.11: "all alone stands hugely politic."

31. See *The Merry Wives of Windsor* I.iii.46: "He hath studied her well and translated her well out of honesty into English"–where "English" probably plays on "ingle" ("a catamite") and "to ingle" ("to fondle"). See also Sonnet 129.13: "All this the world well knows, yet none knows well"; and 154.9: "This brand she quenched in a cool well by."

32. *OED*, s.v. *measure*, 20; s.v. *tread*, 8.b and c. (See also J.S. Farmer and W.G. Henley, *Slang and its Analogues* (London:1890-1904), s.v. *tread*.)

33. See *A Booke of Ayres*, XVII.13-16: "Then come, sweetest, come,/ My lips with kisses gracing:/ Here let us harbour all alone,/ Die, die in sweete embracing"; *The Second Booke of Ayres*, XVII.5-7: "Come quickly, come, the promis'd houre is wel-nye spent,/ And pleasure, being too much deferr'd, looseth her best content.// Is shee come? o, how neare is shee" (notice the potential punning on hour/whore and content/cunt [see below]); and *The Fourth Booke of Ayres*, XXIII.13-14: "O come, while we may,/Let's chaine Love with embraces." Compare *Much Ado About Nothing* V.ii.24-25: *Margaret*. "Well, I will call Beatrice to you, who, I think hath legs." *Benedick*. "And therefore will come"; and *Twelfth*

Night III.iv.29-30: *Olivia:* "Wilt thou go to bed, Malvolio?" *Malvolio.* "To bed? Ay, sweetheart, and I'll come to thee." See also Sonnet 136.1: "If thy soul check thee that I come so near"; 154.12-13: "but I, my mistress' thrall,/ Come there for cure"; and 56.10-11: "where two contracted new/ Come daily to the banks"—where *contracted* ("betrothed," "drawn together") may also carry the more graphic suggestion ("cunt") generally available in Shakespeare in any word containing the sound *con, cun*, etc. (compare Sonnet 20.7; 26.7; 53.5; 58.3: "Or at your hand th'account of hours to crave" where, in its proximity to "account," the hours/whores pun may also be intended; 75.7; 136.10; and also the "country matters" passage in *Hamlet* III.ii.105-106), and where *banks* means "ground bordering a body of water" but may also suggest, as it commonly does in Renaissance pastoral love poetry, what it suggests in *A Midsummer Night's Dream* II.ii.39-40: "find you out a bed,/ For I upon this bank will rest my head."

34. Compare Virgil's *Ecologue* VII.77-78: "*Necte tribus nodis .../...'Veneris...vincula necto.'*" Campion includes a line from this poem ("*non omnia possumus omnes*") in his preface to *Two Bookes of Ayres*, and translates the same line in "Now winter nights enlarge" as *All doe not all things well*.

35. See also "virgin knot" in Eric Partridge, *Shakespeare's Bawdy* (London, 1947).

36. See Partridge, s.v. "O"; and Sonnet 108.5: "Nothing, sweet boy" and 7: "Counting no old thing old, thou mine, I thine." Shakespeare also seems to intend this sense in *Hamlet* III.ii.105-16 (again the "country matters" passage); *Much Ado About Nothing* II.iii.50-53: "Because you talk of wooing, I will sing;/ Since many a wooer doth commense his suit/ To her he thinks not worthy" and in the title of that play; and *The Winter's Tale* IV.iv.603. See also Thomas Pyles, "Ophelia's Nothing," *Modern Language Notes*, XLIV (May 1949), 322-23; and Paul Jorgensen, "Much Ado About *Nothing*," *Shakespeare Quarterly*, V, 3 (Summer 1954), 287-95.

37. John Stevens, *Music and Poetry in the Early Tudor Court* (London, 1961).

38. The personification is probably more apparent to a modern reader than it would have been to a member of Campion's immediate audience, since "his" and the neuter possessive pronoun "its" were still used interchangeably in seventeenth century English. See the account in *OED*, s.v. *his*.

39. See Genesis 12.18: "Therefore Sarah laughed within herself, saying, After I am waxed old [cf. *yellow waxen*] shall I have pleasure, my lord being old also?" and *1 Timothy* 5.6 (in a passage on widows): "But she that liveth in pleasure is dead while she liveth." Compare suggestions of this sense in Shakespeare's Sonnet 20.13: "But since she pricked thee out

for women's pleasure"; 48.12: "From whence at pleasure you mayst come and part"; and 58.12: "I should in thought control your times of pleasure"; see also *Romeo and Juliet* II.iv.152-53: "I saw no man use you at his pleasure; if I had, my weapon should quickly have been out." See also Campion's *A Booke of Ayres,* XVII.6 (in a seduction poem weighted with sexually suggestive language): "Loves pleasure, deere, denie not" and 22: "Securenes helpeth pleasure"; and *The Fourth Booke of Ayres,* XXIV.1 (in a poem about a virgin's "longing thoughts"): "Faine would I wed a faire yong man that day and night could please me." This sense is still current in modern usage, as in "woman of pleasure" or "to have one's pleasure with a woman."

40. *OED,* s.v. *toy,* II.5., I.1., which gives this example from Spenser's *Epithalamium* (1594): "For greedy pleasure, carelesse of your toyes, thinks more upon her paradise of joyes."

41. Notice that the function *but* could perform, if it were syntactically placed where it could link and mediate between two related but somehow incompatible assertions, is a function pertinent to the logic (but not the syntax) of the sentence in which the adverb *but* appears here. The logic of the sentence we hear hinges on *Though;* the adverb *but* presents a shadow of an alternative syntax that the presence of *Though* makes impossible: "Love and all his pleasures are but toyes, [but toyes]/ *They shorten tedious nights."*

42. For an account of circular closure elsewhere in Campion, see Note 3 of the Appendix. Notice also the parallelism between the poem's final line and the final line in stanza 1: the death-like spells of leaden sleep are analogous to the long tiresome nights of winter—the dead time of year; at the same time, the act of removing sleep (by keeping awake) and the act of shortening long nights (by enjoying the fleeting pleasures of love) are themselves analogous.

Notes: Chapter 3

1. I should defend my inclusion of the six potentially doubtful words in this list: *divine, remove, defence, remorse, read* and *delights.* I will begin with *read.* One cannot be certain that, whatever their vowel sounds, the vowels in *tread* and *read* sounded more alike than they do now. Campion uses neither word for an end-rhyme elsewhere. Shakespeare rhymes *tread* with *overhead* and *red;* he rhymes *red* with *bed, bred, dead, entitled, head, spread; head* only with words that rhyme with it in the twentieth century. He rhymes *to read* with *indeed, proceed, weed* and *breed,* but also rhymes

o'er-read with *dead* (Sonnet 81, 10, 12); he rhymes *read* (the past participle) only with *said* (however, and this just makes the matter more confusing, he rhymes *said* regularly with words that rhyme now with *aid, maid,* etc.). The evidence in fact seems to suggest that different Elizabethan speakers probably pronounced th vowel sounds in words like *tread* and *read* differently, and that these vowel sounds may also have varied from dialect to dialect (see Helge Kökeritz, *Shakespeare's Pronunciation* [New Haven, 1953], pp. 194-203). Compare the common variations in modern American pronunciation of words like "aunt," "bouquet," "either," "often," "route," "tomato" and "vase"; and the vast number of words pronounced differently by a native speaker form New York, Alabama and California. For whatever it is worth, my guess is that Campion meant for *read* to be pronounced "reed"–thus making *tread/read* an imperfect rhyme pair. (For further examples of inexact end-rhymes in Campion, see Note 4 of the Appendix.)

As for the other words with a doubtful long *e*, if in modern American speech the first syllable of *divine* is usually pronounced with the vowel sound of "sit," the likelihood that we are meant to hear long *e* in *divine* seems evident from the musical setting of the two words:

The setting's pivotal note–the high C of *-nie,* around which its melodically equal but opposite first and last three notes play–is itself one of the two notes to which *di-* is set; *-nie* and part of *di-* are thus both sung to the same pitch. The fact that we hear a melodic echo of *-nie* in *di-,* plus the fact that the corresponding syllable of the first quatrain (the second of *ayrie-* is set to the same notes as *di-* and also contains long *e*, works to insure that the potential for hearing long *e* in the first syllable of *divine* will be realized when the song is sung. (The obvious objection to this argument–that Campion's songs have most of their popularity with readers who have never heard them sung–does not invalidate it: see below.)

In the same way, there are several incidental pieces of evidence whose cumulative weight suggests that a listener will hear long *e* in the first syllable of *remove:* the precedence of long *e* in the corresponding syllables of lines 10 and 11 (*hunny* and *Courtly*); the proximity in line 12 of the long *e* in *Sleepes;* and the fact that the relatively stable quarter-note setting of *re-* will tend to make a singer draw out the syllable, pronounce "ree-" rather than "ruh-." Similarly, the words *some defense* in line 15 are sung to exactly the same notes as the words *spels remove* in line 12, and the quarter-note setting of *defense* will have the same influence on it as it had on the *re-* of *remove;* notice also the proximity of the word *speech* in line 15, which invites us to hear its long *e* echoed in the first syllable of *defence.* In the same way, we are invited to hear long *e* in the first syllable of *remorse* because we have just heard it two syllables earlier, in *beauty;* moreover, we will hear the *re-* of *remorse* sung to the same two eighth-notes as the second syllable of *ayrie,* the first of *divine* and (although we do not yet know this) the second of *smoothly.* Finally, the first syllable of *delights* is sung to the same quarter-note as the second of *hunny* in line 10, and the relative stability of its setting will again invite a singer to draw out the syllable, pronounce "dee-" rather than "duh-."

Though much of this evidence is musical (and therefore unable to persuade anyone who does not hear "Now winter nights enlarge" sung), my concern in this chapter is with the patterns of sound that Campion originally intended his listeners to hear. He meant for this song to be sung with its music and its music invites us to hear long *e* in *remove, defence, remorse* and *delights* not only because we hear them sung to the same note patterns as other words containing long *e* but because their settings persuade us to enunciate the questionable syllables clearly. Similarly, a reader who enunciates the words of the poem clearly should have no problem hearing long *e* in the first syllables of *remove, defence, remorse,* etc.

2. For examples elsewhere in Campion of rhyme-like relations (by assonance, etc.) among end-rhyme words that do not formally rhyme, see Note 5 of the Appendix.

3. Notice, however, that phonetic likeness in the penultimate syllables of lines 10 and 12 and lines 18 and 20 helps to establish the phonetic sufficiency of an imperfect (at least to a modern reader) likeness between *Love/-move* and *tread/read* by making the end rhymes in these lines disyllabic rather than monosyllabic: *-ny Love/ remove, -ly tread/-ly read.* Augmenting this effect, the presence of *m* (and, more distantly, *o*) sounds in the preceding syllables of lines 18 and 20 creates a loosely trisyllabic rhyme pair: *comely tread/smoothly read.* Similarly, there are less exact disyllabic and trisyllabic parallelisms that underscore the connection between the rhyme pairs in lines 2 and 4 (*their houres/ayrie towres*) and lines 22 and 24 (*his delights/tedious nights*). For an account of disyllabic and trisyllabic rhymes elsewhere in Campion, see Notes 6 and 7 of the Appendix.

4. See Note 8 of the Appendix for an account of the occurrence elsewhere in Campion of rhyming and rhyme-like relationships (e.g. by anaphora) at the beginning of end-rhymed lines.

5. For an account of rhyme-like relationships at the beginning of lines that do not formally rhyme, see Note 9 of the Appendix.

6. For examples of phonetic anadiplosis elsewhere in Campion, see Note 10 of the Appendix.

7. Phonetic epanilepsis also occurs frequently in Campion; for other examples, see the Appendix, Note 11.

8. There are so many examples of pulsating alliteration in Campion's

songs that it would be pointless for me even to begin to account for all of them. Moreover, no reader would stand for such an account. Therefore, in Note 12 of the Appendix, I have taken the two stanzas from one representative poem and used them to point out and describe some of the more prominent kinds of expanding and contracting sound patterns found in nearly every song.

9. Again, no reader would stand for an account of the phonetic unity of the some two thousand Campion lines I have examined. For brief descriptions of the unity in a few good examples, see the Appendix, Note 13.

10. Like notes in music only less precisely determinable, different vowel sounds have different pitches; we can talk about them in terms of "high" and "low." Consider, for example, the series of descending vowel sounds in the following words: *bee, bit, bate, bet, bat, burn* (remem)*ber, but, balm, boy, ball, bone, boom, bull.* See Catherine Ing, *Elizabethan Lyrics* (London, 1950), p. 181.

11. Notice that an expression like "Let well enough alone" has the same sound in its first two syllables. It may have become proverbial for that reason. Proverbs are in fact full of just the sort of phonetic play I talk about here; consider "Don't cry over spilt milk" and "Haste makes waste."

12. *Youthfull* pulls together and inverts the *f*-plus-*th* sounds spread apart in *o'erflow with* (line 6); it also repeats and increases the time between the *y* and *l* of *yellow* (9), and reverses the *l*-vowel-*f/v* pattern in *Love* (10); moreover, the syllabic ordering of long *u* followed by vowel-plus-*l* in *youthfull* reverses the ordering of these two sounds in *well-tun'd* (7). The *vels* of *Revels* echoes and lengthens the duration of the *fl* conjunction in *o'erflow,* also echoes the *fl* combination in the second syllable of *youthfull* (substituting short *e* for short *u*) and chiasmically echoes the *l*-vowel-*f/v* pattern in *Love;* the *ls* conjunction at the end of *Revels* echoes and contracts similar sounds in *clouds* (3), *blaze* (5), *well-tun'd words* (7) and *lights* (9), and—chiasmically—the voiced and unvoiced *s-l* sequences in *nights enlarge* (1), *towres;/ Let* (4-5), *chimneys blaze* (5) and *cups o'erflow* (6). In turn, *Masks* pulls apart the *ms/z* conjunction in *stormes* (3), roughly duplicates the *m*-plus-*s/z* in *chimneys* and *amaze* (7), and reverses that combination in *stormes* and in *words amaze.* Finally, the *ks* conjunction in *Masks* echoes and contracts *k-s* combinations in *clouds* and *cups,* and expands and inverts the *ks* sounds in *waxen.*

13. Notice, however, that *Masks* does give a hint of the rhyme we expect with line 9 because its final unvoiced *s* repeats the same sound at the end of *lights* and echoes similar *s* sounds at the ends of lines 2, 4, 5 and 7 (*houres, towres, blaze* and *amaze*). Notice also that *Masks* plus the following word, *and,* reinforces this suggestion by repeating a pattern heard previously in the enjambment between lines 2-3 (*houres,/And*) and between lines 5-6 (*blaze/And*).

14. The song's music intensifies this rhyme: because *Sleepes* is set to a pair of eighth notes, B rising to C, a listener actually hears the long *e* sung twice:

Slee-eeps.

15. Though modern singers are loath to lay a dental on the waiting wind, it is likely that a singer in the seventeenth century would have pronounced the *d* in *And*.

16. See Chapter 5, note 8.

Notes: Chapter 4

1. See, for instance, Orlando Gibbons' *The First Set of Madrigals and Motets of 5. Parts,* numbers 7-8 and 10-11, in *English Madrigal Verse, 1588-1632,* ed. E.H. Fellowes (1920; 3rd edition Oxford: 1967), pp. 111-12.

2. Of the 116 songs in Campion's five song-books, 44 are composed of two stanzas, 32 of three stanzas, 22 of four stanzas, 17 of five or more stanzas, and only one of one stanza.

3. *O.E.D.,* s.v. *en-,* B; s.v. *dis-,* 7.c and d.

4. Leonard B. Meyer, *Emotion and Meaning in Music* (Chicago, 1956), pp. 157-58.

5. In Campion, see the following examples: *A Booke of Ayres,* III, XVI, XIX; *The First Booke of Ayres,* XVII; *The Second Booke of Ayres,* XVI; *The Third Booke of Ayres,* XX; and *The Fourth Booke of Ayres,* VII, XIV, XX and XXII. See also the regular recurrence of refrain-like lines—lines that are all but identical—in *A Booke of Ayres,* I, II, IV and VI; *The First Booke of Ayres,* XI; *The Second Booke of Ayres,* XI; and *The Third Booke of Ayres,* XXIX.

6. Compare *The First Booke of Ayres,* V, VII, XII and XIV; *The Second Booke of Ayres,* XIII; *The Third Booke of Ayres,* IV; and *The Fourth Booke of Ayres,* XI.

7. The following Campion songs do not repeat the music together with the words at the end of stanzas: *A Booke of Ayres,* XXIV; *The First Booke of Ayres,* I, II, IV, V, IX, XIII, XV, XVII and XVIII; *The Second Booke of Ayres,* XIX, XX and XXI; *The Third Booke of Ayres,* I, III, IV, VI, VIII, XI, XIV, XV, XXII and XXVII; *The Fourth Booke of Ayres,* XIII, XIX and XXII.

8. David Greer, "Campion the Musician," *Lute Society Journal,* IX, 1967.

9. Campion repeats music to new words in the following songs: *A Booke of Ayres,* III, V, VII, IX, X, XI, XII, XIII, XIV, XVII and XX; *The First Booke of Ayres,* VI, VII, IX, X, XI, XII and XX; *The Second Booke of Ayres,* I, II, III, IV, V, VI, VIII, IX, X, XI, XII, XIV, XV, XVI and XVIII; *The Third Booke of Ayres,* III, VI, VII, IX, X, XI, XII, XIII, XIV, XVI, XVIII, XIX, XXIV, XXV and XXVIII; *The Fourth Booke of Ayres,* II, III, V, X, XVII, XVIII, XXI, XXIII and XXIV. He repeats words to new music in the following songs: *A Booke of Ayres,* I, IV, VI and XVI; *The First Booke of Ayres,* I, XI, XVII and XXI; *The Second Booke of Ayres,* IV, VII, XI, XVII and XXI; *The Third Booke of Ayres,* I, IX, XVII and XX; *The Fourth Booke of Ayres,* I, IV, VI, VII and XXII.

10. Though "feet" in English verse are a figment of their describer's bureaucratic imagination, I will talk about them in this discussion because the rhythmic and melodic patterns I will be describing often, though not always, fall within the foot divisions of the verse meter, and may therefore be easily described in terms of those divisions. For a detailed account of the verse meter of "Now winter nights enlarge," see Chapter 5.

11. Frank Kermode, in his review of Bruce Pattison's *Music and Poetry in the English Renaissance* (*Review of English Studies,* XXV [1949] p. 26), isolates *"amplificatio"* as the rhetorical function that sixteenth and seventeenth century music could most easily simulate. Compare Morley's theory of musical "pictorialism," where certain obvious senses of words and phrases could be given simple musical representation: "When your matter signifieth 'ascending,' 'high,' 'heaven,' and such like you must make your music ascend; and by the contrary where your ditty speaketh of 'descending,' 'lowness,' 'depth,' 'hell,' and others such you must make your music descend" (*A Plain and Easy Introduction to Practical Music,* p. 291). Notice, however, that the settings of *-low* and *wax-* in line 9 of "Now winter nights enlarge" indicate an important corollary to the principle Morley describes here: namely, the resonance between a song's music and the sense of its words may not always be "harmonious." Consider Donizetti. Lucia's music is all sunshine and bluebirds and her words say she is the craziest girl in Scotland and she is celebrating her wedding with a murder. People complain about this (because it doesn't make sense); the same people like *Lucia* (because they like *Lucia*). Discord—ideational as well as acoustic—is as essential to harmony as concord, and the greater the mastered strains the more pleasing the harmony.

It should be noted, finally, that the potential for music to amplify its text goes far beyond mere pictorialism—what Campion in his preface to *A Booke of Ayres* called "such childish observing of words": any relationship between words in a song—phonetic, syntactic, ideational—may be effectively underscored by a rhythmic and/or melodic relationship between the notes to which those words are set. See Appendix Note 14 for some particularly good examples.

12. Although the absence of key signature in the original text would indicate to a modern reader that this song is written in the key of C, Campion's scales were based on a system of natural hexachords beginning on the bottom line of the bass clef. The tonic—or root—of "Now winter nights enlarge" is therefore G, the fifth is D, and so on. See M.C. Boyd, *Elizabethan Music and Musical Criticism,* 2nd ed. (Philadelphia: University of Pennsylvania Press, 1974), p. 250: "When there is no flat in the signature, *ut* ["do"] is G, when one flat in the signature, C, when two flats, F."

13. In addition to the special appropriateness of the root-fifth settings of *Now* (the temporal adverb) and *nights* (the temporal noun) in line 1 and *All* and *all* in line 17, consider the following instances of a coincidence of musical and verbal harmony in "Now winter nights enlarge": in line 11 each noun in the three-part subject (*Revels, Masks* and *sights*) is set to the fifth, D; both the phonetic similarity and the ideational dissimilarity of *Revels* and *leaden* (line 12) are underscored by the fact that one syllable is set to the root and the other to the root an octave higher; similarly, the phonetic likeness and unlikeness of the syllables *-ted Rid-* in line 19 are underscored by the identical rhythm and inverted melody of the eighth-note pairs to which they are set; the phonetic relationship between *Rid-* and *read* in line 20 is marked by the fact that both syllables are set to B and accompanied in the bass by the root; the long *e* pattern in *ayrie, divine, remorse* and *smoothly* is amplified by the fact that the penultimate syllables in lines 4, 8, 16 and 20 are set to the same pair of eighth-notes; finally, the identity *and* the non-identity of *nights* in line 24 and *nights* in line 1 is each asserted by the fact that one is set to the root and one to the fifth.

14. There is an effect of rhyme-like unity and division between the two groups of eighth-notes in bars 5 and 3 (the settings of *their stormes,* etc. and *-ber of,* etc.): their rhythmic patterns are identical and the proportions of their melodic patterns identical initially, but their melodic congruence is broken when the last eighth-note in bar 5 rises a whole step rather than falls.

15. Consider the rhyme-like unity and disunity manifest in the change of key at the conclusion of phrase III: because the third syllables in lines 10 and 21 (*on* and *-ter*) are set in the voice part to A, they are pulled toward the last syllables in those lines (*Love* and *-lights*), also set to A; at the same time, because *on* and *-ter* are accompanied in the bass by the same half-note D that accompanied the preceding syllables (*waite* and *Win-*), they are also pulled in the other direction; similarly, *hun-* and *his* are pulled by the C of their voice part settings toward the C of *Shall* and *And* at the beginning of the lines, and by the A of their bass accompaniment toward the A of *Love* and *-lights* at the end.

16. As lines of verse are measured by this pattern of stressed and unstressed syllables divided into metrical feet, notes in music are divided into bars—measures—that are themselves counted by an alternation of naturally accented and unaccented beats. The metrical foot and the musical bar are thus roughly analogous: each is an essentially abstract unit of division superimposed upon and measuring a series of words or notes the way seconds measure minutes, minutes hours, hours days, days months, and months years.

17. This key notion is a cornerstone in my discussion of rhythm in the next chapter.

18. Like any syllable set to a pair of eighth-notes, *Sum-* is sung at two different pitches: it is melodically insistent because its E is the highest note we have heard since E at the beginning of phrase II; its F is higher than any note since the F sharp in bar 3 of phrase I.

19. The phonetic and ideational coupling of *-lights* in line 9 and *nights* in line 1 is both asserted and denied musically: the two syllables are different rhythmically because one is set to a quarter-note and one to a dotted quarter; they are different but related melodically because they are set to the second and third notes of the triad (*-lights* to B and *nights* to D); they are the same in that each is accompanied in the bass by the root; they are different in that the G in the bass on *-lights* is a single quarter-note and the G in the bass on *nights* is an eighth-note that falls to a second eighth-note, F.

20. The overlapping of formal verse-line divisions by the recurrence of this five-note melodic unit in the middle of phrase II and phrase III is both congruent and incongruent with the syntactic patterning of the lines it joins: it underscores the enjambment between lines 3-4, 7-8 and 9-10, and contradicts the temporary break between lines 15-16, 19-20 and 21-22.

21. Notice the rhyme-like effect of surprise and non-surprise manifest in the premature closure of phrase IV: a listener will be surprised the first time he hears phrase IV conclude on *sights* because phrases I-III each continued beyond that point; he will not be surprised at the same closure on *sights* when the B section is repeated; nor will he be surprised when he hears phrase IV close on the D of *toyes* in stanza 2.

22. "In aesthetic experience emotional pattern must be considered not only in terms of tension itself but also in terms of the progression from tension to release. And the experience of suspense is aesthetically valueless unless it is followed by a release which is understandable in the given context" (Meyer, p. 28).

Notes: Chapter 5

1. For purposes of this study, I assume (1) that the abstract metrical pattern of stress and unstress by which we scan ("measure") lines of verse is analogous to the pattern of downbeat and upbeat in musical bars; (2) that the relative temporal values of syllables in verse is analogous to the fixed durations of notes in music; and (3) that the series of phonetic pitches produced when the syllables of a poem are spoken is roughly analogous to the series of precisely determinable frequencies which constitutes the melody of a piece of music. These assumptions will be developed and tested more fully in the following pages.

2. Ezra Pound, *ABC of Reading* (New York: New Directions, 1960), p. 198.

3. A possible exception to this pattern, *All doe* in line 13, should be mentioned. When we read line 17 by itself, *All doe not all things well,* we might reasonably assume that its first foot should be scanned as an inverted

$$/ \quad x \qquad\qquad\qquad\qquad x \quad /$$

iamb, or trochee: *All doe*. Although the opposite scansion, *All doe*, would give supporting metrical emphasis to the vague but thematically important sexual suggestiveness of "to do," to give *All* greater metrical stress than *doe* would not violate the sense of the line, would emhasize the repetition of *all* in the second foot (which is clearly iambic and where *all* is clearly stressed), and would satisfy the not-unreasonable expectation that the same word in different occurrences will receive the same metrical stress. See, for example, *their* and *their* in lines 2 and 3, *Let* and *Let* in lines 5 and 7, and *Some, Some* and *Some* in line 18-20—all unstressed; and *well, well* and *well* in lines 7, 13 and 17—all stressed. But see also a line such as Tuckerman's *The mother sat, sat knitting with pursed lip* (Sonnet XVI, second series), where the line's meter, caesura, and the relative emphasis given to the second syllable of *mother* and the first of *knitting* make the fifth syllable less strongly weighted than the identical fourth syllable. (Compare the probable unequal weighting of identical words in Shakespeare's *Blow, blow, thou winter wind,* Pope's *Shut, shut the door, good John! fatigu'd I said,* and Keat's *And feed deep, deep upon her peerless eyes.*) Similarly, in "Now winter nights enlarge," *Now* in line 1 has a different metrical stress than *now* in line 5, *hath* in line 15 a different stress than *hath* in line 21, *some* in line 15 a different stress than *Some* in lines 18-20, and *his* in line 21 a different stress than *his* in lines 20 and 22. The meter of this poem—and any poem—describes only the relative stress of a syllable with regard to the syllables which come before and after it in a line; the same syllable may be accented differently in different contexts.

4. Notice that since nine of these twelve disyllables occur as the final word in a line, they give to the end of lines 1, 3, 7, 8, 12, 13, 14, 15, 16 and 22 a kind of metrically emphatic conclusion that may or may not coincide with closure at these points in other systems of organization. For example, the syntax and substance of lines 1, 3, 7 and 13 runs over into the next line, the syntax of lines 8, 12, 14, 15, 16 and 22 is complete.

5. In prose either *well-* or *-tun'd* will be stressed according to the speaker's focus, which can invite us to consider (a) well-tuned words as opposed to ill-tuned words, or (b) well-tuned words as opposed to well-thought words; in (a) the concern is with the adverb, in (b) with the adjective. In "Now winter nights enlarge," the meter tells us which is focal: *well-* (rather than ill).

6. As I said in the Preface, one of the reasons Campion recommends himself for an inquiry into the aesthetics of songs is that he himself thought about aesthetic theory and wrote about it. His *Observations* (1602) is still of interest not only to the literary historian but to anyone who would understand the place of quantity in English versification; his *A New Way of Making Fowre Parts in Counter-point* (1613), with its definition of harmony grounded upon the bass, a definition of music as "simultaneously vertical and linear, as the motion of chords" (Davis, p. 320), indicates that Campion was far ahead of his time in anticipating the great changes in music that would occur later in the seventeenth century.

7. Davis footnotes Campion's subsequent use of "flat or falling accent" as follows: "Campion is writing of the pronunciation of the individual word rather than scansion, and he sees the accent of the individual syllable as a matter of pitch reinforcing stress. Though his terminology is sometimes confusing, it appears that a syllable is either "grave" or stressed, "flat" or unstressed; either "rising" or high in pitch, or "falling" or low in pitch" (p. 315).

8. In rule 13, *hideous* and *various* are cited as examples of trisyllables whose first syllable is quantitatively short; we may therefore assume that *tedious* in line 24 of "Now winter nights enlarge" was meant to be pronounced trisyllabically: "teed-ee-us" rather than teed-jus." However, because the last two syllables in *tedious* occupy only a single, unstressed metrical position—and since Campion set them to only one note—it is clear that the potential two syllables in *-dious* were meant to be run together: "teed-jus." Compare the similar syncopation of syllables in *hidious* and *Morpheus* (*A Booke of Ayres*, IX), *beauteous* (*A Booke*, XX), *glorious* (*The First Booke of Ayres*, I and XI), *impious* (*First Booke*, II), *curious* (*First Booke*, VII, *Third Booke*, III and *Fourth Booke*, IV), *th'obsequious* (*Third Booke*, III), *melodious* (*Third Booke*, XVIII), *th'envious* (*Fourth Booke*, XX) and, again, *tedious* (*Third Booke*, XXVIII). Syncopation also occurs in Campion in *Lesbia* (*A Booke*, I), *mutuall* (*A Booke*, VII), *continuall* (*A Booke*, XV), *higher* (*A Booke*, XVI and *Fourth Booke*, XXII), *heavenly* (*A*

Booke, XVII, *Third Booke,* XV and XXVIII), *being (First Booke,* I), *celestiall (First Booke,* VII and *Second Booke,* III), *Venturer (Second Booke,* XVI), *Flowers (Third Booke,* XV), *dalliance and dalying (Third Booke,* XVI), *heaven (Third Booke,* XXVIII), *inferiour (Fourth Booke,* II) and *paradice* and *Orient (Fourth Booke,* VII). In Shakespeare, *beauteous, curious, envious, glorious, hidious, impious tedious, being, celestial, dalliance* and *mutual* are all syncopated (Kökeritz, "Appendix 1"). However, and this makes matters more confusing, while the metrically uncounted syllables in most of the Campion examples are also unrecognized musically (as in *tedious,* the music slurs two syllables together by setting them to only one note), Campion's setting of certain words invites a singer to pronounce each of its syllables distinctly: *hidious* is set to three notes, *Morpheus* to three notes, *tedious* (in *Third Booke,* XVIII) to four, *Venturer* to four, *Flowers* to two, *heavenly* (in *Third Booke,* XVIII) to three, and *paradice* to three. Compare the similar effect of Ferrabosco's separation of the syllables in *Celia* in his setting of Jonson's

                    Come my   Ce - li - a let   us   prove
(Ayres, VI.).

(Ferrabosco was third generation English, but his setting of *Celia* ["Seel-yuh" in English verse] as a trisyllable suggests that he still thought like an Italian.)

9. For example, in line 1 of this poem, *en-* is unstressed and short, *-large* stressed and long; in line 7, *a-* is unstressed and short, *-maze* stressed and long; in line 11, *Court-* is stressed and long, *-ly* unstressed and short.

10. Notice that the rhythmic slowing of this line is also a result of some even more subtle elements: the difficult-to-articulate conjunction of terminal and initial *r* sounds in *Bare ruined;* the repetition of this same effect with voiced and unvoiced *s* sounds in *birds sang;* the fact that in the moment when we first read the word *ruined* we are not sure it is not to be pronounced monosyllabically (thus upsetting the poem's already established iambic meter by making *choirs*–also a drawled monosyllable– metrically unstressed rather than stressed); and the fact that, when we realize *ruined* is to be pronounced disyllabically, this same confusion is repeated with *choirs,* which could well be another two-syllable word– "kwi-ers"–followed by a then metrically stressed monosyllable, *where* (also emphasized by its phonetic likeness to *Bare*), instead of the drawn out, single-stress monosyllable it eventually proves to be.

11. As I use superscript "x" to mark the relative lack of stress in one syllable of metrical foot and an acute accent to mark a relatively heavy stress, I follow Campion in using superscript "◡" to mark quantitatively short syllables and superscript dash to mark quantitatively long ones.

12. See, for instance, Dowland's setting of

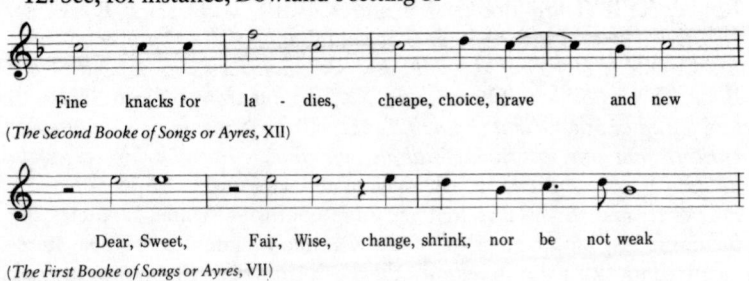

Fine   knacks for   la - dies,   cheape, choice, brave   and new

(*The Second Booke of Songs or Ayres*, XII)

Dear, Sweet,   Fair, Wise,   change, shrink, nor be   not weak

(*The First Booke of Songs or Ayres*, VII)

13. Immediately repeated consonant sounds may be perceived differently by the ear and the eye. The two *m*'s in *Some measures* are separate to the ear as well as the eye; however, in the *ms/sm* inversion of *Poems smoothly* in line 20 we say and hear only one *s*—that is what makes the line suggestive of the sense it carries. Similarly, the ear hears only one *m* in *summer*, only one *n* in *sin no more*, and one *s* in *lies sleeping*.

14. For examples elsewhere in Campion of a quantitatively demanding syllable in an unstressed metrical position, see Appendix Note 16.

15. In contrast, see Shakespeare's *1 Henry IV* II.iii.105 and *Timon of Athens* I.ii.233, where *infinitely* is trisyllabic.

16. Campion often indicates that potentially "extra" syllables are to be syncopated, as in *ev'ry, ev'n, ev'ning, common'st, try'd, cal'd, exil'd, poys'nous, sov'raignes, med'cines*, etc.

17. For examples elsewhere in Campion of a relatively short syllable in a metrically stressed position, see Note 16 of the Appendix.

18. A monosyllable set to a single quarter-note sounds more stable than a monosyllable set to two eigth-notes; however, it is not the notes that are more or less stable but the syllables. *With* in line 8 sounds unstable because it has two successive musical identities; in effect, B-plus-C makes *With*—a known monosyllable—into a disyllable. The phenomenon by which a monosyllable remains a monosyllable in one active system and is simultaneously a disyllable in a second active system is rhyme-like in its physics: *With* both is and is not a monosyllable.

19. Other instances of a falling melodic pattern playing against a word's rising speech accent occur in the settings of *discharge* (3), *o'erflow* (6), *amaze* (7), *divine* (8), *remove* (12), *dispense* (13), *discourse* (14), *defense* (15), *remorse* (16) and *delights* (22). Ten of these eleven disyllables come at the end of a line, where the falling note pattern creates a kind of melodic cadence which in effect supports the formal closure, however brief, which we hear at each of these points. Similar but opposite instances of a rising melodic pattern playing against a word's falling stress pattern occur in the settings of *winter* (1: notice also the phonetic and melodic counterpoint here, the first syllable pronounced with a higher vowel pitch than the second

but set to a lower note), *number* (2), *ayrie* (4), *chimneys* (5), *harmonie* (8), *yellow* and *waxen* (9), *lovers* (14), *measures* and *comely* (18), *knotted* (19), *Poems* and *smoothly* (20), *Summer* (21) and *pleasures* (23). In contrast, instances of a word's falling stress pattern being supported by the falling melody of its setting occur in *hunny* (10), *youthfull* and *Revels* (11), *leaden* (12), *Winter* (22) and *shorten* and *tedious* (24).

20. My use of the word "again" here means to indicate that I have described the same phenomenon before. Notice, however, that if it is understood to refer to a restitution of a previously existing, but since disturbed, pattern, it implies a chronological progress for the perception of the song that is *only* the chronological order of my description. I describe (a) verbal stress, (b) verbal quantity, (c) musical quantity and stress; but the ear does not hear in that or any arbitary sequence in which systems are layered on one another. All systems operate, and are heard, synchronically.

21. The fact that *-on the* and *-ie towres* in line 4 (and parts of two phrases in stanza 2) are set to the same note patterns does not invalidate the special appropriateness of the coincidence of musical and verbal unity in the setting of *harmonie divine*. Since every word casually shares its music with other words and/or syllables, one cannot infer that every effect is the result of an exclusive tactic designed to achieve it. Campion deserves credit for all the effects in the song because it is his song, but the special effect of a particular interaction of words and music may well *not* be reproduced at different points in the song by the interaction of different words and the same music.

22. Remember that the same emphasis fell on *nights* in line 1 and *chim-* in line 5 and will fall on *all* in line 17. To forestall a potential objection to my just claims of special propriety in setting the variously vital syllables *nights, well* and *all* to the fifth (a setting used without special effect for *chim-*), let me say again that an effective interaction of musical and verbal patterning will be effective whether or not it recurs elsewhere in the song when the same music is repeated for new words.

23. Notice that the phonetic unlikeness of the corresponding syllables in line 1 (*Now* and *en-*), line 5 (*Let* and *-neys*) and line 17 (*All* and *things*) in no way diminishes the effectiveness of the coincidence of melodic and phonetic energy at these points in line 13.

24. The unstable setting of the same four eighth-notes helps to play down the relatively strong rhythmic identity of the second foot in line 3 (*their stormes*) and line 7 (*-tun'd words*), and thereby helps to emphasize the subject and verb in line 3 (*clouds* and *discharge*) and the adverb and verb in line 7 (*well-* and *amaze*).

25. While this melodic patterning does not coincide with a phonetic pattern in lines 4, 8 or 20, notice that the penultimate syllables in each of these lines (*ayrie towres, divine, smoothly read*) are set to the same two eighth-notes as *re-* and contain long *e* sounds similar to the one in *re-;*

compare a quarter-note D setting of the penultimate long *e* in line 10
(*hunny Love*) and line 22 (*delights*).

26. Notice the unity and division manifest in the different occurrences of
this root G: it gives the same emphasis that it gives to *tell* to -*charge* in line
3, -*maze* in line 7 and -*fence* in line 15; and unlike *tell,* a monosyllable, each
of these syllables is part of a disyllabic word.

Notes: Chapter 6

1. Gerard Manley Hopkins, "On the Origin of Beauty: A Platonic
Dialogue," in *Poems and Prose of Gerard Manley Hopkins* (London:
Oxford University Press, 1959).